Jim Lindsay

POWER IN THE PORTRAYAL

JEWS, CHRISTIANS, AND MUSLIMS

FROM THE ANCIENT TO THE MODERN WORLD

R. Stephen Humphreys

William Chester Jordan

and Peter Schäfer

Series Editors

Power in the Portrayal

Representations of Jews and Muslims in Eleventh- and Twelfth-Century Islamic Spain

Ross Brann

PRINCETON UNIVERSITY PRESS
PRINCETON AND OXFORD

Published by Princeton University Press, 41 William Street, Princeton, New Jersey 08540
In the United Kingdom: Princeton University Press, 3 Market Place, Woodstock, Oxfordshire OX20 1SY

Library of Congress Cataloging-in-Publication Data
Brann, Ross, 1949–
Power in the portrayal : representations of Jews and Muslims in eleventh- and twelfth-century Islamic Spain / Ross Brann.
p. cm. — (Jews, Christians, and Muslims from the ancient to the modern world)
Includes bibliographical references (p.) and index.
ISBN 0-691-00187-1
1. Andalusia (Spain)—Ethnic relations. 2. Jews—Spain—Andalusia—History.
3. Arabic literature—Spain—Andalusia—History and criticism. 4. Arabic literature—750–1258—History and criticism. 5. Arabic literature—Jewish authors—History and criticism. 6. Jews in literature. 7. Muslims in literature. I. Title. II. Series.
DP52 .B73 2002
946′.8004924—dc21 2001058060

British Library Cataloging-in-Publication Data is available
This book has been composed in Sabon.
Printed on acid-free paper. ∞
www.pup.princeton.edu
Printed in the United States of America
10 9 8 7 6 5 4 3 2 1

In Memory of FKB, n"e

CONTENTS

ACKNOWLEDGMENTS

This is a book about representations of cultural and religious otherness in eleventh- and twelfth-century al-Andalus (Muslim Spain) involving two of its three confessional communities. Although I did not realize it at the time, the project originated in research for a paper I delivered at a Wayne State University/University of Michigan conference on the Jews of Islamic lands. That paper and the encouraging response I received led me to consider representations of imagined and historical figures as the key to a new understanding of several well-known texts of Andalusi provenance.

An earlier version of what is now chapter 5 first appeared in *Princeton Papers in Near Eastern Studies* 1 (1992) and in somewhat different form in the proceedings of aforementioned conference *The Jews of Islamic Lands*, ed. J. Lassner (Detroit: Wayne State University Press, forthcoming). Another conference paper and précis of the material that eventually was expanded significantly into the Introduction, chapter 1, chapter 2, and chapter 3 appeared (with various errors and mistakes) as "Textualizing Ambivalence in Islamic Spain: Arabic Representations of Ismāʿīl ibn Naghrīlah," in *Languages of Power in Islamic Spain*, ed. Ross Brann (Bethesda, Md.: CDL Press, 1997), 107–135, and in slightly different form as "Signs of Ambivalence in Islamic Spain: Arabic Representations of Samuel the Nagid," in *Ki Baruch Hu: Ancient Near Eastern, Biblical and Judaic Studies in Honor of Baruch A. Levine*, ed. R. Chazan, W. W. Hallo and L. Schiffman (Winona Lake, Indiana: Eisenbrauns, 1999), 443–65.

I wish to thank the John Simon Guggenheim Memorial Foundation and the National Endowment for the Humanities, whose support enabled me to devote a period of extended research and reflection on the texts studied in this book, and the Center for Advanced Judaic Studies of the University of Pennsylvania, which afforded me another opportunity for uninterrupted study in which I could complete the research and writing.

Many individuals offered encouragement, comments, advice, critique, assistance, and suggestions on different parts of the work and at different stages in its evolution. In particular I wish to acknowledge the valuable comments, suggestions, and bibliographical assistance of Esperanza Alfonso, Everett Rowson, Maribel Fierro, Raymond P. Scheindlin, Tova Rosen, Angel Sáenz-Badillos, Judit Targarona, Camilla Adang, Munther Younes, David Wasserstein, Maya Shatzmiller, Heather Ecker, and Leslie Adelson.

So too I am extremely grateful to Princeton University Press, the distinguished editors of this new series, to Carol Hagan of Princeton University Press, to Marsha Kunin, copy editor extraordinaire, to two consummate professionals, Alison Zaintz, production editor, and Maria denBoer, who prepared the index, and especially to my editor Brigitta van Rheinberg for giving me the opportunity to publish my work with the Press. I am also indebted to the readers assigned by the Press to evaluate the manuscript. Their comments and bibliographical suggestions were most helpful.

My love and thanks to Allon, Amir, and Eileen for sharing a rich family life with me and for inquiring at timely intervals when I would actually complete the book.

I dedicate this work to the memory of my father, Franklyn K. Brann, *z"l*, for whom cultural "otherness" always seemed intriguing and alluring. He taught me by his example that life is more interesting and society is made better if a person embraces his or her own culture while respecting and learning to appreciate deeply the heritage of people with other backgrounds and different experiences.

ABBREVIATIONS

BT Babylonian Talmud

EI[1] *Encyclopaedia of Islam* (1st ed.) (4 vols.) (Leiden: E. J. Brill, 1913–24)

EI[2] *Encyclopaedia of Islam* (new ed.) (10 vols. to date), ed. H. A. R. Gibb, J. H. Kramers, E. Levi-Provençal, J. Schacht, B. Lewis, and Ch. Pellat et al (Leiden: E. J. Brill, 1960–)

T-S Taylor-Schecter Manuscript Collection, Cambridge Genizah Collection, Cambridge University Library

POWER IN THE PORTRAYAL

INTRODUCTION

Power in the Portrayal

Despite its reputation as a singularly tolerant premodern society and its romanticized popular image as an interfaith utopia shared by the three monotheistic religious communities, al-Andalus, or Muslim Spain of the (European) High Middle Ages as it is more commonly known, was torn repeatedly by tribal and ethnic social cleavages, and socioeconomic struggles and factional rivalries among Andalusi Arabs, Berbers, the *ṣaqāliba* (the so-called Slavs), and Mozarabic Christians. For their part, the Jews of al-Andalus prospered materially under Muslim rule and apparently ranked among the most acculturated and politically complacent groups in the society. They readily accepted Muslim political and cultural hegemony over al-Andalus. And, until the rivalries between "the party kings" (Ar. *mulūk al-ṭawā'if*; Sp. *los reyes de taifas*) of the eleventh century, the Jews seem to have had little or no stake in the various internecine religious and sociopolitical disputes among Andalusi Muslims. Nevertheless, on occasion, encounters between Muslims and Jews in al-Andalus seem to have been highly charged and, it appears, marked by contradiction. On the one hand there were extended periods of sociopolitical calm and mutual economic and cultural productivity; on the other there were sporadic outbreaks of tension, reaction, and deteriorating relations between members of the Muslim and Jewish communities of al-Andalus.

Paradoxically, the supposed contradiction in the nature of relations between Andalusi Muslims and Jews is most evident during the politically turbulent but culturally productive "Golden Age" of Jewish civilization in al-Andalus (c. tenth to twelfth centuries). The very period during which the Jews attained greatest material prosperity, visibility, and influence in Andalusi Muslim society and achieved uncommon cultural productivity in the religious, literary, philosophical, and scientific spheres was also punctuated by three significant intervals of violence increasingly devastating to their religious community.[1] A full-scale and murderous public riot was unleashed against the Jews of Granada and an especially powerful Jewish official in the Zirid administration of that

[1] Only the first of these episodes was directed exclusively against the Jews. Lewis, 1984a, p. 52, observes the irony of the Iberian exception to the rule of tolerance in classical Islam west of Iran.

Muslim state in 1066. The general sociopolitical upheaval surrounding the collapse of *mulūk al-ṭawā'if* rule, and the new pressures exerted on Andalusi Islam by the Christian kingdoms of northern Iberia led to the invasion, occupation, and rule of al-Andalus by Almoravid Muslim revivalists from the Maghrib beginning in 1090.[2] These trends and events brought widespread but temporary desolation to the Jews of al-Andalus.[3] Finally, annexation of al-Andalus to the Maghrib and its incorporation into a single state under the banner of Almohad political revolution, religious reform, and a program of forced conversions swiftly and summarily ended the aforementioned "Golden Age" (c. 1146–47) and all but destroyed Andalusi Jewish communal life.[4]

Inquiry on this complex relationship has relied primarily upon the "direct testimony" of Arabic historical chronicles, biographical dictionaries, *adab* and travel literature, Islamic and Jewish legal codes and responsa, literary-religious polemics, and documentary materials pertaining to the Jews of al-Andalus preserved in the Cairo Genizah.[5] To a lesser extent research has also culled information from Andalusi Arabic and Hebrew poetry and elevated rhymed prose of the period. Yet for all the attention specialists pay to the cultural production of the Jews in eleventh- and twelfth-century al-Andalus, the social and political history of the Andalusi Jewish community, and by extension its place in Andalusi-Muslim society, has remained elusive.[6] That history is occasionally subsumed within the comprehensive narrative of the Jews under the orbit of Islam and presented as conforming to the broader narrative's typical patterns of coexistence and conflict. Alternately, and much more frequently, the history of the Jews of al-Andalus is cast as an aberration from the patterns prevalent in the Muslim East and set apart as the marginal experience of a minority community on the remote

[2] For a summary of this period, see Makki, 1:60–68.

[3] See ibid., pp. 68–77, and Kennedy, pp. 154–88.

[4] See A. S. Halkin, 1953.

[5] On the extent of *genizah* materials pertaining to Iberia, see Goitein, 1967–93, 1:21, 70. On business partnerships among Jews and Muslims in al-Andalus, see ibid., 1:428.

[6] The standard work is Eliyahu Ashtor, *Qorot ha-yehudim bi-sfarad ha-muslimit*; trans. *The Jews of Moslem Spain*. Ashtor's work, while not without many merits, is now regarded as marred by his tendency to fill in many historical gaps and to embellish his narrative presentation. David Wasserstein devotes a chapter of *The Rise and Fall of the Party-Kings: Politics and Society in Islamic Spain, 1002–1086*, pp. 190–223 ["The Jews in the Taifa States"] to the sociopolitical position of the Jews and sociohistorical aspects of their culture in eleventh-century al-Andalus. Similarly, Gerson D. Cohen's still important analysis and interpretation of *The Book of Tradition by Abraham ibn Daud*, Abraham ibn Daud, pp. 149–303, discusses the Andalusi Jewish sociocultural and socioreligious milieu that produced *Sefer ha-Qabbalah* and provided it an audience.

western frontier of Islam.[7] That is, despite the social, legal, religious, political, and cultural structures it shares with Muslim societies of other times and places, eleventh-century al-Andalus and the venture of its Jewish community are thought to present and reflect a most unusual if not unique set of circumstances.[8]

Whether isolated or incorporated into the larger historical picture, the experience of the Jews of al-Andalus has been inflected on an interpretive continuum defined by two fundamentally adverse paradigms, just as that of the Jews of all the lands of classical Islam. Transparently ideological authors with a wide audience in mind along with several social and political historians of the Jews of Muslim lands and a few historians of classical Islam have been engaged in parallel efforts to define the "essential" nature of the relationship between Muslim society and its Jews. Their radically contrasting perspectives regarding the quality of Jewish life under Islam have embroiled some of them in a contentious, high-stakes debate that frames their subject around assessing the extent of "anti-Semitism" in Muslim society.[9] Among those disposed to describe Muslim society in general and Mediterranean Islam in particular, with its characteristic ethnic and religious diversity, as an "interfaith utopia," al-Andalus naturally occupies a central place in the narrative. But those who contest an optimistic view of al-Andalus and the place of Jews in its society also seem to find sufficient evidence to support their assertions to the contrary.[10]

Al-Andalus looms just as large in the inspired lyricism of Ammiel

[7] Stillman, 1979a, pp. 62, 66, 68.

[8] An excellent summary of the ways in which Andalusi Jewish society and culture were unusual is Raymond P. Scheindlin, 1992. Similarly, Wasserstein, 1995, identifies the particular problems the historian faces in studying the elites and elite activities of Jewish scholars, merchants, physicians, and court officials in al-Andalus.

[9] This frame tends to define the issue of Jewish life in Muslim lands comparatively, that is, was Christendom or Islamdom relatively more hospitable or hostile to the Jews? See Mark R. Cohen, 1994, pp. xvii–xix.

[10] See ibid., pp. 3–8; and Stillman, 1979b, pp. xvii, 62–63. For the discussion cum debate, see Mark R. Cohen, 1986, May–June 1991; and Stillman, May–June 1991. Bernard Lewis, "The Pro-Islamic Jews," in Lewis, 1993, pp. 147–48, observes:

> Some romantics, however, like the young Disraeli, seem to have dreamed of such an alliance [between Jews and Turkish Muslims] and seen its fulfillment in the golden age of Muslim Spain, "that fair and unrivaled civilization" in "which the children of Ishmael rewarded the children of Israel with equal rights and privileges with themselves. During these halcyon centuries, it is difficult to distinguish followers of Moses from the votary of Mahomet. Both alike built palaces, gardens, and fountains, filled equally the highest offices of the state, competed in an extensive and enlightened commerce, and rivaled each other in renowned universities."

For a recent study of this aspect of Disraeli, see Rozen.

Alcalay. Alcalay's reading of documents from the Cairo Genizah and his application of S. D. Goitein's notion of "interfaith symbiosis"/"creative symbiosis" reveals "the assumed familiarity of Muslims and Jews, and lack of either animosity or barriers between them as such."[11] Similarly, Nissim Rejwan's vision of Israel's place in the modern Middle East speaks of Muslim Spain as an "unprecedently congenial environment" for the Jews, and of "the Jewish-Muslim encounter in Spain" as "fractious and durable" in nature.[12] Both Alcalay and Rejwan are keenly attuned to the service an edifying narrative of Jewish life under Islam might play in the twenty-first century.

Continuing Goitein's labors and simultaneously revisiting his work and revising some of his conclusions, one set of historians broadly characterizes the relationship of Muslims toward Jews as "tolerant" "benign neglect" bordering on indifference. As expressed by Moshe Perlmann: "For Muslims, Jews and Judaism were an unimportant subject."[13] Jacob Lassner offers an intriguing, supporting observation of what the social historian can expect to learn from reading of the Jew in the Arabic text: "At best the Jews are shadowy figures in the pages of the Muslim chronicles, geographical writings and belletristic texts."[14] Indeed, it appears that most Muslims barely noticed the Andalusi Jews' cultural development and achievement. The Jews' "Golden Age" that was so significant in establishing a powerful sense of communal identity down to the last Andalusi and Maghribi Jewish scholars of the premodern period was a mere blip on the panoramic screen of Andalusi Islam.[15]

Muslim indifference to Jews is explained by Mark R. Cohen and Bernard Lewis, respectively, who have written what are arguably the best comparative study of the Jewish experience under the orbit of Islam and Christianity and the most balanced appraisal of Jewish life under Islam. According to Lewis minorities were "far less noticeable" in Muslim society—a society that is defined by its exceptionally "diverse and pluralistic" character. Furthermore, belligerence toward Jews ap-

[11] Alcalay, pp. 119–94.

[12] Rejwan, p. 52.

[13] Perlmann, 1974, p. 126.

> For Jews, Islam was a subject of considerable importance, not so much in and for public debate but rather in numerous, scattered remarks, references, and allusions intended, on the one hand to weaken known Islamic arguments and objections against Jewish texts, beliefs and customs, and on the other hand, to expose to opprobrium matters felt to be weak points of Islam.

[14] Lassner's remarks appear in his addendum ("Genizah Studies in the United States: Its Past and Future Links to Near Eastern Historiography") to Goitein; Lassner 1999, p. 478.

[15] This important observation belongs to Wasserstein, 1997.

pears to have been "incidental, not essential" in the everyday life of the Muslim because Judaism never posed to Islam the theological challenge it supposedly presented to Christianity.[16] On those occasions when it is manifested, such hostility to Jews is decidedly nonideological but "rather the usual attitude of the dominant to the subordinate, of the majority to the minority."[17] In other words, one tends to read rarely about Jews in Arabo-Islamic sources, but when Jews are mentioned, it is often on account of a real or perceived but geographically and temporally localized problem involving their community or one of its members. That is, at specific times and in particular places, individual Jews, groups of Jews, or the entire Jewish community could be perceived by Muslims as a nuisance, an obstacle, a social, economic, or political threat to the prerogatives of the majority in Muslim society on account of their religious otherness. But even when circumstances strained their relations with Muslim society, the Jews retained the religiously mandated politically protected status of *dhimmīs* so long as they "accepted the supremacy of the Muslim state and the primacy of the Muslims."[18]

Recently, Steven Wasserstrom, a historian of religion, developed another very different approach to Jewish-Muslim interaction that refines Goitein's notion of a "creative symbiosis" connecting Jewish and Muslim cultures and societies. Wasserstrom rediscovers the deepest significance of Goitein's conceptualization in the ebb and flow of structures of thought, religious ideas, and socioreligious movements Jews shared with Muslims in the East during the formative period of Islam.[19] That is, the social and economic contact Goitein documented seems to produce the sorts of cultural interaction Wasserstrom studies. Wasserstrom's work thus crosses the borders many scholars observe strictly between the study of Judaism and Islam on the one hand and the consideration of the various sorts of social, economic, political, and religious-intellectual relationships between Muslims and Jews on the other.[20] Wasserstrom demonstrates just how compromising it can be for scholarship to reflexively separate social and political from cultural and religious history. For Wasserstrom, "*Jew* served as a . . . catalyst in the self-definition of Islam; and *Muslim* likewise operated in synergy with a Jewish effort at self-legitimation."[21]

Reading many of the same sources as their counterparts, another

[16] Mark R. Cohen, 1994, p. 161.

[17] Lewis, 1994a, p. 85.

[18] Ibid., 1992.

[19] In this respect Wasserstrom seems to build on A. S. Halkin's notion of an intellectual-cultural "fusion" among Muslims and Jews. See A. S. Halkin, 1956.

[20] See Udovitch, p. 657.

[21] Wasserstrom, 1995, p. 11.

group of writers,[22] as well as more than a few scholars, depict Jewish life in the lands of Islam, including al-Andalus, as stamped by pervasive degradation and nearly unqualified suffering. They ascribe this oppressive experience to the unyielding hostility toward Jews and Judaism that is supposedly fundamental to Islam going back to its origins in the time of the Prophet.[23] The effort of these scholars, with obvious implications of its own for the contemporary Middle East, is marked by a passionate identification with the Jews' subordinate status, humiliation, suffering, and religious and political aspirations as a social and religious minority in the lands of Islam.

To put the historians' dilemma another way: Should one gauge the nuances of the Jewish condition in Islam according to their Muslim neighbors' most extreme and hostile literary testimonies about them and by the measure of the most violent historical events in which they were victimized by the Muslim majority? Or in venturing an interpretation of the Jewish experience in classical Islam should one give greater weight to other sorts of testimony: (1) the testimony of commonplace documents, (2) the Jews' ingrained literary silences toward Muslims, (3) the extended intervals of relative calm apparently prevailing in relations between the communities, and (4) the Jews' economic prosperity, vigorous institution building, and cultural achievement? As Jane Gerber observes, "so varied is the historical experience of Jews in Muslim lands that virtually any thesis, be it negative or positive, can be buttressed by historical evidence."[24]

In this study, we will purposely set aside the historians' effort to arrive at a meaningful generalization of the Jewish experience in al-Andalus as well as their interest in pinpointing the extent and depth of anti-Jewish sentiment in Andalusi Islam. Similarly, we will relinquish their attempt to utilize primary sources principally in order to "set the record historical straight." Is it possible for us to employ other methods of reading the range of textual "evidence"? William Brinner's keen assessment of the portrait of the Jew in Arabic *adab* literature ("the rich and extremely varied genres of Arabic literature of the European medieval period, roughly from the tenth to the fifteenth centuries") suggests

[22] For an example of this position, see Bat Ye'or, 1985; 1987.

[23] Mark R. Cohen, 1994, pp. 9–14, labels this general approach as "countermyth" to the competing myth of "interfaith utopia." For examples in the scholarly literature, some subtle, others not so subtle, see Gil, 1974; Fenton; Grossman, 1988; Ben-Shammai.

[24] Gerber, 1986, p. 74. So, too, Udovitch, p. 657: "It is exceedingly difficult to formulate meaningful and comprehensive generalizations to characterize the main features of the Jewish experience under medieval Islam." A new synthetic work by Courbage and Fargues, 1997, pp. 1–43, attempts to strike a genuine balance in assessing the welfare of Christians and Jews in the Muslim East and North Africa.

that it is indeed possible. Brinner finds that "the attitude among Muslims [to the Jews] was one of constant ambivalence," an ambivalence reflected in texts: "[H]ow varied, too, are the images of the Jews as projected in that literature, ranging from negative to neutral to positive."[25] Brinner's synthetic observation mirrors an uncensored statement of Jewish ambivalence toward Muslims Goitein discovered in a Genizah document from the turn of the twelfth century—a business letter sent by a son in Fez to his father in Almeria notes: "'Anti-semitism' [Heb. *sin'ah*] in this country is such that, in comparison with it, life in Almeria is salvation. May God in His mercy grant me a safe departure.'" But Goitein adds: "He [the letter writer] mentions, however, incidentally friendly personal relations with Muslims and a lot of business done in the inhospitable country, as well as his intention to proceed to Marrakesh, then (around 1100) the capital."[26]

Various Andalusi-Arabic sources tell of Jews serving as officials of the Muslim state and as physicians tending to the elite strata of Muslim society. We find erudite Jews engaged as discussants with educated Muslims on scientific and literary topics.[27] Less frequently, we encounter Jews as interlocutors with Muslims in open and rational debate or as informants for Muslims about Judaism.[28] So how did the social and literary imagination of Andalusi-Muslim and -Jewish literary religious intellectuals represent their counterparts and rivals, elite members of one another's communities during the eleventh and twelfth centuries? For example, we read the slavishly fawning lyrics of an Andalusi-Arabic poet in praise of a Jewish government official and the positive representation of Jewish intellectuals in an Arabic history of science. These texts

[25] Brinner, p. 229. See also Sadan, 1991.

[26] Goitein, 1967–93, 2:278, on TS 12.435v (ll. 24–27).

[27] For instance, Ibn Bassām, 1:233, relates that a Jew named Joseph ibn Isḥāq al-Isrā'īlī apparently belonged to a literary circle led by the distinguished eleventh-century Andalusi poet Abū ʿĀmir ibn Shuhayd. The master poet is said to have appreciated the Jew's intelligence and literary talent, especially after he bested a Muslim in a poetic contest. See Ashtor, 1992, 3: 98; and Wasserstein, 1985, p. 221.

[28] An interpretation of these aspects of the Andalusi-Jewish experience is offered in Brann, 2000. Apart from several we will study, there are other reports of intellectual encounters between Jews and Muslims in the Muslim West. For example, Joseph ben Judah ibn ʿAqnīn (b. Barcelona, twelfth century), p. 490 (126b), relates an incident (reported to him by the physician Abū Ibrāhīm b. Moril) involving the Andalusi-Jewish physician Abū l-Ḥasan Meir b. Qamaniel. The latter witnessed yet a third Jewish physician present an exoteric view of the biblical Song of Songs before the Almoravid *amīr* Yūsuf Ibn Tāshufīn. Appalled at what he viewed as an ill-informed colleague's foolish performance, Ibn Qamaniel interceded to convince the *amīr* of the sacred text's properly spiritualized reading according to *ta'wīl*, the interreligious hermeneutical method familiar to Muslims and Jews alike. Ibn Qamaniel appeals to the *amīr*'s deep sense of respect as a Muslim for the "author" of the biblical text, namely Solomon, son of David.

seem completely at odds with notorious polemical attacks on the Jews devised in Arabic prose and poetry during nearly the same time and in the same place. Despite differences in tone and approach attributable to genre, the texts we will examine all prove to be concerned with issues of sovereignty, power, and control of knowledge and are reflective of concerns and paradigms internal to Islam for which the Jew serves as a speculum. For their part, Hebrew and Judeo-Arabic texts from the period oscillate between a rare willingness to represent trenchant Muslim foes in a negative light but without reference to their religious identity and a deep-seated reluctance to portray Muslims in any light, almost to the point of silence. That social and textual practice, which amounts to a kind of self-censorship, is indicative of the Jews' underlying cultural as much as social conflict. It appears to be a sign of the Jews' sensitivity to and ambivalence about their status as a subcultural minority in Andalusi society.[29]

The purpose of this study is to examine textual manifestations of the ambivalence with which Andalusi Jewish and Muslim literary and religious intellectuals thought of, or more precisely, imagined one another during the eleventh and twelfth centuries. My aim in analyzing the literary representations of these counterparts and natural rivals is not to advance broad or unsupportable claims for the experience of the Jews under all of Mediterranean Islam. Nor do I hope to settle the historians' questions as they pertain solely to the Jews of al-Andalus during their "Golden Age." My inquiry into the forms and significance of the literary ambivalence Brinner notes will be necessarily programmatic and selective rather than exhaustive. It focuses on a few exemplary figures and a cluster of interrelated texts emanating from or reflecting upon and interpreting paradigmatic moments of the encounter between Muslim and Jewish elites in al-Andalus at the height of Jewish creativity and social and political prominence. My readings of this select group of texts thus makes use of Dominick LaCapra's insight that "what happens to the individual may not be purely individual, for it may be bound up with larger social, political, and cultural processes that often go unperceived."[30] Indeed, I will attempt to demonstrate that the words and behavior of personalities articulated in historical genres and of characters depicted in imaginative literature represent structures of sociocultural and historical signification beyond the figures themselves. That is to say, focused textual study of the sort represented in this work does not signify a turn away from history. On the contrary,

[29] For a fine study of the Andalusi Jews' expressions of ambivalence toward Islam, see Alfonso, 1998.

[30] LaCapra, p. 171.

such study signifies investigation of the traces history leaves in various forms of cultural discourse.

The texts that have come down to us are significant materials for writing the political, social, and cultural history of al-Andalus. Yet they seem insufficiently utilized as sources for exploring the nuances of how Muslims and Jews of al-Andalus imagined one another and sought through their discourses to control one another during the (European) High Middle Ages. Relinquishing some historians' principal methodological concerns with the accuracy and reliability of texts, we will find much to interest us precisely when texts might appear inaccurate and unreliable in the conventional sense.[31] In the words of Brian Stock:

> Accounting for what actually happened is now recognized to be only part of the story; the other part is the record of what individuals thought was happening, and the ways in which their feelings, perceptions, and narratives of events either influenced or were influenced by the realities they faced.[32]

If we apply the poststructuralist methods and insights critical to literary study to a variety of Andalusi texts we are likely to generate new readings of the sources. These readings emphasize the *construction of social meaning* and the reciprocal way in which texts both reflect and shape the attitudes of the society in which they are produced and consumed. For instance, we will want to think about how the texts contribute to fostering both Andalusi-Muslim and -Jewish identity, in large part by examining how they confront and construct religious "otherness." Indeed, study of Muslim and Jewish representations of religious others reveals to the reader more about the cultural situation of the scriptor's textual community than that of the depicted subject. Such issues of identity, otherness, and power relations among social groups, in particular, are frequently played out in textual representations of individuals and events, crisscrossing the imaginary textual boundary between the supposedly objective and the allegedly subjective, the "real" and the imaginary."[33]

W. J. T. Mitchell explains that "representation . . . can never be

[31] Lassner (1999, p. 474) for one, describes medieval Arabic historiography as "a history that should have been, or rather, a history that was or might have been."

[32] Stock, p. 7.

[33] Some of the most important contributions to the discussion of how to approach historical texts as literary texts may be found in collections of essays by Hayden White, *Tropics of Discourse: Essays in Cultural Criticism*. I have benefited especially from "The Historical Text As Literary Artifact," pp. 81–100; "Historicism, History and the Figurative Imagination," pp. 101–120; and "The Fictions of Factual Representation," pp. 121–34.

completely divorced from political and ideological questions; one might argue, in fact, that representation is precisely the point where these questions are most likely to enter a (literary) work. If literature is a "representation of life" then representation is exactly the place where "life," in all its social and subjective complexity, gets into the literary work."[34] The notion of representation thus collapses the aforementioned dichotomy identified with the previously inviolate categories of the "historical" and the "literary." Again, to cite Stock's keen formulation of the two orders of the textual experience:

> The historical is not isolated from the literary as fact and representation. The two aspects of the textual experience are multidimensional, and the objectivity of the alleged events spills over into the alleged subjectivity of the records, perceptions, feelings and observations.[35]

The fabulous aspects of Latin and Arabic accounts of the Muslim conquest of Spain (711),[36] for example, and the marvelous representations of Almanzor (the tenth-eleventh ʿĀmirid dictator of al-Andalus, al-Manṣūr) have been recognized and studied.[37] Similarly, the literary-historical transformation of the twelfth-century Ayyubid leader Ṣalāḥ al-Dīn (Saladin) in the Christian imagination from the Crusaders' "scourge of the Lord" to the epitome of the valiant knight, and the shifting images of Muslims in romance texts have been examined.[38] By contrast, the literary construction of the Jew and the Muslim in Andalusi-Arabic and Hebrew historiography, polemical and *adab* literature, narratives, and poetry has not been studied extensively. We may thus re-read Arabic and Hebrew annalistic, polemical, and literary sources as texts, by reckoning with the conditions of the texts' production and by investigating the conditions of textual meaning. We must reconsider what the texts choose to report and not to report and examine how they relate. That is, we must analyze their discursive language, narrative and rhetorical strategies, and their historically contingent relationship to other forms of cultural discourse.[39]

[34] W. J. T. Mitchell, p. 15.

[35] Stock, p. 16.

[36] See Collins, pp. 17–18, 23–36; and Ṭāha, pp. 84–93.

[37] For example, see the Latin account (preserved as an appendix to the *Historia Turpini*) of al-Manṣūr's affliction with dysentery in Colin Smith, 1988, pp. 76–79.

[38] See Tolan, 1997, pp. 7–38.

[39] The literature of religious polemic amounts to a self-contained genre with its own methods of argumentation and specific subjects. The classic work as it pertains to polemical literature among the three scriptural communities is Mortiz Steinschneider, *Polemische und apologetische Literature in arabischer Sprāche: zwischen Muslimen, Christen*

By eleventh-century al-Andalus, traditional forms of cultural discourse pertaining to religious otherness had penetrated deeply the mental landscape of each community—informing, shaping, and circumscribing the spectrum of ways in which Muslims and Jews could think of one another. Each community, of course, had long since developed a fairly coherent historical and theoretical approach to the other religion, its scripture and theology, including a systematic legal approach to interactions with its adherents. We find abundant expressions of complaint against Islam in late rabbinic midrashim (homiletic literature),[40] *piyyuṭim* (liturgical poetry),[41] biblical commentaries,[42] responsa literature, occasional writings,[43] and works of theology reflecting the sometimes contentious but always intimate relationship between Judaism and Islam in the latter's classical age.

Reciprocally, Qur'anic discourse, *tafsīr*,[44] *ḥadīth*,[45] *fatwā* literature and works of heresiography reflect the disdain for Jews and Judaism sometimes felt by Muslims as well as the Muslims' periodic annoyance with the irksome visibility of prominent Jews in their society. At the same time, all of the Muslim sources, including the most extreme, appear to accept or embrace the presence of the Jew in Muslim society as

---

und Juden. For more recent research see, Adang, 1996; Lazarus-Yafeh, 1992; Stroumsa, 1997. A good summary of the polemical issues, particularly as they pertain to the social position of the Jews of Islam, is found in a chapter devoted to inter-religious polemics in Mark R. Cohen, 1994, pp. 145–51, 154–61.

[40] Late midrashic collections such as the pseudepigraphic *Pirqei de-rabbi eliʿezer*, chapters 31–32, deliver disparaging comments about Islamdom and Muslims in the form of pejorative or caustic references to the biblical Ishmael and his descendants. *Piyyuṭim* and biblical commentaries follow suit in this regard.

[41] Hebrew devotional poetry from al-Andalus provides some excellent examples. Antipathy toward or complaint about Islamdom and Christendom, usually mentioned together, are conventional topoi of this poetry. See Scheindlin, 1999a, pp. 52–53 (Judah Halevi, "*Yaʿalat ḥen*"), pp. 64–65 (Moses ibn ʿEzra', "*Maharu na'*"), pp. 104–105 (Solomon ibn Gabirol, "*Shaʿar pᵉtaḥ dodi*"), and pp. 108–109 (Halevi, "Namta wᵉ-nirdamta"]. Only the latter poem by the twelfth-century poet Judah Halevi speaks solely of Islamdom (l.3 "Hagar's son"; l.6 "desert-ass").

[42] Joseph ibn ʿAqnīn, pp. 274 (70b), 276 (71b), 414 (108a), for example, refers to Islamdom as inimical to the Jews but always in the same breath as Christendom.

[43] Moses Maimonides' statement in *Iggeret Teiman lᵉ-rabbenu moshe ben maimon* (*Epistle to Yemen*), Maimonides, 1952, p. 94 (trans. Stillman, 1979b, p. 241), is perhaps the best-known (certainly the most widely cited) passage from any textual genre concerning the Jews' misfortunes under Islam: "No nation has ever done more harm to Israel [than the nation of Ishmael]. None has matched it in debasing and humiliating us. None has been able to reduce us as they have." For a study of Maimonides' complex attitude toward Islam, see Schlossberg. For a study of an interesting Jewish tradition related to the subject, see Septimus.

[44] See the sources cited in Bashear.

[45] See Vajda, 1937.

a protected subject in accordance with Islamic law.[46] Indeed, Islamic tradition served as an important source of and textual resource for Muslim ambivalence toward the Jews. On the one hand the Qur'ān (9:10) speaks of the *dhimma* (agreement guaranteeing security) extended to non-Muslims in Islam as parallel to *ill*, a "contract of mutual protection." On the other hand, the same *sura* (9:29) (*al-Tawba/Barā'a*) enjoins believers:

> Fight against those who disbelieve in God and the Last Day, who do not account forbidden what God and His Messenger have forbidden, and who do not follow the religion of truth, *from amongst those who have been given the Book, until they pay the jizya in exchange for a benefaction granted to them, being in a humiliated position* (*wa-hum ṣāghirūna*) [emphasis mine].[47]

Built into the very structure of the Jewish position in the lands of Islam, then, is the assurance of their protection and religious autonomy for their community, as well as a socially subordinate status projected in visible and humiliating signs of their subservient condition. Not surprisingly, the apparent ambiguity of Quranic discourse on the proper place of Jews and Christians (actually, *ahl al-kitāb*, "peoples of the Book") in Muslim society is also reflected in two contradictory trends of legal thinking in Islam. Matthias B. Lehmann verbalizes the problem as follows:

> Some jurists tend to stress the mutually obligatory character of the institution of the *dhimma* and the principle of toleration towards non-Muslims; another trend . . . insists on the humiliation of the *dhimmī*s and interprets any attempt of escaping from their humble status as a breach of the 'Pact of 'Umar.'[48]

Apart from the varieties of religious literature and the images of religious otherness painted by religious tradition, the picture turns even messier and arguably more interesting when we reflect on literary representations of Jews and Muslims in eleventh- and twelfth-century al-Andalus.

In the first three chapters of this study I have divided the Arabic texts into "sources nearly contemporary" with the Jewish figures they

[46] Even extreme offenses by Jews against Islam could be overlooked. See Koningsveld, Sadan, and al-Samarrai, pp. 73, 128, 166.

[47] See Bravmann; and Cahen, 1962. Of course, it was left to scholars of traditions and Quranic commentators such as Ibn Kathīr, 3:364–65, to unravel and define the complex relationship of these Quranic utterances.

[48] Lehmann, 1999a, p. 40.

depict and "post–twelfth century sources."[49] This simple division reflecting temporal considerations draws our attention to related and even more significant geographic and cultural-historical considerations. The latter follow directly from the mid-twelfth-century turning point in the history of al-Andalus and the Maghrib and the history of the Jews in the Muslim West. Ibn Saʿīd al-Maghribī, Ibn ʿIdhārī al-Marrākushī, Ibn al-Khaṭīb, and to a certain extent even al-Maqqarī, all wrote during a period in which North African scholars were attempting to formulate or reformulate the identity of Maghribi Islam and Muslim society and culture in relation to al-Andalus and its legacy.[50] Their political, religious, and cultural reevaluation (in which Andalusis held Berbers accountable and North Africans blamed Andalusi moral laxity for the failures of Islam in al-Andalus) was prompted in part by the political demise of al-Andalus as a significant center of Western Islam. The influx of Andalusis into the Maghrib in the wake of the Iberian "Reconquista" was also an important factor. Social and political events that the Spanish later came to call by that name thus resulted in a demographic development that effectively turned North Africa into the guardian, transmitter, and interpreter of Andalusi tradition. This process was never more significant than in the thirteenth century when the political unity of al-Andalus and the Maghrib established during the twelfth century was severed and all that remained of al-Andalus was Nasrid Granada.

Writing during the eleventh and twelfth centuries respectively and thus before these developments, ʿAlī ibn Ḥazm (chapter 2) and Ibn Bassām al-Shantarīnī (chapter 3) served as the most important Andalusi sources for the later North African authorities. Ibn Bassām died just as Almoravid rule was giving way to Almohad control, during a time of heightened concern and anxiety regarding Islamic piety, the legitimacy of Muslim rule in al-Andalus, and the stability of what remained of Andalusi Islam. He served as a transitional source between the era of Andalusi cultural ascendance and the period of Andalusi eclipse and North African supremacy in Western Islam. Other important eleventh-century Arabic sources are examined in chapter 1. Chapters 4 and 5 discuss Jewish "responses," such as they are, to the Jews' social, cultural, and textual condition constructed and suggested by sources of Andalusi-Muslim provenance. Indeed, the topos of the Jews' silence predominates where we find or expect to find representations of Muslim figures in texts authored by Andalusi Jews.

How have scholars read the specific texts in question? In his inimitable fashion the historian Eliyahu Ashtor attempts to write a definitive

[49] See table following notes to Introduction.

[50] See Shatzmiller, 1988, pp. 205–206.

narrative account of the life and times of several prominent eleventh-century Andalusi-Jewish figures, including Ismāʿīl [Samuel] and Yūsuf [Joseph] ibn Naghrīla, for which he relies heavily on two Andalusi-Arabic texts.[51] The Hebrew literary historian Ḥayyim Schirmann, by contrast, is primarily interested in and impressed by the Arabic sources as evidence of Samuel [the Nagid] ibn Naghrīla's social and political prominence.[52] For his part, the philologist-textologist Judah Ratzhaby mines the same (Arabic) sources for reliable details on Samuel and Joseph that are not found in Jewish sources such as Samuel's Hebrew poetry, Moses ibn ʿEzra's *Kitāb al-muḥāḍara wal-mudhākara*, or Abraham ibn Daud's *Sefer ha-Qabbalah*. While focusing principally on expressions of Muslim hostility toward Jews, Ratzhaby further offers a straightforward digest of the Arabic texts, labeling some as accurate and others as completely unreliable.[53]

None of the aforementioned scholars are inclined to treat their Arabic sources as documents of Andalusi-Muslim culture except insofar as they testify to Muslim anti-Jewish attitudes. Instead they only scrutinize the texts according to their respective "commonsense" views of what is conceivably authentic, accurate, and "historical" as opposed to what is manifestly untrue and the fanciful fabrication of a particular Muslim writer. Both Schirmann and Ratzhaby attribute whatever is unflattering, excessive, or offensive in the constructions of Samuel and Joseph ibn Naghrīla to the Muslim authors' trenchant hostility toward the Jews.[54] The sole exception is Joseph's alleged character flaws. Arabic reports of these faults are accepted uniformly as believable by Schirmann, Ratzhaby, and the others because they are "confirmed" by a Jewish text, Abraham ibn Daud's account in *Sefer ha-Qabbalah*.[55]

The parameters and focal points of these studies are biography in the first instance and the history of anti-Semitism in the second. It is thus no coincidence that Schirmann and Ratzhaby attach such importance to Samuel ibn Naghrīla's supposed literary polemic with the Muslim scholar ʿAlī ibn Ḥazm and afford complete credence to the allegation that Samuel actually composed an Arabic treatise attacking the Qur'ān.[56] The image of a supremely emboldened Ibn Naghrīla (the Jew-

[51] Ashtor, 1992, 2:41–189. Ashtor's narrative is based largely on the detailed account provided in *The Tibyān* by ʿAbd Allāh b. Buluggīn (on which see chapter 1) with additional "information" drawn directly from the sources presented by Ibn Bassām in *Al-Dhakhīra* (on which see chapter 3).

[52] Schirmann, 1995, pp. 183–84.

[53] Ratzhaby, 1995.

[54] Schirmann, 1979, 1:234–46.

[55] Abraham ibn Daud, pp. 53–57.

[56] Schirmann, 1995, pp. 197–99. So too, Baron, 1952–83, 5:95, among other works. What survives of the Nagid's polemical work, in their view, is found cited in Ibn

ish Nagid, Samuel or Joseph) mounting a frontal literary assault on the foundation of Islam would appear to serve the particular nationalist and religious purposes of those modern-day scholars themselves. But they are not alone in taking this particular leap of faith as readers of the Arabic sources. Concerning Ibn Saʿīd al-Maghribī's allegation that Joseph planned to turn the Qur'ān into a *muwashshaḥ* (strophic poem/ song) for public performance, Ashtor concludes: "Considering other statements about Joseph in various sources, there is no basis for disqualifying Ibn Saʿīd's account."[57] Even the brilliant polymath Samuel M. Stern essentially reads the texts in the same way. Aside from his contribution to their source criticism, Stern's positivistic assumptions lead him to dismiss the importance of a critical passage in Ibn Bassām, because, he avers, it contains only a "few interesting details but is of no real significance."[58]

David J. Wasserstein stands alone among all the readers of the texts pertaining to the Jews of al-Andalus in general and to Samuel the Nagid/Ismāʿīl ibn Naghrīla in particular. He has made clear that he appreciates how limited the historian is by the paucity of sources and how hampered he is by the various problems they present.[59] Other scholars never saw fit to cast doubts on the assumption that Samuel (the Nagid) ibn Naghrīla actually composed and "published" an Arabic polemical treatise devoted to exposing supposed inconsistencies and theological problems in the Qur'ān. But Wasserstein exercised his typical insight as a reader and arrived at a judicious reckoning of the evidence for and against the universally accepted tradition.[60] Furthermore, Wasserstein recently raised important questions about the nature and extent of Ibn Naghrīla's poetic claims to an unspecified battlefield role in the military campaigns of Zirid Granada.[61]

Is the historian of Islam any more likely to be satisfied with the questions posed and the approaches adopted by social and literary historians of the Jews? Certainly not. She or he will want to know more about the historiography of each of the Arabic textual genres that could explain why, how, and who is borrowing from whom and for what purpose.[62] She or he will note that in general the sort of power Samuel (the Nagid) ibn Naghrīla exercised over Muslims in Granada was not

---

Ḥazm's "*Radd*" ("Refutation"), which undertakes its refutation. But this text nowhere mentions Samuel, as discussed in chapter 2.

[57] Ashtor, 1992, 2:166 and 2:331 (n. 260).

[58] Stern, 1950, p. 141.

[59] Wasserstein, 1997.

[60] Ibid., 1985, pp. 199–205.

[61] Ibid., 1993b.

[62] My thanks to Maya Shatzmiller for her helpful critical suggestions during an early stage of this project about how an Islamicist might approach the texts.

unique to him or even to al-Andalus but was relatively common in Muslim society. For example, at least six other Jewish *wazīrs* served prominently in various *ṭā'ifa* states during the eleventh century.[63] And the careers of the Banū Ruqqāṣa in thirteenth- to fourteenth-century Marinid Morocco and of Hārūn b. Batās in the fifteenth century provide relevant parallels from North Africa a few hundred years after the Ibn Naghrīlas. Additionally, the social historian of Islam will be interested in the role of Jews as tax collectors and their political and social position in the lands of Islam. In such contexts tensions may appear to exist between "foreign" rulers and the local citizens, as with the Fatimids in Egypt and the Zirids in Granada. Along these lines, it is observed in a case study of the *dhimmī* condition in the fifteenth-century Maghrib that "sometimes Muslim rulers would use *dhimmī*s to undertake for them unpopular tasks, such as tax-collection, which only aroused the ire of the taxed population, exposing *dhimmī*s as a community, to violence and despoilment on the death of such a ruler or on other occasions of breakdown of law and order."[64]

From the point of view of the history of Islam, one also would want to consider the episode of Yūsuf ibn Naghrīla's downfall in 1066, say, with that of Ibn Dukhān, a high-ranking Coptic financier in twelfth-century Egypt who was deposed and executed.[65] As in the case of Ibn Ḥazm and Samuel ibn Naghrīla, the episode involving Ibn Dukhān seems to lie at the intersection of personal ambition and politico-religious conflict between members of majority and subcultural minority groups. In Ayyubid Egypt, the discontent of the *'ulamā'* and *fuqahā'* at the elevation of a *dhimmī* to high office in the financial administration of the state apparently coincided with their fear of the Crusaders. As in Zirid Granada, the political prominence of *dhimmī*s in contravention of Islamic law became a touchstone for pious concerns about the well-being of Islam and Muslims as well as a focal point of the personal discontent and frustrated ambitions of Muslim religious elites.

Two sets of themes defined seemingly by their own binary oppositions (learned/ignorant, powerful/weak) circumscribe the parameters of Andalusi (and Maghribi) Muslim constructions of the Jew:

1. (a) The Jew, usually a dignitary working in the state financial administration, a physician giving care to members of the Muslim elite,[66] or a scholar mingling freely among Muslims, possesses learning and expertise useful to and/or admired by Muslims.

[63] Wasserstein, 1985, pp. 209–213.

[64] Hunwick, 1991, p. 135.

[65] See Catlos.

[66] According to the picture of religious minorities in Muslim society drawn by the ninth-century essayist al-Jāḥiẓ, Jews apparently did not become prominent as physicians in Islam until late in the century. See the sources cited by Sadan, 1986, pp. 362–65.

(b) Conversely, said Jew is gravely ignorant of religious truth. Because he is cunning and deceitful, while appearing knowledgeable, he poses an especially dangerous threat to Muslims and Islam.

2. (a) The Jew is empowered because of his knowledge, expertise, or usefulness to Muslims, but such empowerment is against the natural order of Muslim society.

(b) The Jew is enfeebled and humbled by a pious representative of Islam in accordance with God's holy law.[67]

Three of the four themes (insubordination, sedition, apostasy, learning and ignorance) that I have identified as critical to Muslim representations of Jewish figures are found in an anecdote reported in the name of a prominent Mālikī jurist of eleventh-century Qayrawān, Abū ʿImrān al-Fāsī. The anecdote is preserved in *Maʿālim al-imān fī maʿrifat ahl al-qayrawān*, a biographical collection devoted to Mālikī scholars by Abū l-Qāsim ibn Nājī (d. 1435). The text relates an incident in involving al-Fāsī and Abraham ibn ʿAṭāʾ (Abraham b. Nathan), a Jewish physician of high social standing and the Nagid of Tunisia.[68] Because it supposedly originates from the early eleventh-century (eastern) Maghrib rather than al-Andalus, the account suggests that the parameters for Muslim representations of Jews were relatively well established in Western Islam even before production of the Arabic texts we will examine in the first three chapters. More significant still is that the anecdote was preserved and transmitted precisely because it spoke to contemporary eleventh-century Islamic concerns Maghribis shared with Andalusis. In North Africa the times were rife with religious discord, political disorder, and social unrest. The Muslims of the eastern Maghrib (Tunisia) under the sway of the Banū Zīrī had resisted missionary efforts to impose Ismāʿīlī doctrine upon them, rejected Fatimid hegemony, and asserted their independence from Cairo.[69]

Abū ʿImrān al-Fāsī is said to have played a significant role among religious reformers in the genesis of the Almoravid movement before it

[67] Addressing the prominence of Jewish physicians in Ayyubid Egypt, Ashtor-Strauss, 1965, p. 313, observes that entries in *ʿUyūn al-anbāʾ fī ṭabaqāt al-aṭibbāʾ*, Ibn Abī Uṣaybiʿa's standard biographical dictionary of physicians in Islam (down to the thirteenth century), repeatedly report that Jewish physicians were in "a high position" and that they "enjoyed great influence." Such was the importance of physicians in Islam that social status nearly always accompanied its practice, placing Muslims in the intolerable position of dependence upon non-Muslims. Accordingly, al-Ghazālī (d. 1111), the great religious reformer, encouraged Muslims to take up the study of medicine and displace Jewish and Christian physicians. See Lazarus-Yafeh, 1975, pp. 444–45.

[68] Ibn ʿAṭāʾ was apparently the first person to hold the title of Nagid as head of the territorial community. Hayya Gaon conferred the title upon him in 1015. See Goitein, 1967–93, 2: 24.

[69] Abun-Nasr, pp. 83–86.

came to pursue political ambitions in North Africa and al-Andalus.[70] For his part Abraham ibn ʿAṭā' enjoyed influence as a trusted physician in Qayrawān at the court of Bādīs and al-Muʿizz. Like other Jewish officials in the lands of Islam, Ibn ʿAṭā' took full advantage of his professional skill, social stature, and easy access to the *amīr* in order to serve as a protector of the Jewish community and a guardian of its interests.[71] But the text reveals a very different Ibn ʿAṭā' than the commanding figure of *N*^{e}*gid ha-golah* ("Prince of the Diaspora") apparent in documents of Jewish provenance from the Cairo Genizah.[72] In this account, the Jewish dignitary, court physician, and scholar is humbled and denounced by the Muslim jurist. Ibn ʿAṭā' is also terrified and humiliated by Abū ʿImrān al-Fāsī's like-minded sovereign (the *amīr* Bādīs) because the Jew exercised an exemption from the *ghiyār* (distinguishing/differentiation),[73] the sign of non-Muslim identity in the form of distinctive clothing required of *dhimmī* subjects. Because of the symbolic honor associated with clothing in Islam, the Jew's violation of this stipulation of the *dhimma* is especially egregious:

> Al-Muʿizz ibn Bādīs sent his court physician and confidant, Ibn ʿAṭā' the Jew, to Abū ʿImrān al-Fāsī [the jurist] in order to ask for his opinion on a question of Islamic law. When he [Ibn ʿAṭā'] entered the *shaykh*'s [learned religious scholar] home, the *shaykh* thought he was dealing with a court dignitary, and one of his attendants said: "God honors you in that he [the visitor] is among the best of his religious community!" The *shaykh* replied: "What exactly is his religion?" He answered: "It is Ibn ʿAṭā', the Jew." Abū ʿImrān was furious and said to Ibn ʿAṭā': "Don't you know that my house is [as sacred] as my mosque? How dare you enter!" and with that had him thrown out. He [Ibn ʿAṭā'] departed trembling in fear. Since he [Ibn ʿAṭā'] had been without the distinctive mark [of the *dhimma*], the *shaykh* had the edge of his [Ibn ʿAṭā's] turban dyed on the spot and said: "Go back to whoever sent you and tell him to send me a Muslim to receive the response to his question of Islamic law, for I disdain to have you carry back [a message] containing the name of God with even one of His sacred laws."
>
> When the Jew returned to al-Muʿizz he related the affair to him and declared, "By God, my lord, I never thought until today there was any other sovereign in Ifrīqiyā [Tunisia] but you. On occasion

[70] Idris, 1955, p. 54; and 1962, 1:178–79.
[71] Goitein, 1967–93, 2:24.
[72] Goitein, 1965, pp. 166–69; and Hirschberg, 1:112–13, 198–99, 211–13.
[73] On which see Perlmann, *EI*^{2}, 2:1075–76.

I have been present at some powerful outbursts of yours, but I've never known such fear as that which gripped me today." Al-Muʿizz then told him: "In acting as I did, I wanted to show you the power of Islam, the reverence of Muslim scholars, and the signs of sanctity which God has granted them, all for the purpose of converting you to Islam."[74]

For our purposes the text can be read as a paradigmatic confrontation between Muslim and Jew staged between two eminent members of their respective social and religious establishments. The Jew's standing at the *amīr*'s court, earned on account of his medical acumen and sage counsel for the *amīr*, is undone and reversed by the *amīr* himself. As befits a pious ruler, al-Muʿizz ibn Bādīs manipulates his own courtier and restores Muslim society to its properly ordained order.[75] But it is not enough to simply revoke the Jew's privileges. A figure of Ibn ʿAṭā's ilk gives offense to Muslims and appears to undermine Islam because other Muslims deem his intellectual accomplishments and practical skills desirable and useful. In other words the Jew's intelligence and talent seem to compromise the Islamic requirement of his social humiliation in favor of social and political expediency.

In this anecdote as elsewhere, the Jew serves as a relational term for the Muslim, and the dramatic power of the incident stems from a serious concern internal to Islam: the uneasy relationship between the representatives of religious scholarship on the one hand and political authority on the other.[76] Indeed, the policy failures Muslim pietists attributed repeatedly to political authority in Islam turned men of reli-

[74] The passage is from Ibn Nājī, 3:201–202. It may also be found in Idris, 1992, p. 219. See also Idris, 1955, pp. 55–56. I am indebted to my former student Ann Brener for calling my attention to Idris's French article.

[75] There are many parallel reports involving Jewish physicians and their relationships with various Muslim political figures. The latter are obliged to demonstrate their public piety because of their involvement with the Jew. For instance, Muḥammad ibn Aḥmad ibn Marzūq, pp. 314–15 (fol. 92r), relates that Abū l-Ḥasan, the fourteenth-century Marinid sultan, devotee of religious scholarship and architect of the Marinids' *maghribī* empire, once required medical attention in Tlemçen. He received a prominent local Jewish physician and offered him a post if only he converted to Islam. When the Jew declined to convert, Abū l-Ḥasan is said to have refused his services, preferring to remain in pain than be treated by a non-Muslim. Cited by Shatzmiller, 1983, pp. 159–60, 163. See also Shatzmiller, 1978. An incomplete version of the Arabic text appears with a précis in E. Levi-Provençal, 1925. Ibn Marzūq's observations about Abū l-Ḥasan's strictures regarding employment of *dhimmī*s appear on page 30 of the text in Levi-Provençal's article. I wish to thank Esperanza Alfonso for drawing my attention to Ibn Marzūq.

[76] For the most part I have found it unnecessary to reproduce Marshall Hodgson's important terminology, 1:57–60, for differentiating the social, cultural, and political from the religious aspects of Islam. When it is necessary for the sake of clarity, I employ Hodgson's term for the Islamic polity.

gion into political activists.[77] They challenged those holding temporal power to conduct themselves in accordance with Islamic law and to associate themselves unambiguously with the interests of Islam as articulated by representatives of its religious establishment.[78]

That learned and socially prominent Jews with close ties to political authority are the source of much vexation to pious Andalusi Muslims is apparent in a story concerning an unidentified Jewish *wazīr* of eleventh-century Almeria.[79] An important biographical dictionary by the twelfth-century Andalusi Abū Jaʿfar al-Ḍabbī relates that a Jewish savant identified only as the *wazīr* of the ruler of Almeria entered a public bath accompanied by a Muslim youth. Witnessing this untoward intimacy, the Muslim scholar Abū Muḥammad ʿAbd Allāh b. Sahl b. Yūsuf (d. 1087) reportedly became enraged at the *dhimmī*'s uncouth disregard for Islam, whereupon he crushed the head of the Jew with a stone.

The fifth chapter of ʿAbd al-Raḥīm ibn ʿUmar al-Jawbarī's *Kitāb al-Mukhtār fī kashf al-asrār wa-hatk al-astār* (*Revealing the Secrets and Disclosing the Concealed*), a thirteenth-century work devoted to unmasking the tricksters and swindlers around and about the landscape of urban Islam, draws the reader's attention to another agenda. "Disclosing the fraudulence of the Jewish sages" ("*fī kashf* asrār *kadhba aḥbār al-yahūd*") puts the reader on strict notice regarding the chapter's subject, one closely related to our anecdote:

> Know that these people are the most cunning creatures, the vilest, most unbelieving and hypocritical. While ostensibly the most humble and miserable, they are in fact the most vicious. . . . Understand this. They are the most unbelieving and most perfidious of men. They have no belief or religion.[80]

[77] For the Umayyad period, when this pattern was supposedly established in al-Andalus, see Mones. Some of the complexities of the evolving relationship between men of religion and politics in eleventh-century al-Andalus are discussed by M'ḥammad Benaboud, 1994. For a different assessment of this relationship in the *taifa* states, see Wasserstein, 1985, pp. 149–51. Wasserstein contends that Andalusi men of religion were actually associated closely with *taifa* political authorities and as a rule did not assert themselves independently in political life until the end of the period.

[78] Humphreys, pp. 137–39, identifies this kind of activism as one of three paradigms of political behavior Muslims have followed. He observes that these patterns of political action and thought "have grown out of two contradictory and probably irreconcilable attitudes that Muslims have about their religion."

[79] Abū Jaʿfar al-Ḍabbī, pp. 332–33, cited in Wasserstein, 1985, pp. 210–11, and Ashtor, 1992, 2:298, 366.

[80] ʿAbd al-Raḥīm al-Jawbarī, p. 55; Damascus ed. (1885), trans. Perlmann, 1972, p. 316. Perlmann also cites traditions brought by the fourteenth-century North African scholar Ibn al-Ḥājj (al-ʿAbdarī) (ed. 1929), 4:107–114, a treatise on unacceptable innovation, including the following line of verse: "They become physicians and accountants to control our lives and wealth."

Language as truculent and uncompromising as al-Jawbarī, the purpose of which is to invert Jewish learning into utter ignorance, was applied to Andalusi-Jewish figures in several eleventh-century texts, as we shall learn in the second chapter.[81] And *Al-Sayf al-mamdūd fī l-radd ʿalā aḥbār al-yahūd* (*The Extended Sword in Refutation of the Jewish Sages*), a polemical work by the Moroccan scholar ʿAbd al-Ḥaqq al-Islāmī, suggests that the pious agenda directed against learned and thus influential Jews was very much alive at the turn of the fifteenth century.[82]

In times of religious turmoil and political crisis, pious Muslims perceived Islam as failing rather than as triumphant. The *fitna* of eleventh-century al-Andalus and the "Reconquista" of twelfth-century Iberia certainly meet both these criteria. And in such circumstances Muslim hostility toward Jews, especially their erudition and the social status it earns, draws upon a reservoir of negative sentiments toward Jews going back to the first generation of Muslims and the beginnings of Islamic religious scholarship. Even then, the Jew remains a chimerical, slippery character as conceived in texts, a figure whose cultural and religious otherness is inconsistent, mutable, and fluctuating. He is never quite what he appears to be. Like Kristeva's "uncanny foreigner," he serves the Muslim social imagination in times of crisis as the most available and most vulnerable religious "other" upon whom the majority may project its anxiety and hostility.[83] The crisis of Andalusi Islam during the eleventh and twelfth centuries was mediated in part through Arabic literary representations of Jews. Accordingly, we will find in this study that we can read these representations as a textualization of the shifting and ambivalent relations among Andalusi Muslim and Jewish elites.[84]

[81] In particular, we will return to the theme articulated by al-Jawbarī of the Jews as "the most unbelieving" (*ashaddu kufr[an]*) and "They are the most unbelieving and most perfidious of men. They have no belief or religion" (*fa-hum aktharu l-khalq kufr[an] wa-khidāʿ[an] . . . wa-mā lahum qawla wa-lā dīna*).

[82] Esperanza Alfonso, 1998. See Perlmann, 1940.

[83] Penny, p. 128.

[84] Wasserstein, 1985, pp. 142–45, draws attention to the use of *khāṣṣa* (local elites) as a class of Andalusi Muslims and in one important eleventh-century text to *mashyakha* (learned people or communal leaders) in the Jewish community of Granada.

Arabic Sources on Ismāʿīl and Yūsuf ibn al-Naghrīla

Sources Nearly Contemporary

Author:	Ibn Ḥazm Andalusi polymath d. 1064	Ibn Ṣāʿid al-Andalusī *qāḍī*, Toledo d. 1070	Ibn Ḥayyān Cordoba d. 1076	ʿAbd Allāh b. Buluggīn last *amīr* of Zirid Granada d. 1095	Ibn Bassām al-Shantarīnī Seville d. 1147
Text:	1) *Al-Fiṣal fil-milal* 2) *Al-Radd* (*"Refutation"*)	*Ṭabaqāt al-umam*	*apud* Ibn al-Khaṭīb, d.1375 *Al-Iḥāṭa fī akhbār gharnāṭa*	*Al-Tibyān*	*Al-Dhakhīra fī maḥāsin ahl al-jazīra*
Genre:	1) heresiography 2) religious polemic	history of science	historiography	memoir	literary & historical miscellany
note:	1) relates encounter with Samuel (1013) 2) typological construction of Andalusi Jewish courtier		history of Islamic Granada	defense of Zirid dynasty	

Post-Twelfth-Century Sources

Author:	Ibn Saʿīd al-Maghribī Granada&Tunis d. 1286	Ibn ʿIdhārī al- Marrākushī Fez 14th cent.	Ibn al-Khaṭīb *wazīr* of Nasrid Granada d. 1375	al-Maqqarī Tlemçen d. 1632
Text:	*Al-Mughrib*	*Al-Bayān al-mughrib*	*Aʿmāl al-aʿlām*	*Nafḥ al-ṭīb*
Genre:	literary & biographical anthology	historiography	historiography	historical & literary miscellany
note:			source of Abū Isḥāq al-Ilbīrī's *qaṣīda*; history of al-Andalus	

CHAPTER ONE

Force of Character

Three Eleventh-Century Andalusi-Muslim Views of Ismāʿīl ibn Naghrīla (Samuel the Nagid) (*Ṭaqabāt al-umam*; Ibn Ḥayyān al-Qurṭubī *apud Al-Iḥāṭa fī akhbār gharnāṭa*; *Al-Tibyān*)

According to the literary historian and critic Moses ibn ʿEzra' (c. 1055–after 1138) and later chroniclers of Andalusi-Jewish tradition, Abraham ibn Daud (b.c. 1110) and Saʿadia ibn Danān (fifteenth century), there was no greater figure among the Jews of eleventh-century Iberia than Samuel the Nagid (993–1055 or 1056).[1] A reputable rabbinic scholar, Hebrew grammarian, and biblical exegete, and the first truly accomplished and innovative Hebrew poet of the so-called "Golden Age" of Jewish culture, Samuel the Nagid was arguably the most significant Jewish cultural mediator of the eleventh century. The twelfth-century Andalusi-Maghribi Jewish philosopher and biblical exegete Joseph ibn ʿAqnīn, for example, counts Samuel among the pioneering linguists and grammarians (*min ahl al-lugha wal-naḥw*) whose literary endeavors provided the linguistic tools for rabbanite (as opposed to Karaite) rationalist interpretation of Scripture.[2] Judah al-Ḥarizi, the twelfth-century poet and translator from Toledo, devotes two of the *Taḥkᵉmoni's* fifty *maqāmāt* (rhetorical anecdotes [nos. 3 and 18]) to the history of Hebrew poetry, wherein Samuel the Nagid is called "the great prince, chief of all the princes the Jews had, R. Samuel Halevi." Samuel is said to have "displayed a mighty arm in the craft of poetry and his rhetoric was powerful. He brought forth hidden things to light" and was thought to have reset the course and bearing of Arabic-style Hebrew poetry in al-Andalus ("until the great Nagid came upon the scene").[3]

Samuel the Nagid's towering presence and abundant largesse were just as instrumental in legitimizing and supporting the poetic activity, philosophical speculation, and halakhic studies of other literary men. Isaac ibn Khalfūn and Solomon ibn Gabirol and rabbinic scholars such

[1] Moses ibn ʿEzra', pp. 60–62 (ff. 32b–33b); Abraham ibn Daud, pp. 53–56 (trans., pp. 71–75); Saʿadia ibn Danān, 1986, p. 96; and 1856, f. 29a.

[2] Joseph ibn ʿAqnīn, p. 16 (4b).

[3] Judah al-Ḥarizi, 1952, pp. 43, 185; and Schirmann, 1959–60, 2:110, 136.

as Nissim b. Jacob (ibn Shahīn) of Qayrawān and Isaac ibn Ghiyāth of Lucena were among those who benefited from the Nagid's largesse.[4] Samuel was also a highly skilled *kātib* (secretary), known in Arabic historiography as (Abū Ibrāhīm) Ismāʿīl ibn Naghrīla. An exile from the civil turmoil in Cordoba surrounding the collapse of the ʿĀmirid-caliphal state (beginning of the eleventh century), Ismāʿīl began a rise through the ranks of the state chancery of Zirid Granada around 1020 to eventual prominence in the service of successive Berber *amīr*s Ḥabbūs and Bādīs.

As a consequence of the unique range of his communal, literary, and scholarly activities as well as his evident political savvy and opportunism, Samuel's stature grew along parallel tracks in two distinct domains, the specifically Jewish social and cultural milieu and the Muslim civic sphere. In the former, Samuel came to assume the eminent role of Nagid (some time around 1027), the unofficial head of the Jews of Granada and perhaps al-Andalus, whose fame spread to the Jewish communities of North Africa and the Muslim East.[5] In the latter, he functioned as the highest administrative official of Zirid Granada from 1038 until his death in 1055 or 1056. Ibn Naghrīla may have served Granada in some undetermined military capacity as well. According to the forty-one Hebrew "war poems" preserved in his *dīwān* (poetic oeuvre) and their Arabic superscriptions supplied by Samuel's sons, the poet and government officer accompanied the army of Muslim Granada on some twenty military expeditions against its Andalusi rivals. However, the nature and extent of his involvement in Granada's campaigns against its neighboring "party-king" states, unattested in any Muslim source, are open to critical question. It appears that the Nagid may have been more of a self-styled than veritable *dhū l-wizāratayn* (holder of the two forms of authority, the pen and the sword) in Arabo-Islamic parlance.[6] In any case, Andalusi-Jewish tradition regards Samuel the Nagid as a larger-than-life character on account of his singular importance as a protean figure to the Jews of that land and beyond during the eleventh century.

[4] Samuel's exchange of poems with Ibn Khalfūn may be found in Samuel ha-Nagid, 1966, 1:172–94. Ibn Gabirol's poems to the Nagid are available in Solomon ibn Gabirol, pp. 14 (no. 17), 65–66 (no. 115), 73–75 (no. 126), 98 (no. 159), 155 (no. 238). The Nagid's financial support of R. Nissim, Joseph's father-in-law, is reported by Abraham ibn Daud, p. 57 (trans., p. 77), and Saʿadia ibn Danān, 1856, p. 29; of his support for Ibn Ghiyāth, see Abraham ibn Daud, p. 60 (trans., p. 81).

[5] According to Abraham ibn Daud, p. 56 (trans., p. 74), the title was apparently conferred upon Samuel around 1027. On the distinction between the title and the office of Nagid, see Goitein, 1967–93, 2:23–40.

[6] The texts and their superscriptions may be found in Samuel ha-Nagid, 1988; and 1966, 1:3–145. See Schirmann, 1979, 1:149–89.

How does Andalusi-Arabic tradition consider the figure of Ismāʿīl ibn Naghrīla and how do Muslim sources construe the influence the Jewish courtier achieved and the political power he wielded within Muslim Granada? Here too Ismāʿīl ibn Naghrīla, Samuel the Nagid, looms as a unique figure and paradigmatic subject for a study of the image of the Jew in Andalusi-Muslim culture, if only because of the number and variety of Arabic texts in which he is mentioned. Hebrew literary historians and social historians of the Jews have generally handled the Arabic and Hebrew texts in question as direct historical testimony on Ibn Naghrīla's role in the political and communal affairs of both Muslims and Jews.[7] Some historians, notably S. M. Stern, have been concerned with source criticism, that is, with tracing the thread of the textual traditions and analyzing the transmutation of the various Arabic sources concerning Ibn Naghrīla for the purpose of exposing some obvious errors in their transmission.[8] David Wasserstein recently examined how investigation of the Nagid/Ibn Naghrīla has proceeded along strictly divided linguistic and cultural lines, with historians of the Jews relying largely on Hebrew and Judeo-Arabic sources and Islamists depending strictly on Arabic materials. Alone among the readers of these texts, Wasserstein calls for a new approach to the figure of Ibn Naghrīla. He invites scholars to break down the prevalent linguistic and cultural barriers and utilize all of the available sources for arriving at a clearer picture of eleventh-century Andalusi society and culture and Ismāʿīl ibn Naghrīla's place in it.[9] Indeed, the testimony of Jewish and some Muslim sources suggest that such linguistic and cultural borders respected reflexively by modern scholars would have seemed artificial to Samuel and the world of the Andalusi-Jewish elite he represents.[10]

Our principal concern lies less with the important lines of historical inquiry Wasserstein delineates than with the literary construction of the Jew in Arabic texts and their attitude toward Ibn Naghrīla and the Jews. Exactly how have recent readers assessed these texts? Conventional wisdom is divided on this question. Several scholars emphasize that the Muslim chroniclers of al-Andalus regarded Ibn Naghrīla very highly "as a scholar, poet, bibliophile, and astronomer,"[11] especially for his "*modesty, prudence, and munificence*,"[12] that "*Muslim writers . . .*

[7] Ashtor, 1960, 2:72; and 1992, 2:117, refers to Samuel the Nagid's *dīwān* as a "poetic diary." See also Schirmann, 1948.

[8] For example, see Stern, 1963, pp. 254–58.

[9] Wasserstein, 1993b.

[10] See Brann, 2000.

[11] ʿAbd Allāh b. Buluggīn, 1986, p. 205 (n. 111).

[12] Ibid., p. 206.

speak of Samuel with great respect,"[13] or that "*Muslim sources speak favourably of Samuel han-Nagid*" (emphases mine).[14] In this regard, Samuel is typically contrasted with his son and successor Joseph (Arabic: Yūsuf) who is portrayed as arrogant and manipulative, a view that found a surprising echo in Ibn Daud's *Sefer ha-Qabbalah* and subsequent Jewish literature.[15] Other scholars reading the same texts conclude that contemporary Muslim writers (with the singular and notable exception of Ṣāʿid al-Andalusī) speak of Ibn Naghrīla with enmity and utter contempt.[16] A recent reader of *The Tibyān*, one of the texts examined in this chapter, speaks of "ʿAbd Allāh's none-too-friendly portrait of the Nagid." However, the same reader observes: "Yet despite his animus against Hanagid, ʿAbd Allāh also points to some impressive qualities: resourcefulness, political savvy, enormous energy, unwavering allegiance, and coolness in risky situations."[17] Readers have thus treated the texts as opaque statements about Ismāʿīl while disagreeing fundamentally about their meaning and significance.

Andalusi-Arabic discourse on Ismāʿīl ibn Naghrīla does indeed present us with seemingly contradictory figures at whose poles are an intelligent, skilled, and noble Jew deserving of homage, and a vile, foolish, and fiendish enemy of God, Islam, and the Muslims. We can attribute differences in tone and approach among these diverse textual materials in part to their respective literary genres: history of science, historical chronicle, heresiography, religious polemic, and *adab* (literary miscellany). Other critical factors shaping and complicating the representation of the Jew in Andalusi-Arabic texts rest upon the socioeconomic status, intellectual achievement, piety, and position of those who produced and consumed them as well as the temporal and geographic provenance of the sources themselves.[18] Is it nevertheless possible to move beyond the simple characterizations of "favorable" or "unfavorable" when speaking of the Andalusi-Arabic textual representations of Ibn Naghrīla? The constructions of Ibn Naghrīla examined in this and the next two chapters are concerned directly or indirectly with issues of sovereignty and the exercise of power, and all are reflective of matters and issues internal to Islam for which the Jew serves as a mirror. Because "literary figura-

[13] Stroumsa, 1987, p. 769.

[14] Schippers, 1994, p. 54.

[15] The various criticisms leveled against Yūsuf in Andalusi sources are summarized by Tibi in ʿAbd Allāh b. Buluggīn, 1986, pp. 206, 218; Abraham ibn Daud, pp. 56–57 (trans. pp. 75–76). See also Péres, p. 270. The image of Yūsuf/Joseph (ha-Nagid) ibn Naghrīla is discussed in chapter 3.

[16] For example, Stern, 1946b, p. 143 (n. 6), and Allony, pp. 212–15.

[17] Hillel Halkin, pp. 44–45.

[18] Brinner, p. 228.

tions of social realities are scarcely straightforward or innocent,"[19] in the words of Gabrielle Spiegel, we will see that the problem that gave rise to the aforementioned simple characterizations lies in the texts as much as in the readers. Clearly, the construction of Ibn Naghrīla in Andalusi-Arabic literature is unstable and complex rather than determined and unambiguous.

Ṣāʿid b. Aḥmad al-Andalusī—*Ṭabaqāt al-umam*

Let us now turn to the representative texts, first a brief passage found at the close of the final chapter of Ṣāʿid b. Aḥmad al-Andalusī's sketch of a "universal" history of science and culture, *Ṭabaqāt al-umam* (*The Categories of Nations*). Ṣāʿid al-Andalusī (b. 1029) came from a politically prominent family of noble "Arab" lineage and served as a *qāḍī* (religious judge) in the city of Toledo. According to the testimony of *Ṭabaqāt al-umam*, Ṣāʿid was also a historian of science committed to the transconfessional search for truth. Although seemingly uncommon for a person of his station, Ṣāʿid's attitude toward the knowledge religious others possess was also manifested in Baghdad during the ʿAbbasid period of Islam in its classical age when non-Muslim minorities were sometimes considered active participants in the intellectual and cultural life of Muslim society.[20]

Chapter 14 of *The Categories of Nations* is devoted to the eighth and last nation in Ṣāʿid's schematic history of science, namely the Banū Isrāʾīl (Israelites) and their descendants, the Jews. Only a handful of Jews from the Muslim East are mentioned but special attention is paid to the achievements of the Jews of al-Andalus. Because similar emphasis is given to Arabic learning in al-Andalus in chapter 13, the sustained interest in Jewish cultural life (in chapter 14) appears to be a natural extension of the discourse on Andalusi science. All but one of the fourteen Andalusi-Jewish figures mentioned (Ismāʿīl ibn Naghrīla) have some association with Saragossa or Toledo; Ṣāʿid had contact with all but two of them (Ibn Shapruṭ and Ibn Naghrīla), further restricting the survey's field of view. *Ṭabaqāt al-umam*'s very limited scope and its accentuation of Andalusi science led David Wasserstein to think of the work as a "local" history of sorts.[21]

Among the Andalusi-Jewish figures represented are Ḥasdai ibn Shapruṭ (b.c. 915), a physician who, like other trusted men of this profession in classical Islam, served occasional diplomatic, financial, and

[19] Spiegel, p. 5.
[20] See Joel L. Kraemer, 1986, pp. 75–86; and Wasserstrom, 1995.
[21] Wasserstein, 1997.

scholarly functions at the court of the Umayyad caliphs ʿAbd al-Raḥmān al-Nāṣir (d. 961) and al-Ḥakam II al-Mustanṣir (d. 976).[22] Ibn Shapruṭ furthermore utilized his sociopolitical standing and resources to act as the principal advocate for and benefactor of Andalusi Jewish cultural activity, establishing the model for the dual role Samuel the Nagid would play in the eleventh century.[23] Jonah ibn Janāḥ, an aficionado of Arabic and the most significant Hebrew grammarian of the period,[24] and Solomon ibn Gabirol, the neoplatonic philosopher (and Hebrew poet), are among the other figures mentioned in *Ṭabaqāt al-umam*.[25]

Set against the vast corpus of Andalusi-Arabic literature that is virtually silent on the cultural life of the Jews of al-Andalus, *Ṭabaqāt al-umam*'s presentation of Andalusi-Jewish cultural figures and their achievements appears simultaneously striking and modest.[26] Yet each of the figures mentioned is presented in a completely positive light without a hint of the Muslim anxiety and hostility toward Jewish learning we encountered previously in the two anecdotes. For example, *Ṭabaqat al-umam* reports that Ḥasdai b. Isḥāq (ibn Shapruṭ) "was skilled in the practice of medicine, very learned in the legal science of the Jews, and he was the first to open up for those of them who were in al-Andalus their legal and historical and other sciences."[27] *Ṭabaqāt al-umam* reserves superlatives for describing the intellectual accomplishment and sterling character of Isḥāq ibn Qistār (Isaac ibn Yashush), a Jewish physician, Hebrew grammarian, and biblical commentator noted among the Jews for his radically rationalist methods of interpretation. The text reads: "He was skilled in the principles of medicine and understood the science of logic and the opinions of the philosophers; he was of excellent nature and upright manner. I associated with him a good deal and never saw a Jew like him for his learning, his honesty and his perfect character."[28]

In fact, the text's emphatically admiring perspective on these Jewish intellectuals is implied earlier in the chapter when the subject of the discourse shifts imperceptibly from the Banū Isrāʾīl (Israelites) of antiq-

[22] See the entry on Ibn Shapruṭ in Ibn Abī Uṣaybiʿa, part 2, p. 50.

[23] Ibn Shapruṭ is treated extensively and lavishly in Ashtor, 1992, 1:155–227.

[24] For basic bibliography and a summary of what is known about Ibn Janāḥ, see Sáenz-Badillos and Targarona Borras, 1988, pp. 178–80 (Yonah [Abū l-Walīd ibn Marwān] ibn Yanāḥ).

[25] A precis in English of Ibn Gabriol's creativity is Raphael Loewe, *Ibn Gabirol*.

[26] Wasserstein, 1997, p. 190.

[27] Ṣāʿid (ibn Aḥmad) al-Andalusī, p. 88; trans. Wasserstein, 1997, p. 189.

[28] Ṣāʿid al-Andalusī, p. 89; trans. Wasserstein, 1997, p. 190. The *Ṭabaqāt*'s admiring account of Ibn Qistār resembles the entry in Ibn Abī Uṣaybiʿa, part 2, p. 50. See Halkin's comment in Moses ibn ʿEzraʾ, 1976, pp. 138–39 (n. 89) (74a).

uity to the Jews of the Muslim East and, as noted, contemporary al-Andalus. The simple exchange of the term *Banū Isrā'īl* for *Jews* would be taken for granted by an Andalusi Jew but not necessarily by Muslim readers who are the text's intended audience.[29] Polemical issues dividing Islam from Judaism and going back to the Prophet's experiences in Medina as reflected in the Qur'ān and the *Sīra* are critical. Those issues sometimes drive post-Quranic Muslim tradition to draw a distinction between the *Banū Isrā'īl* (Israelites) of antiquity who received a divine dispensation (*al-Tawrāt*) and *al-Yahūd* (the Jews). The latter rejected Jesus' prophethood in late antique Palestine, followed rabbinic teachings and law rather than the aforementioned dispensation, and in the Hijāz during the Prophet's lifetime declined the opportunity to embrace Islam.[30] The perspective that distinguishes Israelite from Jew, or even opposes Israelite and Jew, might have been reinforced for certain Muslim readers because *Ṭabaqāt al-umam* singles out two important figures in Islam—one quasi historical (Kaʿb al-Aḥbār), the other historical (Wahb ibn Munabbih)—as men of exceptional learning. The two scholars were variously credited with transmitting to early Islam much (pre-Islamic) monotheistic and prophetic lore of Jewish and Christian provenance or conversely deemed responsible for introducing into Islam suspect and tainted traditions of Jewish origin.

According to Islamic tradition, the legendary Yemeni Jew Kaʿb al-Aḥbār (Kaʿb of the [Jewish] scholars; d. 652) served ʿUmar as an expert informant surveying the Temple Mount during the second Caliph's visit to Jerusalem in 638.[31] Shortly thereafter, Kaʿb embraced Islam and, according to Islamic historiography, became a principal source for traditions later Muslim exegetes would designate as unreliable by applying the term *Isrā'īliyyāt* (Israelite Lore).[32] Wahb ibn Munabbih (d.c. 738), probably a Muslim of Yemeni-Jewish background,[33] was likewise regarded as a major conduit among the first generations of Muslim scholars for information about creation and monotheistic history before the

[29] Goitein, *EI*^{2}, 1:1020–22.

[30] Lassner, 1990b, pp. 498–507; Kister, 1972.

[31] See the tale as related by Ṭabarī, 1: 2408–09; trans. Lewis, 1974a, 2:3. Another late Muslim source *Muthir al-ghirām* (fourteenth century), trans. Le Strange *apud* Peters, 1985, p. 189, however, reports Kaʿb's Judaizing efforts during that visit. He is supposed to have encouraged the Caliph to maintain two *qibla*s (the original prayer orientation to Jerusalem and the permanent one to Mecca), advice that ʿUmar rejected as blatant Judaizing within Islam.

[32] Many of the various traditional accounts of Kaʿb's conversion are related in Schmitz, *EI*^{2}, 4:316–17. See also, Perlmann, 1953. On *Isrā'īliyyāt*, see Vajda, *EI*^{2}, 4:211–12; and Tottoli.

[33] See J. Horovitz, *EI*^{1}, 4: 1084–85; and Abbott, 1977.

advent of Islam. Here is how *Ṭabaqāt al-umam* defines their role as tradents in early Islam:

> Their scholars [i.e., the Banū Isrā'īl = the Jews] were best informed in the story of creation and in knowledge of the prophets. Muslim scholars such as ʿAbd Allāh ibn ʿAbbās,[34] *Kaʿb al-Aḥbār*, and *Wahb ibn Munabbih* acquired this knowledge from them [emphasis mine].[35]

By recognizing the historical continuity linking the ancient Israelites and their traditions with the Jews of Islam, *Ṭabaqāt al-umam* tacitly accepts the possibility of a contemporary Andalusi-Jewish contribution to scientific-humanistic discourse and signals its potential interest for and acceptability to Muslims.

At the same time, the *Ṭabaqat*'s mention of Kaʿb al-Aḥbār and Wahb ibn Munabbih in the chapter devoted to Andalusi-Jewish science does not stop at representing the Jew as a repository of scientific knowledge and cultural productivity of interest to Muslims. It also depicts such learned Jews as potential converts to Islam. For some Muslim audiences the association of the Jews with these two figures raises concerns over Judaizing influences within Islam and underscores the ambiguous attitude of Muslim scholars toward Jewish learning. For other Muslim readers, mention of these two prominent and erudite Jewish converts served as a model and ideal for Jewish intellectuals in the here and now. The text's other unstated presupposition underscores the virtual integrity of the religious and scientific learning Ṣāʿid al-Andalusī himself pursued: With the exception of Ibn Naghrīla, each of the Andalusi Jews is presented as an expert in specific scientific pursuits *and* in knowledge of Jewish sacred law.

Let us now turn to a seemingly insignificant and laconic passage at the very end of the chapter. The text introduces Ibn Naghrīla by his *kunya* (patronymic) Abū Ibrāhīm. It is a sign of particular respect for him but a violation of one of the stipulations of the Pact of ʿUmar, the

[34] ʿAbd Allāh ibn ʿAbbās also belonged to the first generation of Muslims and is credited with having founded the discipline of Quranic exegesis. Unlike Kaʿb and Wahb, the traditionist Ibn ʿAbbās did not come from a Jewish background. But owing to his interest and expertise in pre-Islamic monotheistic lore, he was called, among other things, *ḥibr al-umma* ("Judaic scholar of the Muslim community"). See Vaglieri. Ironically, Ṭabarī, 1:62, narrates that Ibn ʿAbbās denounced Kaʿb for exerting a Judaizing influence on Islam: "God fight that *ḥabr* [Jewish scholar] and befoul his *ḥabriyya* [tradition of Jewish origin]." See Abbott, 1967, 2:9, cited and discussed by Halperin and Newby, pp. 631–32.

[35] Ṣāʿid al-Andalusī, p. 87; the entire chapter was translated by Joshua Finkel, 1927a.

document that regulates the basic social and legal arrangements between Islam and the non-Muslims residing within its jurisdiction.[36]

> Among them [those learned in the law of the Jews] in al-Andalus was Abū Ibrāhīm Ismāʿīl ibn Yūsuf the Scribe, known as Ibn al-Nagrīla, who served Bādīs ibn Habbūs al-Ṣinhājī, king of Granada and its territory, *as administrator of the state. No one in al-Andalus before him had such learning in the law of the Jews and knowledge of how to use it and to defend it.* He died in the year 448 [1056] [emphasis mine].[37]

The text notes Ibn Naghrīla's preeminent administrative (Ar. *mudabbir*), that is, political, position within Islamic Granada, passing over it without a hint of protest. Just as intriguing is the observation of Samuel's distinctive role within Jewish society and his accomplishments in the domain of Jewish law. He is not only identified as one who possesses expert knowledge of religious law but also as one who strives successfully to implement its observance ("*ʿilm bi-sharīʿa . . . wal-maʿrifa*

[36] On *kunya*, see Goldziher, 1967, 1:242; and A. J. Wensink. The latter indicates that the use of the *kunya* was not honorific if it was employed in order to avoid pronouncing an individual's name. Since the text before us has both Ibn Naghrīla's *kunya* and name (*ism*), the former serves as a sign of special favor. As noted, the Pact of ʿUmar expressly forbids *dhimmīs* from adopting Muslim *kunyas*. See Lewis, 1987, 2:218: "We shall not seek to resemble the Muslims. . . . We shall not speak as they do, nor shall we adopt their *kunyas*." See also Stillman, 1979b, pp. 157–58; and Lewis, 1984a, p. 33. On the need for Muslims to guard against social conformity with non-Muslims as articulated in *ḥadīth* literature see Kister, 1989. For the legal discussion, see Ibn Qayyim al-Jawziyya, pp. 657–63.

[37] Ṣāʿid al-Andalusī, p. 90; trans. Wasserstein, 1997, pp. 191–92. Compare the translations of Finkel, 1927a, p. 54, "Abū Ibrāhīm's mastery of the Talmud and his skill for its vindication were such that none of his predecessors in Spain ever displayed . . ."; Perlmann, 1948–49, p. 271, "he was learned in the law of the Jews and understood how to prevail in disputes on its behalf and to rebut its opponents"; and Salem and Kumar, p. 82:

> Of those [experts in Jewish law] who lived in al-Andalus, we have Abū Ibrāhīm Ismāʿīl ibn Yūsuf al-Kātib, known by the name of al-Ghazal, who worked in the service of al-'Amīr Bādīs ibn Ḥabbush al-Ṣanhājī, the king of Granada and its provinces. He was the director [*mudabbir*] of the state. He knew the Jewish laws and how to defend and protect them more than any other Jewish scholar of al-Andalus.

Also compare to Patai, p. 104:

> And of them was in Andalus Abū Ibrāhīm ibn Ismāʿīl ibn Yūsuf the secretary known as Ibn al-Ghazal, attendant of the Amīr Bādīs ibn Ḥabbūs al-Ṣanhājī, king of Granada and its provinces. He was the governor of the state, and he had knowledge in the *sharīʿa* [religious law] of the Jews, and knew how to lead it to victory, and defend it, more than anybody else among the people of Andalus before him.

bil-intiṣār lahā wal-dhabb ʿanhā").[38] Although it is not rendered explicit, this observation doubtlessly refers to the Nagid's anti-Karaite stance and activity within the Andalusi-Jewish community.[39] Yet the text also projects a singularly important value of Muslim behavior onto a Jewish communal leader and scholar of religious law operating within the context of his own religious community. In his capacity as the Nagid, Ibn Naghrīla here corresponds to the image of a just Muslim ruler whose obligation to uphold Islamic law (*sharīʿa*) ultimately defines his legitimacy before God and consequently in the eyes of Muslim society.[40]

Is it a coincidence that such an image turns up in an eleventh-century Andalusi-Arabic text, even though the subject in question is a non-Muslim? During the eleventh century, the record of the various *mulūk al-ṭawāʾif* (party kings) in observing and maintaining Islamic law was called into question continually by Muslim jurists, scholars, and literary intellectuals. Many go so far as to accuse the "party kings" of breaking faith with Islam, particularly for their excessive materialism, their extensive association with *dhimmīs*, and their habit of elevating non-Muslims to positions of authority in the Islamic state.[41] Yet this was not the first time in Andalusi history for non-Muslims to operate in high government circles or for sectors of Muslim society to respond by expressing opposition to such appointments on religious grounds. The unambiguous testimony of the Qur'ān itself warns Muslims repeatedly to eschew taking non-Muslims as "associates," "confidants," or "partners" ("Let believers not make friends with infidels in preference to the faithful [3:28]"; "Believers, do not choose the infidels rather than the faithful for your friends [4:144]"; "O you who believe, do not take the Jews and Christians as friends [Ar. *awliyāʾ*] [5:51]"; "Believers, do not make friends with those who have incurred the wrath of God [60:13]"; and 5:57, see below). Following these Quranic injunctions, the consensus of Muslim scholars held that Jews and Christians, the "protected communities" under Islam, could not be trusted to serve the interests of Islam or the Muslims. Conversely, evidence from ninth-century Cor-

[38] Ibn Abī Uṣaybiʿa, part 2, p. 50, credits Ibn Shapruṭ (Ḥasday bin Isḥāq) with advanced expertise in Jewish law (*wa-kāna ḥasday bin isḥāq min aḥbār al-yahūd mutaqaddiman fī ʿilm sharīʿatihim*). There is no evidence from any Jewish source attesting to Ibn Shapruṭ's knowledge (as opposed to patronage) of rabbinic scholarship. It appears that Ḥasdai is tailored here to fit the now familiar mold of the Jewish physician-scholar of religious law.

[39] See Abraham ibn Daud, p. 56 (trans., pp. 74–75).

[40] Lewis, 1984b, discusses the ruler's obligation to uphold the *sharīʿa* and the nomenclature used to describe various types of rulers in Islam.

[41] Several Andalusi proof-texts for this pious complaint are discussed in Wasserstein, 1985, p. 280. So too ʿAlī ibn Ḥazm, 1980–83, 3:41, 67, on which see chapter 2.

doba demonstrates that some Mozarabic Christian authorities were just as adamantly opposed to associations with Muslims.[42] And Samuel the Nagid's Hebrew verse from eleventh-century Granada offers poetic "testimony" of the poet's concern that some in the Jewish community disapproved of his consorting with "Muslim princes."[43]

A line of verse quoted by the philosopher Ibn Rushd (Averroes; d. 1198) in the *Middle Commentary on Aristotle's Poetics* (*Talkhīṣ kitāb arisṭūṭālīs fī l-shiʿr*) preserves the faint echo of an Andalusi-Muslim pietist's religious and political complaint against Ḥasdai ibn Shapruṭ. Ibn Rushd cites the line in the *Middle Commentary* for the purpose of illustrating a point of poetics rather than to convey damaging information about well-placed Jews in Andalusi society or to assail Ibn Shapruṭ's role and influence at the Umayyad court of ʿAbd al-Raḥmān al-Nāṣir and his son al-Ḥakam II al-Mustanṣir:

> Now the jurist who said to ʿAbd al-Raḥmān al-Nāṣir before the assembly of the people of Cordoba to stir him up against Ḥasdai the Jew:
>
> Indeed, the one on whose account you were honored,
> This man claims that he is a liar
>
> needed nothing more than this statement to arouse al-Nāṣir's anger against him.[44]

To provoke the caliph's ire against the Jewish courtier, the poet accused Ibn Shapruṭ of having uttered blasphemous remarks about the Prophet Muḥammad. Such remarks, if spoken, would profoundly offend Muslim religious sensibilities and thereby violate another essential stipulation of the Pact of ʿUmar, the document that sets forth the terms according to which *dhimmī*s must conduct themselves in Islamdom.[45] Ibn

[42] For discussion, see Wolf, p. 68.

[43] "*Sheʾeh mini ʿamiti we-ḥaveri*" (ll. 7–11) (Samuel ha-Nagid, 1966, 1:31–34 [no. 7] = Samuel ha-Nagid, 1988, pp. 36–40). Such disapproval may have been forthcoming or imagined. See Brann, 1991, pp. 52–58.

[44] Ibn Rushd, *Talkhīṣ kitāb arisṭūṭālīs fī l-shiʿr*, trans. Butterworth, p. 115; and Stern, 1946b, p. 141.

[45] A new and path-breaking study of the literary form and literary history of the Pact of ʿUmar is that by Mark R. Cohen, 1999. The importance Muslims and Muslim society attached to *al-shurūṭ al-ʿumariyya* (Stipulations of ʿUmar, more commonly known as the Pact of ʿUmar) is underscored by its repeated appearance in diverse genres. Cohen studies some thirty versions such as we find in historical chronicles (Ṭabarī), "mirror of princes" treatises (al-Ṭurṭūshī), *fatwā* literature (al-Wansharīsī), law books (Ibn Qudāma al-Maqdisī), *ḥadīth* collections (Qāḍī ibn Zabr), *ḥisba* and administrative manuals, polemical works (Ghāzī b. al-Wāsiṭī), and edifying literarature (al-Ibshīhī). On

Shapruṭ's alleged utterance against the Prophet would also reflect very badly on ʿAbd al-Raḥmān al-Nāṣir's lineage as the citation itself signifies. It would thus strike a blow against the Caliph's political and religious legitimacy as much as Ibn Shapruṭ's position and influence.[46]

Whatever ʿAbd al-Raḥmān al-Nāṣir's private orientation in matters of Islamic piety, official Andalusi sources documenting and memorializing his public-behavior poem represent the Umayyad caliph a paragon of Islamic virtue. ʿAbd al-Raḥmān al-Nāṣir's letter to provincial governors informing them to henceforth refer to him by the caliphal title and Ibn ʿAbd Rabbih's 445-line epic poem articulate Islamic political legitimacy in religious terms.[47] A caliph sensitive to the demands of Islamic piety simply could not tolerate any such public blasphemy against the Prophet, for it is a crime against Islam punishable by death.[48] Andalusi *fatāwā*, as well as the so-called Mozarabic martyrs crisis of mid–ninth century Cordoba, demonstrate the willingness of the Umayyads to impose the capital sentence on non-Muslims when forced to do so.[49] And since it seems completely unlikely that Ibn Shapruṭ would deliberately jeopardize his own political standing and well-being, Ibn Rushd's tradition probably reflects the efforts of Ḥasdai's enemies at court to traduce him. The report is accordingly an instructive representation of the particular political vulnerability of Andalusi-Jewish courtiers.

Grievances and charges such as this were by no means peculiar to tenth- or eleventh-century al-Andalus. Andalusi traditions critical of *dhimmī*s and their Muslim sponsors were kept alive, and similar criticism was sounded in fourteenth-century Marinid North Africa.[50] In the same way, the ruler's betrayal of Islamic values and the *sharīʿa* in showing preferences to Jews and Christians was heard in the Muslim East, usually by demonstrating for readers the liberties well-placed *dhimmī*s took contrary to Islam. For instance, Ghāzī ibn al-Wāsiṭī (thirteenth century) transmits an account of the ʿAbbasid Caliph al-Ma'mūn's [b. 786] confrontation with an influential but brazen Jew and similar sto-

---

the stipulations of the Pact of ʿUmar as reflected in several specifically Andalusi texts, see chapters 2 and 3.

[46] To the best of my knowledge this alleged incident is not reported in any other Muslim or Jewish source.

[47] The text of the letter preserved in various sources is translated in Wasserstein 1993a, p. 11. Ibn ʿAbd Rabbih's *urjūza* is found in Aḥmad ibn ʿAbd Rabbih, 4:501–527; trans. Monroe, pp. 74–129.

[48] Fierro, 1990.

[49] On this episode and its representation in texts, see Coope; Wolf; and Fierro, 1990, pp. 109–110.

[50] See chapter 3.

ries.[51] Appointment of non-Muslims to high government office was thus a persistent source of complaint in Islam of which Andalusi sources present variations on a theme.[52] Against the background of such complaints, *Ṭabaqāt al-umam* portrays Ibn Naghrīla as supremely "learned in the law of the Jews and [in] knowledge of how to use it and to defend it" and as "administrator of the [Islamic] state." This portrait of Ibn Naghrīla therefore serves as a doubly ironic commentary on the frequently troubled relationship between religious learning and political authority in Andalusi Islam as much as a comment on the Andalusi-Jewish scene. The eleventh century was, after all, a period in which the guardians of religious knowledge found themselves in frequent conflict with those who exercised sovereign political power in the various Muslim principalities of al-Andalus. In the name of Islam, the *ʿulamāʾ* and *fuqahāʾ* thus sought to assert their influence over society, often in ways that clashed with the perceived interests of the state and in opposition to the real or imagined political influence of Jews such as Ibn Naghrīla.[53]

Ibn Ḥayyān al-Qurtubī—*apud Al-Iḥāṭa fī akhbār gharnāṭa* (Ibn al-Khaṭīb)

A somewhat more fully drawn portrait of Ibn Naghrīla emerges in a tradition reported in the name of the great Andalusi historian Abū Marwān Ibn Ḥayyān al-Qurṭubī (987–1076).[54] It is transmitted in *Al-Iḥāṭa fī akhbār gharnāṭa*, a chronicle of Granada compiled by the fourteenth-century Andalusi scholar and Naṣrid *wazīr* Ibn al-Khaṭīb (1313–1375):

> This cursed man was a superior man, although God did not inform him of the right religion. He possessed extensive knowledge and tolerated insolent behavior with patience. He combined a solid and wise character with a lucid spirit and polite and friendly manners. Endowed with refined courtesy, he was able to utilize any circumstances to flatter his enemies or to disarm their hatred with his kind conduct. He was an extraordinary man. He wrote in

[51] Ghāzī ibn al-Wāsiṭī (thirteenth century), ("*Radd ʿalā ahl al-dhimma wa-man tabaʿahum*,") ed. Gottheil, text, p. 396; trans., pp. 429–30. On public opposition to Jewish officials in Fatimid Egypt, see Fischel, 1937, pp. 88–89; and Goitein, 1967–93, 2:374–76. For study of *dhimmī* public service in general see Tritton, pp. 18–36; Fattal, pp. 232–63; and Mark R. Cohen, 1994, pp. 65–68. Ibn Qayyim al-Jawziyya, 1:208–203, treats the prohibition of *dhimmī*s exercising authority over Muslims.

[52] Lewis, 1984a, pp. 28–30.

[53] Fierro, 1994; and Benabboud, 1994.

[54] Ibn Ḥayyān is said to have been a staunch supporter of the Umayyad caliphate and thus a critic of the *ṭāʾifa* kingdoms that replaced it. The portrait of Ibn Naghrīla brought in Ibn Ḥayyān's name (see below) gives no hint of this ideological orientation.

both languages: Arabic and Hebrew. He knew the literatures of both peoples. He went deeply into the principles of the Arabic language and was familiar with the works of the most subtle grammarians. He spoke and wrote classical Arabic with the greatest ease, using this language in the letters which he wrote on behalf on his king. He used the usual Islamic formulas, the eulogies of God and Muḥammad, our Prophet, and recommended to the addressee to live according to Islam. In brief, one would believe that his letters were written by a pious Muslim. He was excellent in the sciences of the ancients, in mathematics as well as astronomy. Also in the field of logic he possessed ample knowledge. In dialectics he even prevailed over his adversaries. Despite his lively spirit he spoke little and reflected much. He assembled a beautiful library. He died on the 12th of Muḥarram, 459 A.H. The Jews decorated his coffin and bowed in deference [as it passed by]. They held fast to him in their anguish and mourned him publicly.

He [Ismāʿīl ibn Naghrīla] had encouraged his son Yūsuf, whose *kunya* was Abū Ḥusayn, to read books. He brought together for him masters and literary intellectuals from all directions who instructed him and taught him. He made him stick with the precious art of writing and so trained him for his first job as secretary of Buluqqīn, his master's son who was a candidate to succeed [his master], easing his way in the fundamentals of his work. When Ismāʿīl died on the aforementioned date, Bādīs approached Yūsuf. Bādīs demonstrated his satisfaction with him as a replacement for his father in [Bādīs'] service.[55]

Apart from its perfunctory rhetorical reference to Samuel's "accursed" religious identity, Ibn Ḥayyān (*apud* Ibn al-Khaṭīb), like *Ṭabaqāt al-umam*, appears to cast Ibn Naghrīla in an uncommonly favorable light. The text attributes to the learned Jewish court secretary (*min akmala l-rijāl ʿilm[an] wa-ḥilm[an] wa-fahm[an]*) every conceivable trait of a noble and aristocratic character such as were valued in al-Andalus and all of Islam in its classical age.[56] According to this highly stylized portrait of a court secretary, Ibn Naghrīla is said to demonstrate refined manners, disarming resourcefulness in dealing with associates and enemies, linguistic skill and eloquence, and a command of literary and scientific knowledge and learning. Finally, Ibn Ḥayyān's report on Ibn Naghrīla also proceeds to relate a few details of the meticulous

[55] Ibn Ḥayyān, quoted by Lisān al-Dīn ibn al-Khaṭīb, 1973, 1:438–39. I have modified slightly the translation of Schippers, 1996, p. 80.

[56] Ibn ʿAbd Rabbih, 4:171–72, sketches the ideal qualities of the court secretary.

intellectual preparation and administrative tutelage Ismāʿīl endeavored to provide Yūsuf, his son and eventual successor as Nagid of the Jews and as *wazīr* of Zirid Granada.[57]

Ibn Ḥayyan's depiction of Ismāʿīl is as significant for what it neglects to report as for what it relates. The tradition transmitted in his name by Ibn al-Khaṭīb alludes to but makes no explicit mention of Ibn Naghrīla's pivotal role in the financial and political administration of Zirid Granada. In this respect, the text can be said to portray Ibn Naghrīla as a "mere" court secretary, a singularly gifted and important *kātib* to be sure, but certainly not as a central actor in the exercise of the power of the Islamic state. In Andalusi-Arabic usage *kātib* can be synonymous with *wazīr* but there is little in the description of Ibn Naghrīla's responsibilities to suggest that he in fact occupied an executive office. This striking omission in Ibn Ḥayyān's account of Ibn Naghrīla is however balanced and rectified in advance by the previous source Ibn al-Khaṭīb transmits in *Al-Iḥāṭa*. It is a brief but critical citation from *Al-Bayān al-mughrib fī akhbār al-maghrib* by the thirteenth-century North African scholar Abū l-ʿAbbās Aḥmad ibn ʿIdhārī:

> Ibn ʿIdhārī al-Marrākushī said in his book entitled *Al-Bayān al-mughrib*: Bādīs threw his support behind his father's secretary and *wazīr* Ibn Naghrīla, the Jew, and the subordinate tax-collectors from his religious community. *They gained stature during his tenure and behaved arrogantly toward the Muslims* [emphasis mine].[58]

Unlike Ibn Ḥayyān, Ibn ʿIdhārī's terse notice identifies Ibn Naghrīla as an essential political figure in Zirid Granada. *Al-Bayān al-mughrib* treats Ibn Naghrīla as though his career were a case in point of the harm that comes to Islam when a non-Muslim attains a position of influence and authority over Muslims and the Islamic polity. The text reports that the lower-level Jewish functionaries who accompanied Ibn Naghrīla amassed wealth and displayed contempt toward Muslims, contrary to Islamic law and against the stipulations by which *dhimmī* subjects are required to abide in the lands of Islam.[59]

To return to Ibn Ḥayyān: The passage transmitted in *Al-Iḥāṭa* presents Ibn Naghrīla as the veritable embodiment of courtly virtues and secre-

[57] It is an effort that is reflected in Samuel's own poetry. See Samuel ha-Nagid, 1988, pp. 47–49, 50–53, 60–63, 64–66, 73–74, 142–43, and especially 87–88, which addresses Joseph's education. A translation of the latter poem appears in Cole, p. 54.

[58] Ibn al-Khaṭīb, *Al-Iḥāṭa*, 1:438 and the parallel text, Ibn ʿIdhārī al-Marrākushī, 3:264.

[59] At issue is the absence of deference and humility *(dhull)* that the Qur'ān and Islamic law require Jews and Christians to display toward Muslims as an obligation of the *dhimma*.

tarial skills. Most significantly, Ibn Naghrīla is lauded for his exquisite use of the appropriate Arabic formulas of Islamic piety in his correspondence on behalf of the Zirids.[60] What with the words of the inimitable Qur'ān flowing from his stylus if not literally from his lips, Samuel's Jewishness is something of a marvel to behold, nearly more apparent than real. Signs of Ibn Naghrīla's cultural otherness are limited to his knowledge of Hebrew language and literature such that the social self very nearly appears to supplant the "real" self. Reference to any form of behavior contrary to Islam and abhorrent or incomprehensible to Muslims is suppressed. Much like the image of the noble Moor in the *Poema de Mio Cid* (c. 1207), the figure of Ibn Naghrīla in Ibn Ḥayyān is less a Jew than a Jew inscribed in the text, an emblem of an idealized *dhimmī* who is a Muslim in all but name.[61]

But there is another way an Andalusi Muslim might comprehend Ibn Ḥayyān's portrait of Ibn Naghrīla. Because the boundaries he seems to cross are inherently ambiguous, what one reader might construe as Ibn Naghrīla's cultural assimilation to Muslim society another might understand as his infiltration of Islam. That is to say, like all boundaries and borders, they both separate and unite.[62] Much as the figure of Abraham ibn ʿAṭā' in the anecdote related in the Introduction, Ibn Naghrīla so closely resembles an educated aristocratic Muslim in his discourse and demeanor that he blends in imperceptibly with the community of Muslims. Apart from literary and historical texts such as these, reports preserved in the documents of the Cairo Genizah in fact testify to instances of individual Jews "passing" as Muslims.[63] This sec-

[60] The legendary vignette (Abraham ibn Daud, pp. 54–55; trans., pp. 72–73) relating Samuel's accidental "discovery" in a Malagan spice shop is a significant illustration of the ecumenical importance of the rhetorical ideal of life. For the Jews of the Christian kingdoms of northern Iberia, it also illustrated the importance of expert knowledge of Arabic. Stern, 1950, pp. 135–38, identified an Andalusi-Arabic parallel to Ibn Naghrīla's rise to power in a tale of how al-Manṣūr's eloquence and stylistic gifts hastened his own ascent to power. In chapter 3 I attempt to give another, very different reading of the anecdote.

Saʿadia ibn Danān, 1856, f. 29a; 1986, p. 96, furthermore relates that the Nagid composed a seven-line panegyric in seven languages ("each verse in a different language") for the *amīr* Ḥabbūs. So too the famous "ethical will" of Judah ibn Tibbon to his son: "you know that the great men of our people attained their greatness and many virtues only because of their ability in writing Arabic. You have already seen what the Nagid, of blessed memory, said about the greatness he achieved through it. . . . *The achievement of his son as well was due to it*" (emphasis mine); trans. Abrahams, 1:59.

[61] Here I have benefited from reading Israel Burshatin, "The Moor in the Text: Metaphor, Emblem, and Silence," in Gates, 117–39.

[62] See Lotman, p. 136. Ibn al-Khaṭīb, the author/editor of *Al-Iḥāṭa*, must also have been struck that Ibn Naghrīla, a previous prime minister of Granada and fellow poet, was also a Jew.

[63] Goitein, 1967–93, 2:286.

ond reading of Ibn Ḥayyān's figure of Ismāʿīl would also reinforce the Muslim reader's sense of the Jew's serious violation of the stipulations of the *dhimma*—the very conditions established by Islam in order to draw unmistakable and inviolate social, political, and religious boundaries between Muslims and their Christian and Jewish subjects. Viewed this way, with his real self masked by the social self, the figure of Ibn Naghrīla might appear all the more dangerous to Islam. As Jonathan Z. Smith argues:

> While the "other" may be perceived as being LIKE-US or NOT-LIKE-US, he is in fact most problematic when he is TOO-MUCH-LIKE-US, or when he claims to BE-US. It is here that the real urgency of a "theory of the other" emerges. This urgency is called forth not by the requirement to place the "other" but rather to situate ourselves. . . . This is not a matter of the "far," but of, preeminently, the "near." The problem is not alterity, but similarity . . . at times even identity. A "theory of the other" is but another way of phrasing a "theory of the self."[64]

Accordingly, the reader might easily grasp that Ismāʿīl (and others like him) represents a threat to Islam because of the ease with which he lurks among Muslims, disguised as it were and operating nearly unnoticed within the Muslim *umma*. Like the legendary figure of Kaʿb al-Aḥbār and the more historical figure of Wahb ibn Munabbih depicted in the literature of Muslim traditionists, Ibn Naghrīla thus occupies an ambiguous position in the text. If the reader does not take Ibn Naghrīla for a gifted and assimilated ersatz-Muslim courtier he can just as easily regard him as a Jewish infiltrator operating covertly within Islam or with equal justification as a Jew entrenched in a position of authority over Muslims and the Muslim state. In either case, Ibn Naghrīla trespasses inviolate social and political boundaries Islam imposed on its Jewish subjects.

Concern for the weakening of these boundaries was very much on the minds of Muslim pietists of the eleventh century.[65] For instance, the Mālikī authority Abū l-Ḥasan al-Qābisī (d. 1012) sought to circumscribe social and intellectual interactions between Muslims and Jews (and Muslims and Christians). According to al-Qābisī such contacts foster religiously impermissible pedagogical exchanges between Muslims and *dhimmī*s regarding revealed scripture. Such encounters, in his opinion, had already produced certain undesirable Judaizing behaviors

[64] Jonathan Z. Smith, p. 47. Brinner, pp. 228–29, drew my attention to Smith's essay.

[65] We shall return in chapter 3 to the motif of the Jew as an ersatz Muslim when we read several passages from *Al-Dhakhīra fī maḥāsin ahl al-jazīra*, a twelfth-century Andalusi source by Ibn Bassām.

among Maghribī Muslims.[66] Opinions and rulings such as those expressed by al-Qābisī signify not only apprehension of the proximity of Jew to Muslims but also of Judaism to Islam. Nor was the latter a figment of the pious imagination. The connection is made clear in al-Shahrastānī's perspective that Judaism is the religion most closely resembling Islam.[67] And there are numerous Sunni traditions decrying the violation of Islam introduced by the penetration of Jewish traditions and behaviors among Muslims.[68]

With the conclusion of Ibn Ḥayyān's tradition, Ibn al-Khaṭīb returns to Ibn ʿIdhārī al-Marrākushī's *Al-Bayān al-mughrib* as his source for the next chapter of *Al-Iḥāṭā*:

> Ismāʿīl left behind a son, named Yūsuf, who had never known the humility of the *dhimma*, nor the filthy situation in which Jews must normally live. He was a good looking man, sharp of wit. He started to improve his situation with enthusiasm. He collected taxes and extracted money and appointed Jews to all kinds of functions.[69]
>
> The original location of his grave—and that of his father—is known even today by the Jews who consecutively transmitted this in their circles. Before the gate of Ilbira, at the distance of a bow-shot, across the road. On his grave is a piece of limestone, roughly shaped. He was famous because of his rank in enjoying a delicate life, his refined behavior, elegance and literacy. These qualities added to his reputation so that he deserves mention with important intellectuals and unique men. He had the same stature except for his religious beliefs.[70]

There is a noticeable difference in tone and a subtle difference in approach between this entry, a document of thirteenth-century North Africa, and Ibn Ḥayyān's nearly contemporary eleventh-century Andalusi report. References to the "humility of the *dhimma*," and "the filthy situation in which the Jews must normally live," are mostly absent in the contemporary eleventh-century sources except for Ibn Ḥazm's *Al-Fiṣal fī l-milal* and *Al-Radd* and Abū Isḥāq al-Ilbīrī's poetic diatribe (see chapter 2).[71] But such bracing expressions are highly typical of slightly

[66] Abū l-Ḥasan al-Qābisī, 301, cited by Speight, pp. 185–86.

[67] Wasserstrom, 1997, pp. 147–48.

[68] Kister, 1989, "Do Not Assimilate Yourselves," including the appendix by Menahem Kister, pp. 354–56; and Uri Rubin, 1997, p. 84.

[69] Ibn al-Khaṭīb, p. 439; trans. Schippers, 19996, p. 80.

[70] Ibn al-Khaṭīb, p. 440.

[71] To cite but two parallels from Abū Isḥāq al-Ilbīrī's *qaṣīda*, "*Alā qul li-ṣinhājatin*," in Lisān al-Dīn ibn al-Khaṭīb, 1956, p. 233, and Garcia Gómez, 1944, pp.

later sources produced in North Africa. By comparison, Ibn Ḥayyān's sole reference to Ibn Naghrīla as a "cursed man" on account of his religion seems an instance of restrained, obligatory, and almost mechanical rhetoric. *Al-Bayān al-mughrib*'s (Ibn ʿIdhārī) turns of phrase in this regard are more specific and critical to the text's perspective on the transfer of office and power from the senior to junior Ibn Naghrīla in Zirid Granada.

If we read *Al-Bayān al-mughrib* carefully we will notice a subtle variation between the text's terse statement regarding the effects of Samuel's term of office and its parallel formulation concerning the consequences of Joseph's incumbency. The first passage speaks of Jewish status and displays of arrogance toward Muslims ("They [the Jews] gained stature during his [Ismāʿīl's] tenure and behaved arrogantly toward the Muslims"). These are offenses against Islam to be sure. But the second excerpt speaks of the Jews' extracting money wrongfully from Muslims, the proliferation of secondary Jewish administrative appointments, and the extraordinary personal benefit Ibn Naghrīla derived in implementing the various aspects of his political program ("He started to improve his situation with enthusiasm. He collected taxes and extracted money *and appointed Jews to all kinds of functions*" [emphasis mine]). The transfer of power from father to son thus reflects the incremental nature in Ibn ʿIdhārī's view of the harm done to Islam during the Ibn Naghrīlas' successive administrations.

The text of Ibn al-Khaṭīb's *Iḥāṭa* encloses the Andalusi Ibn Ḥayyān's seemingly admiring yet ambiguous account with a later, uncompromising thirteenth-century Maghribi source that is arguably more consistent with an Islamic historical judgment on the careers and agenda of the Jewish *wazīrs*. In the third chapter we will encounter a similar textual strategy in two textual segments devoted to Ismāʿīl from Ibn Bassām's twelfth-century *Al-Dhakhīra*, but for now we turn to a related approach to the Ibn Naghrīlas found in another but distinctive eleventh-century Andalusi text.

ʿAbd Allāh b. Buluggīn—*Al-Tibyān*

The third nearly contemporary text we will consider in this chapter takes a very different approach to Ibn Naghrīla. *Al-Tibyān (Exposition on the Downfall of the Zirid Dynasty in Granada)* by ʿAbd Allāh b. Buluggīn, the last *amīr* of Zirid Granada (r. 1073–90), is an autobio-

---

149–50: "Through him, the Jews have become great and proud and arrogant—they, who were among the most abject" *(min al-ardhalīn)* (v. 5); "Put them back where they belong among the lowest of the low" *(asfala l-sāfilīn)* (v. 10); trans. Lewis, 1993, p. 169.

graphical source of sorts noteworthy for the immediacy of its detailed narration and its unusual candor.[72] Deposed and exiled to North Africa (alongside other "party-kings" such as al-Muʿtamid ibn ʿAbbād of Seville) by the Almoravids during the upheavals in al-Andalus at the end of the eleventh century, ʿAbd Allāh composed a revisionist historical memoir in defense of the fallen Zirid dynasty. In the process of bolstering the dynasty's record, the text of *The Tibyān* makes Ismāʿīl out to be a perspicacious political operator who conducts his affairs responsibly in the interests of the Zirid ruler and the Islamic state.

Before we examine several aspects of *The Tibyān*'s portrait of Ismāʿīl, we should establish what we reasonably can claim to know about Ibn Naghrīla's rise in the Zirid state.[73] Following years of service as a *kātib* (secretary) for Abū l-ʿAbbās ibn al-ʿArīf and his son Abū l-Qāsim, *kātib*s (or *wāzir*s) of finance under Ḥabbūs b. Māksan, Ibn Naghrīla drew closer to the *amīr*'s inner circle of advisors and officials. His mentor Abū l-ʿAbbās died and Abū l-Qāsim proved ill equipped for discharging his responsibilities, providing Ismāʿīl with even greater opportunity for advancement. Then, when the *amīr* Ḥabbūs died in 1038, Ibn Naghrīla sided with Bādīs b. Ḥabbūs (r. 1038–1073) over his brother Buluggīn in the matter of succession. Bādīs' succession was secured and under the new *amīr* the Jewish courtier came to play an even more significant and eventually, it appears, central role in the administration of the Zirid state.[74]

Bādīs's confidence in and reliance upon Ismāʿīl only increased as the *amīr* confronted a succession of internal and external threats to his rule. On the internal front, for instance, Bādīs' cousin Yiddīr b. Ḥubāsa had ambitions of his own and never seems to have accepted Bādīs' accession to head of state upon his uncle Ḥabbūs' death.[75] Yiddīr lost no time in scheming (1038) to depose Bādīs, apparently supported in his efforts by disgruntled elements among the Ṣanhāja Berbers. With their backing, Yiddīr supposedly attempted to initiate a coup by murdering Bādīs. But Ibn Naghrīla supposedly came to Bādīs's aid, apparently by duping the

[72] ʿAbd Allāh bin Buluggīn, 1986, pp. 55–77 (Chapters 3 and 4); (Ar. text) ʿAbd Allāh bin Buluggīn, 1955, pp. 30–57.

[73] En route to higher office, Samuel/Ismāʿīl apparently suffered a typical reversal of fortune for a civil servant. The precise details of a temporary demotion are altogether fuzzy. See the Nagid's poems "*Yᵉdidutakh bᵉ-tokh libbi*," Samuel ha-Nagid, 1966, 1:192–94, a reply to a poem by Isaac ibn Khalfūn regarding Samuel's dismissal from a government post, and "*Shᵉmaʿ ha-sar*," Schirmann, 1959–60, 1:150, on the occasion of the Nagid's pardon for whatever may have led to the dismissal.

[74] See Wasserstein, 1989, pp. 197–98.

[75] Yiddīr's father, Ḥubāsa (d. 1012), was Ḥābbus's brother.

conspirators and foiling their plot against the new *amīr*.[76] On the external front, an Andalusi *wazīr* named Aḥmad ibn ʿAbbās of the neighboring *taifa* Almeria was already unremittingly hostile to Ismāʿīl's influence with the Zirids during Ḥabbūs's reign. Ibn ʿAbbās agitated passionately against Bādīs's Jewish associate and ultimately against Bādīs himself. For his part, Zuhayr, the Slav ruler of Almeria, dissolved his alliance with the Zirids and sought to topple Bādīs in order to annex Granada to his own kingdom.[77]

According to *The Tibyān*'s account, Ismāʿīl's resourceful intervention in Yiddīr's conspiracy against Bādīs helped bring down the insurgents. This episode was every bit an instance of political intrigue that was typical for the time and place and for which the principal parties' religious or ethnic identity was secondary. Ibn Naghrīla had acted against Yiddīr and his confederates and against Ibn ʿAbbās and Zuhayr because they were Bādīs's political enemies rather than because they were Muslims. Yet his opponents could, whenever they wished, point to his religious otherness in order to provoke renewed opposition to the *amīr* and his Jewish *wazīr*.[78] For example, the poet Muḥammad ibn ʿAmmār, a boon companion of al-Muʿtamid ibn ʿAbbād, ruler of Seville and another of Bādīs's adversaries, praised his patron by denigrating the Zirids' associations with parties of non-Andalusi origin:

> A people who are considered to be nothing but Jews, though they are called Berbers, have been reduced to nothing by your sword![79]

By the same token, the elder Ibn Naghrīla appears to have earned the lasting trust and admiration of the Zirids, as reflected in *The Tibyān*'s appreciative account of his loyal and invaluable service to ʿAbd Allāh's grandfather Bādīs.

As in *Ṭabaqāt al-umam, The Tibyān* introduces Ismāʿīl respectfully by his Arabic *kunya*:

[76] ʿAbd Allāh bin Buluggīn, 1986, pp. 55–56; (Ar. text) ʿAbd Allāh bin Buluggīn, 1955, p. 31.

[77] For two accounts of the history of the Zirids in Granada including these episodes, see Idris, 1964; and Handler.

[78] The Nagid relates his and Granada's final reckoning with Yiddīr (1041) in two very long poems, "*Sheʾeh mini ʿamiti we-ḥaveri*," Samuel ha-Nagid, 1966, 1:31–34 (no. 7) = Samuel ha-Nagid, 1988, 1:36–40 and "*Leʿvavi be-qirbi ḥam*," Samuel ha-Nagid, 1966, 1:35–38 (no. 9) = Samuel ha-Nagid, 1988, 1:41–44. These lyrics are noteworthy for the way in which they establish a correspondence between the poet's personal adversaries and the enemies of Israel. The literary construction of Muslims in the Nagid's poetry is studied in chapter 4.

[79] "*Adiri l-zujāja*," (l.31), in Aḥmad ibn Muḥammad al-Maqqarī, 1:656; trans. Monroe, p. 192.

> Abū Ibrāhīm the Jew was a secretary to Abū l-ʿAbbās, secretary of Ḥabūs. On the death of Abū l-ʿAbbās, who left a number of sons, Ḥabūs put the eldest in his father's place and employed him in the same capacity. The son of Abū l-ʿAbbās, however, was characterized by a youthful frivolity which made him unsuitable for service with the ruler. And so it was that Abū Ibrāhīm the Jew was able to scheme against him. Devoting himself entirely to the ruler's service. . . . And so Abū Ibrāhīm kept on in this vein until he established his position, and his service and untiring efforts to collect revenue were plain for all to see.[80]

Following this introduction of Ibn Naghrīla and its brief account of how the shrewd and ingratiating Jewish secretary initially caught the *amīr*'s attention, *The Tibyān* relates the events of 1038 and the attempted coup against Bādīs. In this critical episode the opportunistic Ibn Naghrīla is no longer merely an effective servant of the *amīr*; rather he has become indispensable to the economic foundation and political survival of Bādīs's regime:

> Badis was grateful to Abū Ibrāhīm for this and was thus assured of his loyalty and trustworthiness. From that day Abū Ibrāhīm was attached to the service of Bādīs, who in most of his deliberations sought his advice concerning his kinsmen.
>
> The Jew possessed the kind of astuteness and diplomacy that were consonant with the times in which they lived and the people intriguing against them. Badis therefore employed Abū Ibrāhīm because of his utter lack of confidence in anyone else and the hostility of his kinsmen. Moreover, Abū Ibrāhīm was a Jewish *dhimmī* who would not lust after power. Nor was he an Andalusian against whom he needed to be on his guard lest he scheme with non-Berber princes. Bādīs also needed money with which to placate his kinsmen and to maintain his royal position. He therefore simply had to have someone like Abū Ibrāhīm to secure for him the money which he needed to realise his ambitions. *Abū Ibrāhīm, however, was not accorded any power over Muslims in any issue whether right or wrong.* As most of the subjects in Granada as well as the tax-collectors were only Jews, Abū Ibrāhīm would collect money from them and give it to Bādīs. Bādīs would hand over extortionists to an extortionist thereby extracting from them resources with which to fill the treasury, for supplying the

[80] ʿAbd Allāh bin Buluggīn, 1986, p. 55; (Ar. text) ʿAbd Allāh bin Buluggīn, 1955, pp. 30–31.

needs of the kingdom which had a better claim on the money [emphasis mine].[81]

The Tibyān's account of Ibn Naghrīla's role in the affairs of the Zirid state in general and its specific assertions concerning the limits of his political ambition represents a brilliant if transparent piece of political self-justification. The text attempts to offer several interrelated explanations for Bādīs's appointment of the Jewish *wazīr*.[82] We can break down the rationale for Ibn Naghrīla's appointment into four categories. (1) Ibn Naghrīla was inherently worthy for the post of *wazīr*. (2) His appointment brought political and financial benefits to the Zirids and Granada. (3) Bādīs faced a complete lack of reliable alternatives to consider for the roles Ibn Naghrīla played. And mentioned almost as an aside: (4) there was an extraordinary concentration of Jews in Granada who were over-represented in the population. *The Tibyān* goes out of its way to emphasize Ismāʿīl's loyalty, intelligence, and diplomatic gifts as well as the appointment's political and material benefit to the regime. Yet the text would have the reader believe that, whatever its returns, the appointment of the Jewish *wazīr* was a matter of urgent political pragmatism and necessity rather than policy or choice.

Bādīs's hands are represented as tied by "the times in which they lived," that is, the internecine sociopolitical struggles among the Muslims of eleventh-century al-Andalus in general and Granada in particular. The text thus cites opposition to Bādīs's regime from among the Ṣanhāja Berbers ("the hostility of his kinsmen"). It further notes the potential for interference in Granada's internal affairs by representatives of other Andalusi principalities acting in concert with Granadans of Andalusi Muslim families ("Nor was he an Andalusian against whom he needed to be on his guard lest he scheme with non-Berber princes."). These observations are intended to suggest that Ibn Naghrīla was the most capable and safest available candidate for office. The designation of Ibn Naghrīla as *kātib/wazīr* thus appears to be an instance of economic interests and political expediency, perhaps even political survival, dictating policy in clear violation of Islamic law.

It is well known that *dhimmī* appointments of the sort that brought Ibn Naghrīla to power were a salient and enduring characteristic of the politics of the *ṭāʾifa* states.[83] Yet they were not new to Islam in eleventh-

[81] ʿAbd Allāh bin Buluggīn, 1986, p. 56; (Ar. text) ʿAbd Allāh bin Buluggīn, 1955, pp. 31–32.

[82] By Tibi's reckoning (ʿAbd Allāh bin Buluggīn, 1986, p. 207, n. 120), the text offers six such explanations. From the text's point of view the most important of these is that the Jews of Granada were not allied with the Andalusi Muslims.

[83] Wasserstein, 1985, p. 192.

century al-Andalus. There was abundant de facto historical precedent for such appointments in classical Islam, despite the prohibition of Islamic law. From the administrative continuity instituted by the first caliphs to latter ʿAbbasid and Fatimid practices, Muslim rulers regularly "employed Jews, Christians or certain non-Arab clients versed in it (bookkeeping). . . . Afterwards, royal authority flourished. . . . Bookkeeping remained in the hands of clients, Jews, and Christians" in the words of Ibn Khaldūn.[84] As documented in various *fatāwā*, even appointments of a far lesser order than Ibn Naghrīla's could arouse the resentment and outrage of Muslim pietists. A thirteenth-century jurist in the Muslim East responds to a believer's query regarding what a devout Muslim must do when "a Jew has been appointed inspector of coins in the treasury of the Muslims." The jurist's reply could hardly be more definitive:

> It is not permissible to appoint the Jew to such a post, it is not permitted to leave him in it, and it is not permissible to rely on his word in any matter relating to this. The ruler, may God grant him success, will be rewarded for dismissing him and replacing him with a competent Muslim, and anyone who helps procure his dismissal will also be rewarded. . . . you should not adopt outsiders, that is, unbelievers, and allow them to penetrate to your innermost affairs. "They will spare no pains to corrupt you" [Qur'ān 3:114].[85]

The Tibyān goes out of its way to assert and reassert that the Jewish official (Ibn Naghrīla) naturally accepted working within the limits circumscribed for *dhimmī* subjects by Islam: "*Abū Ibrāhīm was a Jewish* dhimmī *who would not lust after power. . . . Abū Ibrāhīm, however, was not accorded any power over Muslims in any issue whether right or wrong* [emphasis mine]."[86] This perspective runs contrary to the Hebrew poetic account of the Nagid's political and military exploits and the extent of his political and financial functions described in other Arabic sources. Yet *The Tibyān*'s disclaimer betrays its unique agenda: It aims to minimize Ibn Naghrīla's role in the highest affairs of state in order to salvage Bādīs's (ʿAbd Allāh's grandfather) sullied reputation as an impious Muslim.[87]

[84] Ibn Khaldūn, 2:8–9 (chapter 3 section 32).

[85] From *Al-Manthūrāt*, by the thirteenth-century *ḥadīth* scholar Muḥyī l-Dīn Yaḥyā ibn Sharaf al-Nawawī, in Goldziher, 1894, p. 94; trans. Lewis, 1984a, 2:228–29.

[86] An interesting parallel to the disparity between the Zirid policy of appointing Jews to executive office and the requirements of Islamic law is the gap between Alfonso X of Castile's practice and the stipulations of the *Siete Partidas*. See Carpenter, 1986, p. 30.

[87] ʿAbd Allāh bin Buluggīn, 1986, p. 211; Ibn al-Khaṭīb, 1956, p. 232.

ʿAbd Allāh mounts additional arguments in defense of the Zirids' Islamic piety as though the dynasty were always in compliance with Muslim sensibilities such as the *muftī* articulates unambiguously in the cited text. *The Tibyān* draws the reader's attention to the supposedly overwhelming Jewish presence in Granada: "As most of the subjects [*raʿāyā*] in Granada as well as the tax collectors [*ʿummāl*] were only Jews, Abū Ibrāhīm would collect money from them and give it to Bādīs."[88] In contrast with *Al-Bayān al-mughrib*, *The Tibyān* here emphasizes that most of the state funds Ismāʿīl ibn Naghrīla raised came directly from Jews, not Muslims. It therefore suggests that Ismāʿīl's exercise of authority was very nearly a function of the internal autonomy Islam grants every Jewish community to manage its affairs in exchange for keeping its provisions of the *dhimma*, including, of course, payment of taxes to the Muslim state. For our purposes, it matters little whether the Jewish residents of eleventh-century Granada actually amounted to a majority of the local citizenry.[89] The significance of *The Tibyān*'s demographic claims lies in its construction of Granada as a virtually Jewish enclave.[90] At this point in *The Tibyān*'s narrative, the figure of Ismāʿīl all but drops out of view as if to authenticate the text's assertions of his limited field of administrative authority and activity. Ismāʿīl is mentioned only two more times,[91] just prior to the report of his death and the transfer of office to his son, Yūsuf.

The Tibyān's portrayal of Yūsuf ibn Naghrīla in the second half of chapter 3 and in chapter 4 is another matter altogether.[92] Unlike his

[88] Tibi (ʿAbd Allāh bin Buluggīn, 1986, p. 206, n. 118) discusses the critical translation of *raʿāyā* (sing. *raʿiyya*) as "subjects."

[89] On that community, see Spivakovsky, which questions the reliability of the traditions characterizing it as a "Jewish town."

[90] From the famous comments of Natronai Gaon, the geographer al-Idrīsī, and Ibn Abī Uṣaybiʿa we learn that Muslims and Jews shared similar traditions regarding the Jewish character and supposed demographic domination of neighboring Lucena (Ar. al-Yussāna). See Ashtor, 1992, 1:308–10, and note 441.

[91] ʿAbd Allāh bin Buluggīn, 1986, p. 60; (Ar. text) ʿAbd Allāh bin Buluggīn, 1955, pp. 36–37.

[92] My interest in the figure of Yūsuf/Joseph in *The Tibyān* is restricted to how he serves as a counterpoint to Ismāʿīl, in large part because of the Andalusi and Maghribi conflation of the two Ibn Naghrīlas after Ibn Bassām's *Al-Dhakhīra* (see chapter 3). Much more could be said about *The Tibyān*'s extensive treatment of Yūsuf. Tibi (ʿAbd Allāh bin Buluggīn, 1986, p. 218, n. 192) neatly sums up the Andalusi criticisms of Yūsuf: (1) he attacked Islam in writing; (2) colluded with Ibn Ṣumādiḥ against Bādīs; (3) he favored the Jews with appointments and thereby extended Jewish power over Muslims; (4) he hoped to establish a state for the Jews in Almeria with himself as ruler; (5) he dominated Bādīs; (6) he sequestered Bādīs from the people and turned him into a hedonist.

worthy and respectable if cunning father,[93] Yūsuf is represented as a completely Machiavellian and rapacious figure without scruples or loyalties. Accordingly, he is excoriated for various misdeeds including his reputed role in Buluggīn b. Bādīs's (ʿAbd Allāh's father and Bādīs's designated heir) death following a drinking bout at Yūsuf's home.[94] This textual opposition between father and son is encapsulated in *The Tibyān* by the very terms it employs for the two figures. Samuel is usually deemed "Abū Ibrāhīm," "Abū Ibrāhīm the Jew," and only infrequently "the Jew." When his death is reported and mentioned a second time, Samuel is accorded a title of respect normally reserved for a communal leader or for a learned religious authority in Islam, "the *shaykh* Abū Ibrāhīm." By contrast, Joseph is never even mentioned by name let alone by his *kunya* or a title of honor but always as "the son of Abū Ibrāhīm," as if to remind the reader of the gap separating the two as well as their connection, or more frequently *dhālika l-yahūdi* ("that Jew") and *al-khinzīr* ("the swine"; "the Jew, swine that he was") just as he is labeled with abusive epithets in Abū Isḥāq al-Ilbīrī's invective.[95] His mention at critical moments of narrative tension also brings forth imprecations such as "May God curse him!"[96] Finally, it is worth noting another significant opposition marking off father from son in the narrative. Ismāʿīl foiled a plot against Bādīs and saved the *amīr*'s life. Yūsuf concocted several plots of his own against Buluggīn, whose life he is said to have taken by poison, and against Bādīs, whom he sought to topple.

Whereas the father is represented as cautiously respecting the boundaries imposed on *dhimmī*s by Islam, the son is portrayed as offering only lip service to this requirement of Islamic law ("I am only a *dhimmī* whose sole ambition is to serve you and collect money for your treasury").[97] In painstaking detail, the narrative relates Yūsuf's various duplicitous intrigues against routinely gullible Muslims (Bādīs; ʿAlī and ʿAbd Allāh ibn al-Qarawī; Buluggīn b. Bādīs; Ibn Ṣumādiḥ) at whose expense he consolidated his power and control over the apparatus of

[93] ʿAbd Allāh bin Buluggīn, 1986, p. 56; (Ar. text) ʿAbd Allāh bin Buluggīn, 1955, p. 32: "Bādīs would hand over extortionists to an extortionist" is nearly the only sour note pertaining to Ismāʿīl and his period of service.

[94] ʿAbd Allāh bin Buluggīn, 1986, p. 63; (Ar. text) ʿAbd Allāh bin Buluggīn, 1955, p. 41.

[95] Chiefly, "ape" (*qird*) (Ibn al-Khaṭīb, 1956, p. 233, ll. 7, 31) in accordance with the well-known Qur'anic topos (2:65–66), on which see Brinner, pp. 235–39; Rubin, 1997; Lichtenstadter; and Viré.

[96] ʿAbd Allāh bin Buluggīn, 1986, p. 66; (Ar. text) ʿAbd Allāh bin Buluggīn, 1955, p. 44.

[97] ʿAbd Allāh bin Buluggīn, 1986, p. 61; (Ar. text) ʿAbd Allāh bin Buluggīn, 1955, p. 38.

the Zirid state. Ismāʿīl is said to have worked in concert with and relied upon two of Bādīs's trusted *wazīrs*, brothers named al-Qarawī ("[A]nd it was their judgement that counted whenever trouble loomed. The *shaykh* Abū Ibrāhīm supported them and counted on their assistance").[98] Yūsuf, however, supposedly manipulated ʿAlī ibn al-Qarawī ("Abū Ibrāhīm's son . . . insinuated himself into ʿAlī's favour by lavishing substantial sums of money upon him") for his own venal designs before turning against him.[99]

Bādīs is said to have endeavored, as he had with Ismāʿīl, to curtail the Jew's range of operations and activities ("Al-Muẓaffar would never allow the Jew to accuse a Muslim of any offence, nor did he place him in a position to do so").[100] But Yūsuf continued to realize his political ambitions through cunning ruses, bribery, pretense, and exploiting the weaknesses of Muslims. *The Tibyān* respects Abū Ibrāhīm's (Ismāʿīl) cunning and savvy as we have seen. Thus, *The Tibyān*'s first references to a Jew's mendacious character and insatiable designs for exercising power over Muslims and lording it over them refer exclusively to Yūsuf ibn Naghrīla: "And so by his boastfulness and mendacity, the Jew gave people the impression that he wielded power. But such power as he had was achieved only by subterfuge and machination."[101] In *The Tibyān*'s construction of events Yūsuf manages to outwait the isolated and aging *amīr* Bādīs and ultimately consolidate power in Granada:

> By this time my grandfather had grown old and more disposed to peace and quiet. With advancing years and the death of his son, he lost all zest for territorial expansion and delegated all powers to the Jew who therefore could exercise just as much authority as he wished.[102]

Yūsuf ibn Naghrīla subsequently hatches a plot with Ibn Ṣumādiḥ of Almeria to wrest control of Granada from the Zirids, with disastrous results for himself and the Jews.

The entire portrait of Yūsuf thus stands in counterpoint to the previous passage devoted to Ismāʿīl. The latter figure's limited aspirations together with his unusual skills and political savvy assured him success

[98] ʿAbd Allāh bin Buluggīn, 1986, p. 60; (Ar. text) ʿAbd Allāh bin Buluggīn, 1955, p. 36. The Qarawīs appear to have been converts to Islam. See Tibi (ʿAbd Allāh bin Buluggīn, 1986, p. 208, n. 126) and the sources cited there.

[99] ʿAbd Allāh bin Buluggīn, 1986, p. 60; (Ar. text) ʿAbd Allāh bin Buluggīn, 1955, p. 37.

[100] Ibid.

[101] Ibid.

[102] ʿAbd Allāh bin Buluggīn, 1986, p. 65; (Ar. text) ʿAbd Allāh bin Buluggīn, 1955, p. 42.

and afforded him longevity at the Zirid court according to the text's reconstruction. By contrast, *The Tibyān* seems to posit that Yūsuf's excessive ambition and haughty character, whatever his administrative qualifications and skill, doomed him during a period of heightened political and religious unrest.[103]

The Tibyān's apologetic denials, rationalizations, and excuses notwithstanding, Bādīs was well known for holding to the policy of relying on non-Muslims to handle many of Granada's affairs of state. The text is in fact much more open and direct in the case of the Christian minister who succeeded Yūsuf in the administration:

> When he could see that they were united against him, al-Muẓaffar, feeling the pressure of these disastrous events and finding no one with whom he could feel comfortable, sent for the Christian Abū l-Rabīʿ.[104]

These Zirid policies are the subject of the lines of passionate and memorable political satire composed by the poet Khalaf b. Faraj al-Sumaysīr of neighboring Almeria (eleventh century). The complaint is reminiscent of Abū Isḥāq al-Ilbīrī's verses directed to the Ṣanhāja as well as the anti-Zirid theme found in the verse of Ibn ʿAmmār.[105] Here is al-Sumaysīr's scatologically minded lyric:

> Every day is worse than the one before;
> urine is replaced by excrement.

[103] There is a story in *The Tibyān* (ʿAbd Allāh bin Buluggīn, 1986, p. 72; [Ar. text] ʿAbd Allāh bin Buluggīn, 1955, p. 51), concerning Yūsuf's zealous sensitivity as a Jew who is above the requirements of the *dhimma*. The tale also involves another confrontation between a Muslim and a Jewish physician in Yūsuf's entourage and speaks to the issues raised in the anecdote related in the introduction:

> One day I was in the presence of al-Muẓaffar who had set out for one of his country houses [*mutanazzahāt*]. He was accompanied by al-Nāya, and the Jew came behind. Spotting a Jewish physician of the *wazīr*'s, al-Nāya ordered him to be subjected to humiliation and to dismount in the presence of the Ruler. Al-Nāya went out of his way to be extremely rude and abused the Jew disgracefully. The Jew [i.e., the *wazīr*] took a serious view of the scene and complained to Ibn Arqam, "There you are, see—I've had enough of this humiliation—I can't stand it any longer. If only you could do something for me I should be only too delighted. But if you can't I shall have no option but to join forces with other princes."

[104] ʿAbd Allāh bin Buluggīn, 1986, p. 84; (Ar. text) ʿAbd Allāh bin Buluggīn, 1955, p. 66.

[105] Text in Ibn al-Khaṭīb, 1956, p. 231 (vv. 3–4); trans. Lewis, 1993, p. 168:

> Your chief has made a mistake
> which delights malicious gloaters.
> He has chosen an infidel as his secretary
> when he could, had he wished, have chosen a believer.

Now, it is becoming Jewish,
  sometimes becoming Christian.
And he [the *amīr*] will incline toward Magians
  if he were granted long life![106]

According to *The Tibyān*'s account of the terrible events of December 1066, the rage of the Andalusi-Muslim street was finally directed against the Jewish population of Granada as a direct consequence of Yūsuf's excesses and his provocations against Islam and the rights of Muslims.[107] Whatever its actual dimensions and causes, the murder of Yūsuf and the ensuing assault on the Jewish community of Granada was a singular event in the history of al-Andalus to whose discursive traces we will turn in the third chapter.[108]

In sum, the eleventh-century representations of Ismāʿīl ibn Naghrīla we have read in this chapter are varied. The texts are evasive in their incomplete reporting of Ismāʿīl's extraordinary powers, restrained in their critique of his exercise of political authority, and sympathetic to the point of being respectful. Ismāʿīl appears to be the embodiment of the pragmatic tolerance concerning which Bernard Lewis writes: "This distinction between a man's religious affiliation, which might be disapproved, and his professional competence, which might be useful, was rarely expressed but often applied."[109] Where circumstances direct Muslim sensibilities to call for textual ire and outrage directed against Ibn Naghrīla, these sentiments are reserved for or displaced entirely onto Yūsuf. Ismāʿīl is left virtually unscathed, a model Jew in the service of the Muslim *amīr* and state.

We have not found a uniform image of the Jew in the Andalusi texts but an inconsistent, mutable, and fluctuating construction of his otherness. Much like the treatment of Jews (and Muslims) set forth in the Alfonsine texts *Siete Partidas* and *Cantigas de Santa Maria*,[110] we

[106] Text in Aḥmad b. Muḥammad al-Silafī, p. 84. The passage in which these lines of verse appear is discussed briefly by Simon. My thanks to Angel Sáenz-Badillos for pointing me to the latter article. Tibi (ʿAbd Allāh bin Buluggīn, 1986, p. 222, n. 218) glosses the poem and thereby censors the scatological imagery.

[107] ʿAbd Allāh bin Buluggīn, 1986, p. 75; (Ar. text) ʿAbd Allāh bin Buluggīn, 1955, p. 54: "All sections of the population from top to bottom had a detestation of the underhanded ways of the Jews and the widespread changes they had wrought for the worse."

[108] Moses ibn ʿEzra', p. 67; Abraham ibn Daud, pp. 56–57 (trans. p. 76). On the entire episode, see Schirmann, 1979, 1:234–45.

[109] See Lewis, 1984a, p. 30, concerning a story (reported by Ibn Qutayba) involving the caliph ʿUmar I, Abū Mūsā the governor of Kūfa, and a Christian secretary.

[110] Carpenter, 1992, p. 63.

have seen that divergent textual strategies for making sense of or objectifying the historical figures signify an unstable construction of the Jew in eleventh-century al-Andalus. In the next two chapters, we will encounter representations of the figure of Ibn Naghrīla involved in political sedition against Andalusi Islam such as *The Tibyān* ascribes to Yūsuf. We will also encounter a new but related motif that is nowhere to be found in the three texts we have studied to this point: Ibn Naghrīla's religious subversion of Islam.

CHAPTER TWO

An Andalusi-Muslim Literary Typology of Jewish Heresy and Sedition

Al-Fiṣal fī l-milal wal-ahwā' wal-niḥal and
Al-Radd ʿalā ibn al-naghrīla al-yahūdī
(ʿAlī ibn Ḥazm)

L'enfer, c'est les autres. —JEAN PAUL SARTRE

The figure of Samuel ibn Naghrīla turns up again in a heresiographical text by Abū Muḥammad ʿAlī ibn Ḥazm (994–1064), the outstanding but highly idiosyncratic Andalusi-Muslim literary and religious intellectual of the eleventh century. Ibn Naghrīla is also taken to be and may well be the suggested subject in another fiercely polemical work by Ibn Ḥazm. Both texts draw a fundamentally different portrait of Ibn Naghrīla than either *Ṭabaqāt al-umam*, Ibn Ḥayyān, or *Al-Tibyān* examined in the previous chapter. They are of interest not only because of their extensive treatment of Samuel and the Jews of eleventh-century al-Andalus but also on account of Ibn Ḥazm's personal acquaintance with the subject of his remarks.

Our primary interest in re-reading the report of an early religious and intellectual encounter between the youthful Ibn Ḥazm and Ibn Naghrīla lies in analyzing the figure of Samuel ibn Naghrīla represented in the Andalusi-Muslim text. We will adopt the same approach in examining the textual tracings of a second purported clash of a literary nature between the two scholars on another occasion. Other students of Ibn Ḥazm and Ibn Naghrīla have already sought to utilize these sources for again and again going over details of Samuel's biography and ʿAlī's checkered career, or to establish what can be known about the turbulent events of eleventh-century al-Andalus.[1] Similarly, we are not principally concerned here with exhaustive analysis of the views of Judaism elaborated in polemical terms by Ibn Ḥazm and other Muslim heresiogra-

My thanks to David J. Wasserstein for his generous critique on an earlier version of this chapter.

[1] For biographical sketches of Samuel, see Schirmann, 1997, pp. 183–204; and 1951, pp. 99–126; Samuel ha-Nagid (Sáenz-Badillos and Targarona), 1988, 1:ix–xli; Levin, 1973, pp. 38–72; and Stern, 1950.

phers. That is likewise a subject studied amply of late.[2] Our concern for Andalusi Muslim views of Judaism rests on how they contribute to the textual idioms Muslims utilize to construe and construct the Jew in a particular cultural environment and at a specific historical moment. That is, we are interested in Muslim views of Judaism insofar as they inform the complex attitudes of Muslims toward Jews in eleventh-century al-Andalus. Our inquiry centers on the significance of these materials as social texts and in the ways traditional Islamic polemical views of Judaism and Jews are inflected in the literary construction of the Andalusi Jew.

During a period of profound social and political unrest shortly after the disintegration of the unified Islamic state in al-Andalus (1013), Ibn Ḥazm and Ibn Naghrīla were forced to flee Cordoba on account of the Berber rioters who sacked the capital. Ibn Ḥazm made his way to Almeria; Ibn Naghrīla sought refuge in Malaga.[3] As had been his practice in Cordoba, Ibn Ḥazm consulted and often debated other Andalusi religious scholars and literary intellectuals, including Jews and Christians. In this way he came into contact with Samuel in 1013, presumably in Almeria. Although no mention of it is made in any contemporary Jewish source,[4] a report of their meeting and debate is preserved in Ibn Ḥazm's monumental heresiography *Al-Fiṣal fī l-milal wal-ahwā' wal-niḥal* (*Book of Opinions on Religions, Sects, and Heresies*). Usually, readers assume this work to have been written between 1027 and 1030, about the time Ibn Ḥazm first abandoned political life, but it may well have been from another period in Ibn Hazm's career. In any case, it incorporates material from another, now lost, polemical work refuting Judaism and Christianity entitled *Iẓhār tabdīl al-yahūd wal-naṣārā lil-*

[2] Wasserstrom, 1985, studies religious polemics between Jews and Muslims, including Ibn Ḥazm. So too, Adang, 1996, and Adang's more narrowly focused 1994 study.

[3] This experience is the subject of the Nagid's lyric "*N^eshamah me-asher tit'aw g^edu'ah*" Samuel ha-Nagid, 1966, 1:209–10 (no. 67); trans. Cole, pp. 5–6.

[4] Polemical materials in general and their specific arguments in particular achieved wide circulation in Iberia among Muslims, Christians, and Jews. For instance, Petrus Alfonsi, an Aragonese-Jewish convert to Christianity who may have known Ibn Ḥazm's writings, employed critical ideas of Muslim origin in his polemics against the Jews. In particular, Alfonsi's *Dialogi contra Judaeos* speaks of rabbinic (as opposed to biblical) Judaism as heretical and blasphemous. See Tolan, 1993, pp. 12–27. It is assumed that Solomon ibn Adret, a thirteenth-century rabbi of Barcelona and purported author of *Ma'amar yishma'e'l*, became acquainted with the substance of Ibn Ḥazm's literary attacks on Samuel the Nagid and the Jews through their dissemination in Christian intellectual circles. See Zucker, and the other sources cited by Lazarus-Yafeh, 1992, p. 6. Camilla Adang's study of *Ma'amar yishma'e'l* is forthcoming in *Judios en tierras de Islam: Intellectuales musulmanes y judios en contacto, al-Andalus y el maghreb*, ed. M. Fierro (Madrid: Casa de Velazquez/Consejo Superior de Investigaciones Cientificas).

tawrāt wal-injīl (*Exposure of Jewish and Christian Falsifications in the Torah and Gospels*).[5]

Al-Fiṣal fī l-milal devotes much of its first and second books to an extended discussion of the respective faults of Judaism and Christianity. This intervention is entitled "the obvious contradictions and clear lies in the book which the Jews call 'Torah' and in others of their books, as well as the four Gospels, which will demonstrate convincingly that they have been corrupted and are different from what Allah, praised be He, has revealed."[6] In more than three hundred pages of acerbic comments in this major subdivision, *Al-Fiṣal* expresses repeated contempt for Judaism and antipathy toward its adherents.[7] The text's disdain for Judaism proceeds from completely familiar Islamic theological objections to the articulation and practice of the other monotheistic tradition. *Al-Fiṣal fī l-milal's* primary objections against Judaism are:

1. the Torah's "unreliable transmission" (*tawātur*) and "textual corruption and alteration" (*taḥrīf/tabdīl*) going back to ʿEzra' the Scribe's initial forgery in postexilic times[8]
2. the Torah's abrogation (*naskh*) by the perfect divine dispensation revealed to Prophet Muḥammad.[9]
3. the Hebrew Bible's manifest anticipation (*aʿlām*) of the Prophet

The Jews are said to have tried desperately (and very nearly successfully) to suppress from their text references and allusions to the Prophet Muḥammad, just as they sought previously to expunge scriptural references to the prophet Jesus.[10] Furthermore, *Al-Fiṣal* discovers

[5] See Perlmann, 1948–49, p. 270. Palacios, 1:5ff., regards *Al-Fiṣal fī l-Milal* as an exercise in "comparative religion." Contrary to Goldziher, 1878, p. 364, Adang, 1966, p. 65, discerns a trajectory in Ibn Ḥazm's attitude toward Judaism and the Jews. In her view *Iẓhār tabdīl al-yahūd* occupies an intermediate position between the more scholarly tone of other materials in *Al-Fiṣal fī l-milal* and the extreme vitriol of *The Refutation (Al-Radd)*. In this case the *Iẓhār* would have been written second and incorporated into the text of *Al-Fiṣal fī l-milal*. David Wasserstein tells me in a personal communication that his forthcoming translation and study of *The Refutation* proposes a different dating of these works than the one that has been assumed since Palacios.

[6] Lazarus-Yafeh, 1992, pp. 26–27.

[7] Perlmann, 1948–49, p. 271, refers to the relevant sections of *Al-Fiṣal fī l-milal* as "the only extensive work written by a Muslim author on the subject; it is the only work of anti-Jewish polemics written by one of the great minds of Islam."

[8] Qur'ān 2:73, "Woe to them who write the scripture with their hands and say: 'this comes from Allah.'"

[9] Qur'ān 2:91, "When they are told, 'Believe in what God has revealed,' they reply: 'we believe in what God has revealed to *us*.' But they deny what has since been revealed, although it is the truth, corroborating their own scriptures."

[10] Qur'ān 7:157, "I will show mercy . . . to those that shall follow the Apostle—the Unlettered Prophet—whom they shall find described in the Torah and the Gospel."

abundant evidence of ideas in the Hebrew Bible (the passages are mostly from Genesis and Exodus) contrary to reason and objectionable to Islam and monotheism as understood by religious intellectuals in the eleventh century (as opposed to Israelite antiquity).[11]

Hava Lazarus-Yafeh classifies *Al-Fiṣal*'s enumeration of the Jews' falsifications of what God actually revealed to them by Moses as (1) chronological inaccuracies (e.g., "I have never seen anyone as ignorant of mathematics as the person who compiled the Torah for them"),[12] (2) theological impossibilities (e.g., "This passage contains an atrocity. . . . It says in this passage that Jacob fought with God. Heaven forbid that God should be compared with His creatures, and far be it from us to think that He would engage in wrestling matches"),[13] and (3) the preposterous or morally offensive behavior of biblical figures whom Islam regards as prophets (e.g., "Marvel at the enormous impiety of these people [the Jews] and at the lies which their forebears fabricated for them concerning God and His prophets").[14]

Al-Fiṣal fī l-milal does not confine its assault on Judaism and the Jews to biblical literature. Ibn Ḥazm's religious sensibility seems even more offended by the rabbis' homiletic literature (*midrash aggadah*), a genre of imaginative religious discourse riddled with countless anthropomorphisms (*tajsīm*) no philosophically minded religious intellectual could accept literally.[15] In this regard it should be recalled that Ibn Ḥazm was a *Ẓāhirī* theologian who rejected esoteric readings of the Qur'ān and *ḥadīth* (traditions of the Prophet), the sacred texts of Islam.[16] *Al-Fiṣal* thus launches an exposé of the Jews' "counterfeit" postbiblical tradition, a collection of theologically absurd materials fabricated by the talmudic rabbis, some of which seem to be criticized already in the Qur'ān.[17]

Qur'ān 61:6, "And of Jesus the son of Mary, who said to the Israelites: 'I am sent forth to you from God to confirm the Torah already revealed, and to give news of an apostle that will come after me whose name is Aḥmad.'"

[11] These polemical issues are studied extensively in Adang, 1996, pp. 184–91, 216–22, 237–48; Pulcini, 1998, and in brief, Powers, pp. 109–121.

[12] Ibn Ḥazm, 1982b, (*Al-Fiṣal fī l-milal wal-ahwā' wal-niḥal*), 1:241.

[13] Ibid., 1:232; trans. Adang, 1996, p. 238.

[14] Lazarus-Yafeh, 1992, pp. 32–34. *Al-Fiṣal fī l-milal*, 1:239; trans. Adang, 1996, pp. 239–40 ("By God, I have never seen a religious community which, while accepting the concept of prophethood, ascribes to its prophets what those infidels ascribe to theirs!"). Adang's classification of the polemical issues *Al-Fiṣal fī l-milal* raises against the Hebrew Bible adds "contradiction between [biblical] passages."

[15] Perlmann, 1948–49, p. 278.

[16] On the Ẓāhirī school and its doctrine, see Goldziher, 1971.

[17] An example of such a critique is Qur'ān 5:64, "The Jews say: 'God's hand is chained.' May their own hands be chained! May they be cursed for what they say! By

Apart from investigating the doctrinal issues *Al-Fiṣal* explores for its own polemical purposes, readers have long been struck by the abrasive manner in which the text transfers rejection of the belief (Judaism) onto the believers themselves (the Jews):

> They, both the ancient and the contemporary, are altogether the worst liars. Though I have encountered many of them, I have never seen among them a seeker [of truth], except two men only.[18]

In this respect, *Al-Fiṣal* (and Ibn Ḥazm's *Refutation*) significantly amplifies the Quranic proof-text regarding the Jews' tendency toward discursive mendacity (Qur'ān 5:41–45 "and those Jews who listen to lies. . . . They tamper with words out of their context. They listen to falsehoods and practice what is unlawful.").[19] For all *Al-Fiṣal*'s reputation for harping on the Jews' deceitfulness, the topos can turn up unexpectedly in Andalusi-Arabic sources. An excursus on astrology in *Al-Tibyān* by ʿAbd Allāh b. Buluggīn includes the following comment on the Jews' liturgical calendar:

> Furthermore, don't the Jews say that they are Saturnians? There is no doubt about this. Don't you see they adopt Saturday as their holiday, which is Saturn's day, and that their character conforms with what Saturn stands for, namely miserliness, dirt, wickedness, cunning and deceit?[20]

---

no means. His hands are both outstretched: He bestows as He will." Halperin, 1988, pp. 467–68, has identified one of the rabbinic sources of this topos with *Lamentations Rabbah* on chapter 2, verse 3. My attention was drawn to Halperin's book by Gordon Newby, p. 59. Many rabbinic homilies in fact represent God as in some way constrained by rabbinic authorities. See, for example, the famous midrash regarding God's response to a halakhic debate between Rabbi Eliezer and Rabbi Joshua (BT *Bava Meṣiʿa'* 59b) in which the rule of the majority of scholars, not a heavenly voice, is said to decide the *halakhah*.

[18] Ibn Ḥazm, 1982b, 1:249; trans. Perlmann, 1948–49, p. 279.

[19] See the similar formulation regarding lying and the Jews in Ibn Hazm ("*Al-Radd ʿalā ibn al-naghrīla al-yahūdī*"), 1981, 3:57 (no. 35): "Realize, o people . . . that the Jews are the most offensive religious community and the one to which lying comes most easily. Of the many I have known in my life I have never met a single one of all those I encountered who avoids vile lying—except for one man." David J. Wasserstein has prepared an English translation of the text of "*Al-Radd*" that is to appear in the *Raphael Loewe Festschrift*, ed. Nicholas de Lange. "*Al-Radd*" has now been translated into Hebrew by Hannah Shemesh in Lazarus-Yafeh, ed. 1996, pp. 83–118.

[20] ʿAbd Allāh bin Buluggīn, 1986, pp. 181–82; (Ar. text) ʿAbd Allāh bin Buluggīn, 1955, pp. 188–89. The passage also comments on the supposed relationship between the Christians' and Muslims' holy days and communal characters. On this medieval astrological tradition, see Shinar and the bibliography cited there. On the Saturnine motif in particular, see Idel.

To give a sense of just how far Ibn Ḥazm extends and magnifies the Quranic topos taken up in Muslim tradition and inherited by Muslim society, consider briefly the treatment it receives by Ibn Khaldūn, the fourteenth-century North African polymath and historian of Andalusi origin. Ibn Khaldūn ascribes the Jews' deceitful conduct mentioned in the Qur'ān to their unique social and political history. He asserts that the Jews have fallen

> under the yoke of tyranny and learned through it the meaning of injustice. . . . One may look at the Jews and the bad character they have acquired, such that they are described in every region and period as having the quality of *khurj*, which according to well-known technical terminology means "insincerity and trickery." The reason is what we have just said.[21]

According to Ibn Khaldūn's historically minded reading of the Qur'ān, the Jews' shortcomings as individuals and as a community are thus socially conditioned acquired traits rather than inherent defects in Jews' "genetic" constitution and character. By contrast, Ibn Ḥazm, much like the fifth chapter of al-Jawbarī's *Kitāb al-muhktār* (cited in the Introduction), essentializes the Jews' faults as the innate and defining vices of the entire religious community throughout their history.

For a heresiographical and polemical text to take issue with doctrinal claims put forward by a rival monotheism and to reject its tradition as invalid is perfectly understandable. That, after all, is the purpose of such a text. In fact, similar rhetorical excesses abound in *Al-Fiṣal fī l-milal's* vitriolic treatment of Christianity and Christians.[22] For instance, Ibn Ḥazm's dispassionate exposé of the inconsistencies found in the four canonical New Testament Gospels leads inexorably from textual critique to condemnation of the religious community possessing that text: "[All this shows that] the [Christian] community is altogether vile."[23] The correspondence in *Al-Fiṣal's* treatment of religious minorities under Islam and their respective doctrines is thus indicative of a trademark polemical style for which Ibn Ḥazm was legendary in Islam.[24]

Vehement polemic and invective was thus not a register Ibn Ḥazm reserved specifically for literary assaults on Judaism and the Jews.

[21] Ibn Khaldūn, 3:306. See Bland.

[22] Pulcini, pp. 134–38.

[23] Ibn Ḥazm, 1982b, 2:74 (*Al-Fiṣal fī l-milal*); Constable, 1997, p. 83. Abu Laila, 1987, p. 111, cites a spirited debate from around 1027–30 (reported in *Al-Fiṣal fī l-milal*, 2:108) between Ibn Ḥazm and a Christian judge and notable of Cordoba. Adang, 1996, p. 254, n. 3, provides a partial listing of the many instances in which *Al-Fiṣal fī l-milal* exhibits abusive epithets for Christians.

[24] See Ibn Khallikān, 3:325–30.

Rather, he tended to confront all of his discursive opponents, including Muslims not belonging to the Ẓāhirī *madhhab* (school of Islamic legal interpretation) such as the Mālikī jurists of al-Andalus, by articulating his arguments in extravagantly hyperbolic and often venomous language. The style in which *Al-Fiṣal* delivers its blanket condemnation of the Jews thus appears to be embraced in Ibn Ḥazm's works as a function of an established but distinctive Arabic discursive form going back to the ʿAbbasid age in the ninth-century Muslim East.[25] For example, *Radd ʿalā l-naṣārā* (*Refutation of the Christians*) by the master essayist al-Jāḥiẓ,[26] is said to be linked as political and religious propaganda to the Caliph al-Mutawakkil's (r. 847–861) policies toward non-Muslim secretaries employed in the state chanceries.[27] The abundance of quotations from al-Jāḥiẓ's works in Andalusi letters points to his powerful stylistic influence in Arabic prose literature.[28] In al-Andalus itself, this style is evident in the famous *Risāla* of Ibn Gharsiyya and its five refutations, texts in which "Arab," that is Andalusi Muslims, and "non-Arab," that is Muslims of "Slav" background, engage in exuberant yet highly learned mudslinging of the scatological kind.[29]

At the same time, our rhetorical sensibility as readers differs markedly from our eleventh-century counterparts. One can appreciate that only a degree of *Al-Fiṣal*'s caustic argumentation against Judaism and its reviling of the Jews can be reasonably attributed to the requirements of the genre or even the author's preferred style. *Al-Fiṣal*'s comments such as, "They are the filthiest and vilest of religious communities, their unbelief horrid, their ignorance abominable," seem to zigzag from social to religious to intellectual denunciation of the Jews and tend to find a conspicuous place as rhetorical flourishes at the end of specific polemical arguments.[30] Ibn Ḥazm's irascible temperament, loss of political of-

[25] See Sadan, 1986, p. 353ff.

[26] Finkel, 1927b.

[27] C. Pellat, 1990, pp. 84–85. See the excerpt from Ṭabarī trans. in Stillman, 1979b, pp. 167–68.

[28] Ch. Pellat, 1956.

[29] *The Shuʿūbiyya in Al-Andalus: The Risala of Ibn Garcia and Five Refutations*, translation, introduction, and notes by James T. Monroe. Nor can we ascribe such discursive practices solely to Muslims. Christian polemical writings against Islam, including Mozarabic writings, resort to a contentious polemical style of their own. See Norman Daniel, 1993, pp. 220–76; and Burman.

[30] Ibn Ḥazm, 1982b (*Al-Fiṣal fī l-milal*), 1:247; trans. Perlmann, 1948–49, p. 279. So, too, *The Refutation* employs various epithets to brand the text's Jewish interlocutor as utterly stupid (e.g., "*Al-Radd*," Ibn Ḥazm, 1981, 3:45 (no. 8) "*hādhā l-māʾiq al-jāhil*"; 48 [no. 14] "*hādhā l-khasīs al-māʾiq*" "this vile dolt") or as unbelieving and ignorant ("*Al-Radd*," 3:50 (no. 19) "*hādhā l-zindīq al-jāhil* "this ignorant heretic"). In *The Refutation* such epithets usually appear at the beginning of a section and introduce

fice and influence, as well as his passionately personal response to the crises of Andalusi-Muslim society and Andalusi Islam all seem to have contributed to his notorious literary attacks on the Jews, Christians, and others with whom he disagreed. Yet, we should not underestimate or dismiss his deeply felt aversion to religions other than Islam. Indeed, Ṣāʿid al-Andalusī, whose comments on Jewish physicians, scientists, philosophers, and literati in *Ṭabaqāt al-umam* have not a hint of religious, political, or social animus, came from the same privileged and erudite background as Ibn Ḥazm, his exceptional teacher.

Beyond their patently rhetorical function and stylistic trademark, what is the substance of *Al-Fiṣal*'s seemingly ad hominem attacks against the Jews? On the face of it, *Al-Fiṣal*'s accusations of Jewish duplicity and assertions of the Jews' filth all seem determined by the textual corruption Islam posits and Ibn Ḥazm finds in the Hebrew Bible. The idea of the Torah's textual inaccuracies (accounting for the apparent rather than real discrepancy between what God gave to Moses and had Muḥammad recite) gives way in numerous instances to charges of the Jews' deliberate tampering with the text. In many cases, they are accused of tampering with God's word to blasphemous effect. For example, regarding the befouled origins and impious and immoral behavior attributed to prophetic figures in the Hebrew Bible, *Al-Fiṣal* exclaims: "God forbid that Moses and Aaron, David and Solomon would come from such birth and this is what necessarily proves that *this [Bible] was invented by a heretic [zindīq] who made fun of [revealed] religion(s)*" (emphasis mine) (Ar. *wa-hādhā yashhadu ḍurūrat[an] annahā min tawlīdi zindīqa mutalāʿib bil-diyānāt*).[31] The Jews' various other forms of error, ignorance, and stupidity evident in their corruption of Scripture are one thing. Unlike these offenses, the Jews' penchant for lying and their inclination for employing impious language, blasphemous images, and sacrilegious motifs in their distorted version of the Torah transforms merely idiotic, errant, or contemptuous beliefs and behavior into an altogether more serious category of offense. Judaism represents an affront to Islam and a danger to Muslim society.

Consider *Al-Fiṣal*'s apprehension of "materialist-atheist" opinions in the biblical Book of Psalms (103:15–16, "his days are as grass, as a flower of the field") and in other biblical and rabbinic writings. This particular accusation is critical to the conjunction of *Al-Fiṣal*'s repudia-

the polemical argument. They serve as a rhetorical link between the scriptural polemics of the work's body and its social and politically minded introduction.

[31] Ibn Ḥazm, 1982b (*Al-Fiṣal fī l-milal*), 1:231; Lazarus-Yafeh, 1992, p. 34. See also the references to the rabbis as "*mustakhafīn bil-dīn*," Ibn Ḥazm, 1982b (*Al-Fiṣal fī l-milal*), 1:320.

tion of Judaism and its revulsion for the Jews in Muslim society. Concerning this Jewish theological transgression, Ibn Ḥazm observes that:

> Indeed, the religion of the Jews tends strongly toward that, for there is not in their Torah any mention of the next world, or of reward after death. . . . *They combine materialism, plurality in deity, anthropomorphism, and every stupidity in the world* [emphasis mine].[32]

Accordingly, *Al-Fiṣal fī l-milal* and the so-called *Refutation of Ismāʿīl ibn Naghrīla, the Jew*, another text authored by Ibn Ḥazm (examined later in this chapter), identify two Jewish physicians and Ibn Ḥazm's unnamed Jewish courtier and adversary in the latter text as *mutadahhirūn* or *min ahl al-dahr* (free-thinking heretics).[33] This branding proves central, rather than incidental, to both texts' construction of the Jews in general.

Who exactly were the *dahriyya* and did their views hold any appeal for Jewish intellectuals during the classical age of Islam? Apparently, the *dahriyya* were "holders of materialist opinions of various kinds, often only vaguely defined."[34] In the Muslim East, Saʿadia Gaon al-Fayyūmī confronts their opinions and refutes their ideas about Creation, referring to the *dahriyya* as "proponents of the eternity of the world,"[35] as does David al-Muqammiṣ, a tenth-century theologian with likely ties to the Karaites.[36] At the turn of the thirteenth century Moses Maimonides defended the monotheistic view of Creation against such ideas, although he does not explicitly mention the doctrine or the group by name.[37]

According to *Al-Fiṣal*, there were essentially three distinct types of religious relativists-agnostics who espoused the doctrine of *dahriyya*. Ibn Ḥazm identifies one type with Ismāʿīl ibn Yūnus al-Aʿwar and another with Ismāʿīl ibn al-Qarrad, the two aforementioned Andalusi-Jewish physicians:

[32] *Al-Fiṣal fī l-milal*, 1:309; trans. Perlmann, 1948–49, p. 279. On the accusation of materialism and anthropomorphism, see Goldziher, 1967–73, 2:173.

[33] Ibn Ḥazm, 1981, (*Al-Radd*) 3:42 (no. 2) ("*min mutadahhirat al-zanādiqa al-mustasirrīn bi-adhall al-milal wa-ardhal al-niḥal min al-yahūd*" [a man who belongs to the "materialist heretics"' who conceal themselves among the most abject of religions and most detestable of religious doctrines, namely Judaism]); French translation by Fierro, 1992a, p. 81.

[34] Goldziher-(Goichon), EI^2, 2:95–97.

[35] Saʿadia Gaon, pp. 39, 75–78, 411.

[36] Stroumsa, 1989, pp. 101, 105, 111, 123, 139. See Wolfson, p. 505.

[37] Moses Maimonides, 1963, 2:282–85 (Chapter 13).

> One group maintains the general equivalence of proofs of everything under dispute. They will neither affirm nor deny the existence of the Creator or of prophecy; nor will they affirm or deny any religion or heterodoxy. They merely say: We are absolutely certain that the truth abides in one of these opinions but that it is not apparent to a single soul, and is neither evident nor discernible at all.
>
> The utterances of Ismāʿīl ibn Yūnus al-Aʿwar, the Jewish physician, are definite indications that he held this view, for he endeavored to support it, though he did not openly profess it.
>
> The second group maintains the equivalence of proofs in matters that do not refer to the Creator. This group affirms the existence of the Creator and concludes that He is certainly and beyond doubt, the real Creator of everything. Beyond that, it neither affirms nor denies prophecy, and neither accepts nor rejects any established religion. . . .
>
> Ismāʿīl ibn al-Qarrad, the Jewish physician, certainly held this view openly when we had a disputation with him. Whenever we invited him to embrace Islam, and sought to dispel his doubts and refute his arguments, he would say: "Conversion from one religion to another is buffoonery."[38]

Apparently, extreme rationalists with relativistic intellectual orientations did not believe it was possible to prove by rational arguments the truthfulness of one revealed religion over others. But they were by no means confined to the ranks of the Jews. Their skepticism resembles opinions attributed to prominent Muslim heretics especially the ninth-century heresiarch Ibn al-Rāwandī who was deemed "the pillar of heresy."[39] In this respect Ibn al-Rāwandī functioned less as an individual with a reputation for embracing a particular heretical outlook or theological error than as a typological figure embodying many intellectual heresies against

[38] Ibn Ḥazm, 1982b (*Al-Fiṣal fī l-milal*), 5:193; trans. Perlmann, 1949–50, pp. 281–82.

[39] Kraemer, 1986, pp. 189–90; Stroumsa, 1987, p. 767; Lewis, 1953, pp. 43–63, reprinted Lewis, 1993, pp. 275–93 as "The Significance of Heresy in Islam." Lewis (p. 285) says that it in later Islamic times, *zindīq* "was generalized to cover all holders of unorthodox, unpopular, and suspect beliefs, *particularly those considered dangerous to the social order and the state*" (emphasis mine). He goes on to observe (p. 287) that *ilḥād* is "more or less synonymous with *zandaqa* in its later more generalized application" and that "in the first few centuries of Islam the *mulḥid*—deviator—is the man who rejects all religion, the atheist, materialist, or rationalist type of the notorious Ibn al-Rāwandī."

Islam, a figure who "attacked revealed religions in general and Islam in particular."[40]

Even if Ibn Ḥazm identified certain Andalusi Jews as harboring ideas heretical to Islam, the reader must question what Muslim heresies such as those attributed to Ibn al-Rāwandī have to do with Judaism. The answer is found in *Al-Fiṣal*'s critique of classical (that is rabbinic) Judaism, which comes at the very end of its lengthy treatment of Judaism:

> God willing, we shall now mention a small part of the many sayings of their rabbis, from whom they have taken their Book and their religion and to whom they trace back the transmission of their Torah, the books of their prophets and all their laws, so that anyone endowed with intelligence can see the extent of their depravity and mendacity, and that it will become clear to him that *they were liars making light of religion* [emphasis mine].[41]

Following the conclusion of its detailed exposé of Jewish falsifications of Scripture, *Al-Fiṣal* goes much further than other polemical texts against Judaism by identifying the intellectual skepticism of religious materialists of classical Islam as the very essence of rabbinic Judaism. In this view, the Talmud was compiled by "[atheist] heretics". "Marvel at and realize that they are heretics; they have no [monotheistic] religion" ("*fa-ʿjabū* Ar. *li-hādhā wa-ʿlamū' annahum mulḥidūn lā dīna lahum*").[42] *Mulḥidūn* (heretics),[43] the Arabic term used here, is derived from the verb *alḥada* that appears in the Qur'ān 7:180 as follows: "God has the Most Excellent Names. Call on Him by His Names and keep away from those that pervert (*yulḥidūna*) them." Discussing the semantic range of *alḥada* and related words in its semantic field, Ian Netton notes that "the Arabic verb *alḥada* has a range of meanings which include 'to deviate from the right course, digress from the straight path; to abandon one's faith, apostasize, become a heretic.' But in the above Quranic

[40] Kraemer, 1982, p. 168.

[41] Ibn Ḥazm, 1982b, *(Al-Fiṣal fī l-milal)*, 1:320 ("*miqdārahum min al-fisq wal-kidhb fa-yalūḥu lahu annahum kā'nū' kadhdhābīn mustakhifīn bil-dīn*"); trans. Adang, 1996, pp. 98–99.

[42] Ibn Ḥazm, 1982b, (*Al-Fiṣal fī l-milal*), 1:325; Perlmann, 1948–49, p. 278. Recall that al-Jawbarī, p. 55, uses identical language to assert that Jewish scholars "have no belief or religion." Jeremy Cohen, p. 355, discusses the views of the thirteenth-century Dominican friar Raymond Martin. Martin assailed the foundation of postbiblical Judaism by deeming the rabbis' notion of a divinely given Oral Torah "nothing other than the insanity of a ruined mind." To this citation, Cohen glosses, "a mind that has willfully opted for the false over the true."

[43] See Corriente, p. 477 (*l-ḥ-d*), and Dozy, 1967, 2:518 ("*jaʿalū' yulḥidūna fī amrihi*" = "ils se mirent a abanner son parti").

quotation it is quite clear it is blasphemy which is intended by this verb." Netton further observes that because "such nouns as *kufr* (unbelief), *shirk* (polytheism), and *ilḥād* (heresy) share a common semantic field"[44] pinpointing their usage (to say nothing of translation) is inexact and often extremely difficult.[45]

Sarah Stroumsa outlines the same semantic field somewhat differently:

> In Islamic heresiographical literature heretics of all shades and colors were labeled rather loosely as *zanādiqa* (sing. *zindīq*), a term which could refer to dualists (especially Manicheans) as well as to philosophers or theologians whose doctrinal audacity irked their *bien pensants* Muslim adversaries. Another term, *malāḥida* (sing. *mulḥid*), was sometimes used more specifically to denote apostates or heretics who radically opposed the contemporaneous idea of religiosity. According to the muʿtazili scholar Zamaḫšarī (d. 539/1144), for example, a person was labeled a *mulḥid* not when he abandoned one religion for the sake of another, but only when he adopted a system which deviated from all religions. But *mulḥid* was also used more vaguely, to designate other kinds of religious deviations, or as a synonym of *zindīq*.[46]

Al-Fiṣal's allegations of Jewish *zandaqa*, its references to the rabbis as *mulḥidūn* in general and to the Andalusi Jews' espousal of *dahriyya* in particular, effectively connect the Jews and Judaism to intellectual heresies against Islam attributed to figures such as Ibn al-Rāwandī. In this respect, it certainly helped that traditions surrounding Ibn al-Rāwandī from the Muslim East relate of the heresiarch's purported conspiracy with a certain Jew named Ibn Lāwī or alternately of his father's allegedly Jewish origins.[47]

To return to Ibn Ḥazm and the rabbis of classical Judaism: Among other affronts to religion, the rabbis of late antiquity were responsible for corrupting Paul of Tarsus. Specifically, they induced him into professing the divinity of Jesus (*"ittafaqū ʿalā an rashaw' būlas al-binyāmīnī laʿanahu llāh wa-amarūhu bi-ẓhāri dīni ʿīsā ʿalayhi l-salām*; "they agreed

[44] Netton, pp. 3–5. However, Arberry, 1986, p. 193, translates the same Quranic passage as "leave those who *blaspheme* His Names." In *Blasphemy: Verbal Offense against the Sacred, from Moses to Salman Rushdie*, p. 31, Levy observes a nearly identical semantic shift and conceptual link in Christendom between blasphemy, a verbal offense against God, and heresy, a deviation from correct belief that is an offense against society and its religious establishment.

[45] See Madelung, *EI*², 5:546, where *mulḥid* is likewise defined as "deviator, apostate, heretic, and atheist."

[46] Stroumsa, 1999, p. 5, and the sources cited there.

[47] Ibid., pp. 75; 198, and the sources cited there.

Rabbis Bribed Paul to propogate divinity of Jesus

to bribe Paul the Benjaminite, may God curse him, and charged him with propagating the religion of Jesus, peace be upon him").[48] The Jews thereby exercised a subversive influence upon the very formulation of Christianity and are ultimately accountable for introducing the single most important doctrine separating Christian error from Muslim truth. Even more to the point for *Al-Fiṣal*'s contemporary Andalusi-Muslim audience, the rabbis' successors continued to practice sedition of the religious kind when Islam appeared on the historical scene. According to *Al-Fiṣal* (following a well-entrenched Sunni tradition), ʿAbd Allāh ibn Saba', a Jewish convert from the Yemen, sought to undermine Islam from within its very ranks.[49] He supposedly introduced the Shīʿa to Islam and taught the extremist doctrines (*ghulāt*) some of that group's radical adherents espouse. Notable among the extravagant ideas of some Shīʿa was the divinity of ʿAlī (the prophet's cousin and son-in-law and the fourth caliph).[50]

In the larger scheme of Islamic heresiography, ʿAbd Allāh ibn Saba', like Ibn al-Rāwandī, is far from a solitary, subversive heresiarch operating freely within Islam while maintaining close ties to the Jews. A longstanding practice of the discipline of Islamic heresiography and a standard feature of its literary genre attributes to Jewish figures various heresies *within* Islam. Steven Wasserstrom observes that "it would be difficult to find a Muslim heresy that was not at one time or another traced back to a Jewish originator. Thus, to cite only a few, the origination of Ismaʿilism was ascribed to Maymun al-Qaddah; the Fatimids were said to have been further inspired by Yaʿqub ibn Killis; the idea of a Created Qur'an was ascribed to Labid; and the heretic Jahm ibn Saf-

Jews responsible for every heresy

---

[48] Ibn Ḥazm, 1982b *(Al-Fiṣal fī l-milal)*, 1:325. See Perlmann, 1948–49, p. 278; Adang, 1996, p. 105.

[49] Ibn Ḥazm, 1982b *(Al-Fiṣal fī l-milal)*, 1:325–26; Hodgson, *EI²*, 1: 51.

[50] Ibn Ḥazm, 1982b *(Al-Fiṣal fī l-milal)*, 1:325–26; Perlmann, 1948–49, p. 278. In this respect, the figure of ʿAbd Allāh ibn Saba' stands very nearly opposite that of ʿAbd Allāh ibn Salām (d. 664), a prominent Arabian Jewish convert to Islam whom tradition accorded the status of a Companion of the Prophet. Whereas Sunnī traditions portray the former as a seditious force in early Islam, Muslim sources depict the latter as a font of Islamicized monotheistic lore akin to Kaʿb al-Aḥbār and Wahb b. Munabbih. See Guillaume, pp. 240–41; Ibn al-Nadīm, 1:42; Horovitz, *EI²*, 1:52. On this aspect of ʿAbd Allāh ibn Salām, see Wasserstrom, 1995, pp. 175–80. And yet, as we observed briefly in the previous chapter, figures such as Kaʿb al-Aḥbār and Wahb ibn Munabbih must be regarded as unstable figures in Islam. Some authorities embraced them and the traditions reported in their name and therefore viewed them as paradigmatic early Jewish converts to Islam. However, other Muslim traditionists regarded them and their traditions with suspicion or as typological models of subversives internal to Islam.

wan was said to have been taught by Aban b. Maymun who was taught by Talut b. Aʿsam, 'the Jew who bewitched Muhammad.'"[51]

The canonical biographies of the Prophet and the major works of Islamic historiography provide extensive narratives of Muḥammad's increasingly hostile relations with various Jewish adversaries in Medina after 622. Muḥammad and the nascent *umma*'s struggle with the three main Jewish tribes of Yathrib/Medina and their Arab confederates in fact informs many of the Medinese *sūra*s of the Qur'ān. Among their alleged affronts to the Prophet and challenges to his authority, the Jews purportedly encouraged the Medinese "hypocrites" (*munāfiqūn*) among their Arab allies to renounce the Islam they had adopted out of political convenience.[52] So, too, a Jew who is said to have bewitched Muḥammad of his male potency (or alternately, the Jew whose daughters bewitched the Prophet) is identified as Labīd b. Aʿsam. Since Labīd is sometimes labeled a "hypocrite" (*munāfiq*), suggesting that he was a convert to Islam, the sources place him variously inside and outside the community of Muslims.[53] Such narratives established the Jew as a truly problematic figure in early Islam. And by virtue of the Jews' collective presence and influence in Medina and the role they initially played as part of the Medinese *umma*, Islam transformed the Jew from *an associate to an outsider*. The Jew thus became a figure critical to the delineation of social, political, and religious boundaries in Islam and a potential source of political sedition and/or religious subversion.

The interface of religious, social, and political issues dividing Muslims and Jews suggested in our texts goes back to the ways in which Muslims remembered the events of seventh-century Medina and the Prophet's complex encounter with the Jews of that oasis town. Quranic proof-texts cautioning Muslims to avoid fraternizing with non-Muslims, in particular Qur'ān 3:118, doubtlessly reflect the Prophet's struggle against the political alliance of Medinese Jews and the so-called Hypocrites (*munāfiqūn*) whose embrace of Islam was conditional and temporary.[54] To *Al-Fiṣal*'s Andalusi Muslim audience, the following

[51] Wasserstrom, 1995, pp. 157–58, and the sources cited there.

[52] Guillaume, p. 239, "But in secret they were hypocrites whose inclination was towards the Jews because they considered the apostle a liar and strove against Islam." The *Sīra of the Prophet* further relates, pp. 239–40: "It was the Jewish rabbis who used to annoy the Prophet with questions and introduce confusion, so as to confound the truth with falsity. . . . The first hundred verses of the Sura of the Cow came down in reference to these Jewish rabbis and the hypocrites of the Aws and Khazraj, according to what I have been told, and God knows best."

[53] Guillaume, p. 240. See Lecker.

[54] Kister, 1986, pp. 61–96, especially p. 88.

Quranic passages would also seem to speak directly to the sinister religious influence non-Muslims exert over the community of believers:

> Believers, do not make friends with any but your own people. They will spare no pains to corrupt you. They desire nothing but your ruin. Their hatred is evident from what they utter with their mouths, but greater is the hatred which their breasts conceal. (3:118)[55]

> Many among the people of the Book wish, through envy, to lead you back to unbelief, now that you have embraced the Faith and the truth has been made plain to them. (2:109)

Qur'ān 5:51–56 further addresses the seductive appeal Christians and Jews hold for the weakest elements among Muslims. The latter scurry to curry the favor of the non-Muslims who in turn demean and mock Islam with apparent impunity:

> Believers, take neither the Jews nor the Christians for your friends [Ar. *awliyā'*] They are friends with one another. Whoever of you seeks their friendship *shall become one of their number. . . . You see the fainthearted hastening to woo them. . . .*

> Believers, do not seek the friendship of the infidels and those who were given the Book before you, *who have made of your religion a jest and a pastime* [emphasis mine].[56]

Several of the Andalusi texts within our field of view invoke this salient topos of Muslim polemics. *Al-Fiṣal fī l-milal* assails the Jews' scripture by noting that "*this [Bible] was invented by a heretic [zindīq] who made fun of religion*[s]") (emphasis mine).[57] *The Refutation* expresses the hope "that God the Exalted will hold sway over whoever takes Jews as associates and befriends them and makes them intimates of their entourage."[58] And Abū Isḥāq al-Ilbīrī's invective forewarns the Zirids of Granada, "Go, tell all the Ṣanhāja. . . . Your chief has made a mis-

[55] This is the Quranic proof-text brought by Al-Nawawī, *Al-Manthūrāt*, cited in chapter 1, pp. 72 and 73, n. 85.

[56] So, too, Guillaume, p. 246, "These hypocrites [Jewish rabbis who took refuge in Islam] used to assemble in the mosque and listen to the stories of the Muslims *and laugh and scoff at their religion*."

[57] Lazarus-Yafeh, 1992, p. 34. Ibn Ḥazm, n.d. (*Al-Fiṣal fī l-milal*), 1:231.

[58] Ibn Ḥazm, 1981 ("*Al-Radd*"), 3:67 (no. 61): "My hope is strong, my expectation reinforced that God the Exalted will hold sway over whoever takes Jews as associates and befriends them and makes them intimates of their entourage, just as He prevailed over the Jews [in the past]. Let them hear the word of God [Qur'ān 5:51, 3:105, 60:1]."

take / which delights malicious gloaters. . . . He *laughs at us and our religion*" (emphasis mine).[59]

Following these Quranic injunctions, Muslim scholars sought to draw a clear line of ritual differentiation between Islam and its rival monotheistic religions, to delineate certain socioreligious boundaries between Muslims and non-Muslims as a means of self-definition and to root out supposedly Christian and Jewish "influences."[60] Later, when Islam was well established, the religious practices of some Muslims that were considered undesirable could always be censured by attributing their origins to Jewish customs or beliefs. Alleged associations with Judaism were thus turned into a vehicle for intra-Muslim polemics. There is a time-honored Sunnī tradition of ascribing certain Shīʿī convictions to a supposed connection between the Shīʿa and the Jews, one that is reflected in *Al-Fiṣal*'s aforementioned comments regarding ʿAbd Allāh ibn Saba'.[61] Ibn Ḥazm also expressed concern in his legal writings about supposed Jewish "influence" on the practice of certain Islamic religious rites of the Mālikī *madhhab* that was predominant in al-Andalus.[62]

Curiously, Ibn Ḥazm would have his readers believe that his feelings toward non-Muslims were more uniformly hostile than he seems to have displayed toward them in his many apparently cordial social encounters and interactions. Consider anecdotal remarks such as we read in Ibn Ḥazm's reports about the Jewish physicians (and to a certain extent about Ibn Naghrīla himself). These suggest that on the personal level Ibn Ḥazm practiced the Quranic injunction, "Be courteous when you argue with the People of the Book, except with those among them who do evil. Say: 'We believe in that which is revealed to us and which was revealed to you. Our God and your God is one. To Him we surrender ourselves' (Qur'ān 29:46)." For these associations and other relationships Ibn Hazm maintained with Andalusi Jews as well as his excessive and misplaced interest in their scripture, ʿAlī's apparently competitive and religiously minded cousin Abū l-Mughīra ʿAbd al-Wahhāb (d. 1029) supposedly took him to task and questioned his Islamic piety.[63]

[59] Text in Ibn al-Khaṭīb, 1956, pp. 231–33; trans. Lewis, 1993, pp. 167–74.

[60] Kister, 1989.

[61] See Steven Wasserstrom, 1994. Of course, such maneuvers were by no means confined to the ranks of Muslims and Islam. Levy, p. 43, notes that Athanasius, bishop of Alexandria at the time of the Nicea Council and the promulgation of the Nicene Creed, describes his adversaries as "Arian heretics" or, synonymously, as "Jewish blasphemers." Athanaius labeled interchangeably those with whom he disagreed as "Jews," "heathens," "antichrists," and "blasphemers."

[62] Adang, 1995.

[63] Ibn Bassām, 1:163.

Al-Fiṣal fī milal amplifies greatly these paradigmatic, traditional associations of Jews with subversion against Islam. Following a structure of Muslim thought established early in Islam, the text collapses any meaningful distinction between the religious danger the Jew presents to Muslims because of his heretical views (*irtidād* = apostasy) and his political insubordination against Muslim society and the sovereign authority of Islam (*ridda*).[64] This sociopolitical and religious construct is articulated even more sharply in *The Refutation* (on which see below) and was absorbed subsequently from Ibn Ḥazm's works by the Maghribi historiographical literature on the Ibn Naghrīlas studied in the next chapter.

Among its comments on Judaism in general and its exposé of the manifold defects of the Hebrew Bible in particular, *Al-Fiṣal fī l-milal* uncovers the intellectual foibles of Jewish scholars Ibn Ḥazm heard defend their "corrupted" scripture. In one of many textual riffs on the baseness and idiocy of the Jews, *Al-Fiṣal* introduces Ibn Naghrīla as "the most knowledgeable and the most accomplished debater among the Jews [*aʿlamuhum wa-ajdaluhum*], Ismāʿīl b. Yūsuf the Levite, the secretary (*al-kātib*)."[65] It is scarcely surprising that Ibn Ḥazm would acknowledge Samuel's merits in the context of this report, if only because so excellent a disputant as ʿAlī surely deserved to be matched against an intellectually worthy though religiously misguided opponent. Furthermore, the reader cannot help but be impressed by the relative ease with which Ibn Ḥazm appears to vanquish even his most learned interlocutor among the Jews. This is not *Al-Fiṣal*'s only passage apparently excepting individual Jews from its otherwise blanket condemnation of the Jewish character.[66] Elsewhere, *Al-Fiṣal* speaks of the tenth-century rabbinic polymath Saʿadia al-Fayyūmī (Gaon) and other learned Jews of the Muslim East as astute dialectical theologians.[67] And it concedes a measure of genuine intellectual respect to Ibn Ḥazm's two Jewish informants and disputants from his days in Almeria, whom he identified as adherents of the *dahriyya*. An anecdote related in *Ṭawq*

[64] Levtzion, pp. 6–7.

[65] Ibn Ḥazm, 1982b (*Al-Fiṣal fī l-milal*), 1:245. Lazarus-Yafeh translates "*al-kātib*" in this passage as "famous author" but I think it makes more sense to read the passage as identifying Ibn Naghrīla according to the standing by which the wider Andalusi-Muslim audience would best know him, that is, as a scribe or secretary.

[66] Perlmann, 1987, 11:396, characterizes the encounter very differently: "They met when they were in their early twenties, but the meeting was not conducive to mutual respect and appreciation."

[67] Ibn Ḥazm, 1982b (*Al-Fiṣal fī l-milal*), 3:207 ("*Naʿm wa-yuʾtīhim al-qūwa wal-tadqīq fī l-fahm kal-fayyūmī saʿīd bin yūsuf*"). See Adang, pp. 106–107.

al-ḥamāma fī l-ulfa wal-ullāf (*The Ring of the Dove on Companions and Companionship*), Ibn Ḥazm's famous treatise on the manners and psychology of love, further accords Ismāʿīl ibn Yūnus al-Aʿwar respect as a physician and physiognomist with whom he kept company. There is no trace of disdain for al-Aʿwar as a *mutadabbir*:

> I was seated one day in Almeria at the shop of Ismāʿīl ibn Yūnus, the Jewish physician who was also a shrewd and clever physiognomist. *We were engaged in a social gathering* [*wa-kunna fī l-lamma*] when Mujāhid ibn al-Hasīn al-Qaisī said to him, pointing to a certain man named Hatim—he was familiarly known as Abū l-Baqa'—who was withdrawn from the rest of us, "What do you say about this man?" He [Ismāʿīl] looked at him for a brief moment, and then said, "he is passionately in love." Mujāhid exclaimed, "You are right; what made you say this?" Ismāʿīl answered, "Because of an extreme confusion apparent in his face. Simply that; otherwise all the rest of his movements are unremarkable. I knew from this that he is in love, and not suffering from any mental disorder."[68]

Ibn Ḥazm's reports of convivial relationships and courteous encounters with Andalusi Jews did not deter his expression of profound hostility for their religious community. Aside from its imputations of religious insolence and blasphemous language and motifs in the Hebrew Bible that render the Jews loathsome to Muslim society, there is another way to read *Al-Fiṣal*'s disdain for their religious community. By labeling as mendacious all but two Jews, "ancient and contemporary," *Al-Fiṣal* in effect renders their written and spoken discourse as irritating, perhaps even troubling, but undeserving of serious attention. It thus serves to dismiss and silence the Jews and to marginalize Ibn Naghrīla ("the most knowledgeable and the most accomplished debater among the Jews") as unrepresentative of his religious and textual community. An even more blunt articulation of this polemical and rhetorical strategy is *Ifḥām al-yahūd* (*Silencing the Jews*), a tract by Samau'al al-Maghribī, a twelfth-century Jewish convert to Islam residing in the Muslim East but also of Andalusi background.[69] Moses Maimonides, a refugee from Almohad persecution in al-Andalus and North Africa, testifies to the resonance and reality of this topos in Jewish experience. His famous *Epistle*

[68] Ibn Ḥazm, 1986 (*Ṭawq al-ḥamāma fī l-ulfa wal-ullāf*), p. 67. I have modified slightly the translation of Arberry, 1953, p. 45.

[69] Samau'al al-Maghribī. The elaboration of this motif in a twelfth-century imaginative Jewish text is studied in chapter 5.

to Yemen expressly counsels the Jewish community "to bear its suffering [under Islam] *in silence* [my emphasis]."[70]

Al-Fiṣal's account of one of Ibn Ḥazm and Ibn Naghrīla's apparent disputations speaks directly to a pious Muslim's satisfaction in silencing his Jewish opponent. The passage concerns a longstanding crux (since explained by ancient Near Eastern cognate usage) of Gen. 20:12 wherein Abraham marries his "sister" ("the daughter of my father") Sarah. For Ibn Ḥazm, the literal sense of the tale is degrading to the prophet Abraham who would, of course, never commit incest or any other moral offense. Ibn Naghrīla is said to argue for a less than literal reading of the biblical passage but is deftly countered by Ibn Hazm who concludes the report: "With that my adversary *became upset and said nothing more* [Ar. *fa-khuliṭa wa-lam ya'ti bi-shai'[in]*] [my emphasis]."[71] A similar encounter between Ibn Ḥazm and an unidentified Jew also reported in *Al-Fiṣal* concerns the story of Judah's adultery with Tamar in Gen. 38 (an illicit union from which the Islamic prophets David and Solomon would ultimately descend). *Al-Fiṣal*'s report of this discussion likewise concludes with a dismissive rhetorical clincher: The Jewish interlocutor turns *quiet and morose*, defeated utterly by the powerful argument of his Muslim adversary ("*fa-sakata khazyān kāliḥ[an]*" "he lapsed into silence, shamefaced and sullen").[72]

One of the crucial points of engagement in the literary report of Ibn Ḥazm's debate with Ibn Naghrīla brings the political subtext of *Al-Fiṣal*'s anti-Jewish discourse into sharper focus. It is the famous discussion regarding the historical significance of Gen. 49:10 ("The scepter shall not depart from Judah, nor the ruler's staff from between his feet till Shiloh [i.e., 'tribute'] come [to him]").[73] Ibn Ḥazm's account appears in the subchapter entitled "The Torah Foretells the Conferring of Authority to Judah's Descendants." *Al-Fiṣal*'s critique of the pertinent biblical passages emphasizes the Jews' historic *loss of sovereignty*:

[70] Moses Maimonides, 1952, p. 96; trans. in Abraham Halkin, 1985, p. 127. As Goitein observed, 1967–93, 2:284, "Worship of the non-Muslim denominations under Islam had to be inconspicuous." Strictly speaking, the Pact of ʿUmar expresses the Christians' acceptance of conditions imposed upon them while living under Islam. But the same stipulations were also applied to the Jews of Islam. The document states, "We shall not display our crosses or our books in the roads or markets of Muslims. We shall only use our clappers in our churches very softly. We shall not raise our voices in our church services or in the presence of Muslims, nor shall we raise our voices when following our dead." Trans. Lewis, 1993, p. 218.

[71] Ibn Ḥazm, 1982b (*Al-Fiṣal fī l-milal*), 1:225. The details of this polemic are discussed by Adang, 1996, p. 219.

[72] Ibn Ḥazm, 1982b (*Al-Fiṣal fī l-milal*), 1:238–39. Pulcini, pp. 61–62, discusses the details of this polemic.

[73] Ibn Ḥazm, 1982b (*Al-Fiṣal fī l-milal*), 1:245.

> This verse is untrue because the scepter departed from Judah and leaders from his offspring,[74] but the One sent [*al-mabʿūth*], whom they await, did not come. The kingdom of Judah found its end in the time of Nebuchadnezzar more than one thousand five hundred years ago, except for a short time only under Zerubavel b. She'altiel. I have repeated this passage to one of the Jews' most learned polemicists, namely Ishmū'āl b. Yūsuf al-Lāwī, the famous author known as Ibn al-Naghrāl, in the year 404 A.H.[1013]. And he said to me: "The Exilarchs [*ru'ūs al-djawālit*] are the offspring of David and from the sons of Judah and they have leadership and kingdom and authority in our days." But I told him: "This is a mistake, because the Exilarch cannot exert power on the Jews or on anybody else and it is therefore a title only, but no reality."[75]

The literary report of this discussion in fact proved critical to future polemical efforts Muslims (and Christians) undertook against the Jews and their particular aspirations for communal redemption. The seventeenth-century Morisco text *Kitāb Nāṣir al-Dīn ʿalā 'l-Qawm al-Kāfirīn* [*The Supporter of Religion against the Infidel*] by Ahmad ibn Qāsim al-Ḥajarī (d. after 1640), for example, broadens *Al-Fiṣal*'s historically-minded critique of the idea of any temporal Jewish authority:

> In the first book of the Old Testament, in Chapter Forty-Seven, it is said that our lord Jacob used to mention to his sons what would happen to them in this world. He said about the Jews: "They will rule and be in authority in this world until Shiluh comes." The Christians say that Shiluh was our lord Jesus-peace be upon him!—but the truth is that they held the kingship for more than forty years after him. In reality, it did not stop completely until the Prophet came—may God bless him and grant him peace!—because they waged war and committed evil against him in Khaybar. After that no war of the Jews against anyone is mentioned any longer.[76]

Samau'al al-Maghribī's interpretation of the biblical verse in *Ifḥām al-yahūd* differs markedly from Ibn Ḥazm, addressing principally the mes-

[74] This passage avers that leadership of the Jews ("leaders from his offspring") departed from the House of David. But in a passage devoted to Israelite genealogy in *Jamharat ansāb al-ʿarab (Geneaology of the Arabs)*, 1982, p. 506, Ibn Ḥazm asserts that the leaders of the Jews down to his day and age do indeed descend from David.

[75] Ibn Ḥazm, 1982b (*Al-Fiṣal fī l-milal*), 1:245–46; trans. Lazarus-Yafeh, 1992, pp. 98–99. Ironically, Samuel the Nagid, following Ḥasdai ibn Shapruṭ, seems to have been partly responsible for moving the Jews of al-Andalus away from dependence upon (if not allegiance to) the Eastern rabbinical authorities. See Horowitz.

[76] Aḥmad ibn Qāsim al-Ḥajarī, pp. 170–71.

sianic-religious as opposed to messianic-political significance of the prophetic verse.[77]

For the Jews of al-Andalus as elsewhere, belief in the uninterrupted continuity of the "House of David" was a necessary and certain article of faith. Seemingly relegated to the margins of a political history dominated by Islam and Christendom, the Jews at least could look to the figure of the Exilarch or "Head of the Exile" (Heb. *ro'sh ha-golah*; Aram. *re'sh galuta'*; Ar. *rā's jālūt*). The dignity of this office and figure provided them a sign of hope in the biblical messianic promises of their eventual political restoration (recorded in the Hebrew Bible).[78] Benjamin of Tudela's (twelfth-century) account of his visit to Baghdad is also indicative of the symbolic investment Jews placed in the figure of the Exilarch. In this blend of realia and fantasy we find a vivid depiction of the dignity of the *ro'sh ha-golah*. The Muslims of Baghdad, for whom the biblical David is a venerable prophet, pay tribute to the Exilarch referring to him as "*sayyidnā bin dāwūd*."[79] According to Benjamin's imaginative reconstruction, the ceremonious recognition of the Exilarch as a genuine sovereign and equal at the caliph's court represents the literal realization of the biblical prophecy voided by Ibn Ḥazm. Here Benjamin offers words of encouragement for the manifestly disempowered Jews of his age:

> And the Head of the Captivity is seated on his throne opposite the Caliph, in compliance with the command of Muhammad, to give effect to what is written in the Law—"The scepter shall not depart from Judah."[80]

Benjamin of Tudela's message of comfort notwithstanding, Ibn Ḥazm was correct in assessing the actual authority of the Exilarch during the eleventh century. As S. D. Goitein has shown, the Exilarch's power, like the caliph's, had long since declined. The *ro'sh ha-golah* was reduced to little more than an ecumenical figurehead and limited to dispensing honorific titles.[81] Real communal authority rested in the hands of the Talmudic academies and their heads, the *g^{e}onim*. Ibn Ḥazm's rejoinder to Samuel concerning the Exilarch goes further still,

[77] Samau'al al-Maghribī, text, p. 23; trans., pp. 41–42.

[78] On the history of this office during the High Middle Ages, see Grossman, 1984.

[79] Benjamin of Tudela, ff. 61–63 (Engl. trans., pp. 39–41).

[80] Benjamin of Tudela, *Sefer massaʿot*, f. 62; (Engl. trans., p. 40). For a discussion of Benjamin's world and his message of consolation, see the introduction by Signer, pp. 13–33.

[81] Goitein, 1967–93, 2:17ff. On Muslim attitudes toward the Exilarch, see Goldziher, 1884; Fischel, 1938; and on the specifically Shīʿī interest in this figure, Wasserstrom, 1994.

stripping the Jews of even the appearance of temporal power and wresting from them the semblance of hope for the future.[82] We should be careful not to make too much of the apparent distinction between the political and religious issues dividing Andalusi Muslims and Jews raised in *Al-Fiṣal*. As we shall see in examining aspects of Ibn Ḥazm's *Refutation* and in the next chapter treating *Al-Dhakhīra fī maḥāsin ahl al-jazīra* by Ibn Bassām, for Muslims and Islam the political is nearly always grounded in and informed by the religious. Perhaps the reader can sense in Ibn Ḥazm's rejection of the chain of symbolic Jewish political authority a sign of an Andalusi-Muslim's dismay over the demise of the Umayyad caliphate in the eleventh century and his profound disgust at the pathetic succession of Umayyad pretenders to that once dignified office.[83]

What of the other text in which Ibn Ḥazm mounts a frontal assault against Judaism, the Jews, and an unnamed opponent bearing a certain resemblance to Ismāʿīl ibn Naghrīla? A comparison of the representation of Ibn Naghrīla in *Al-Fiṣal fī l-milal* with the figure of Ibn Ḥazm's literary adversary in the so-called *Radd ʿalā ibn al-naghrīla al-yahūdī* (*The Refutation of Ibn Naghrila, the Jew*, hereafter *The Refutation*) is instructive. The reader finds no ambiguity or contradiction in *The Refutation* between the articulation of Ibn Ḥazm's religious thought and political sentiments and reports of his personal behavior and attitude toward the Jews. The intellectually resourceful, although greatly mistaken Ibn Naghrīla in *Al-Fiṣal* is displaced in *The Refutation* by a variously obtuse, base, and diabolical but unnamed Jewish figure identified traditionally with Ismāʿīl ibn Naghrīla, or alternately with his son and successor Yūsuf.[84] Incorporating the same arguments and language em-

[82] There are good reasons why Jewish messianism might appear seditious even if its prospects for realization were beyond reason. See chapter 5.

[83] On which, see Wasserstein, 1993, pp. 192–93.

[84] In his introduction to Ibn Ḥazm, "*Al-Radd*," 1981, 3:17, Iḥsān ʿAbbās reasons that the pamphlet's author was not Ismāʿīl but Yūsuf ibn Naghrīla for whom such an impudent effort would supposedly have been more in character. ʿAbbās thus attempts to solve the problems associated with ascribing the work to the first Ibn Naghrīla. Arabic historiography does paint a more crass and insolent picture of the son than the father making Yūsuf a more likely candidate for authorship in ʿAbbās's thinking. Yet no mention is made of Yūsuf as the author in any other source. See also Ashtor, 1960, 2:354, n. 116; Fenton, p. 91; and the other sources cited by Stroumsa, 1987, p. 770, n. 28. By contrast, Arnaldez, p. 40, surmises that Samuel wrote his treatise in response to Ibn Ḥazm's critique of the Hebrew Bible and rabbinic Judaism in *Al-Fiṣal fī l-milal*. According to Arnaldez's scheme, "The Refutation" would have been Ibn Ḥazm's counterresponse.

ployed in *Al-Fiṣal*,[85] *The Refutation* embraces established traditional elements from *tafsīr* and *ḥadīth* literature in its defense of Islam and polemic against Judaism, and further evokes Quranic proof-texts cautioning Muslims to avoid fraternizing with Jews and Christians (*ahl al-dhimma*). Read in the context of the tribulations of eleventh-century Andalusi Islam, *The Refutation* is a religious polemic that sets a new standard for vilification of another religious group, and so it is very much a social text and a piece of political propaganda.[86]

Ibn Ḥazm supposedly undertook writing *The Refutation* when he learned a Jew had written a book exposing alleged inconsistencies and logical contradictions in the Qur'ān.[87] Unable to obtain a copy of the sacrilegious text, Ibn Ḥazm reports that he had to rely on the work of another Muslim scholar who had already come to the defense of Islam in refuting the arguments put forward by the Jew.[88] Without actually identifying the offending party, Ibn Ḥazm signals his familiarity with the Jew and his intellectual limitations in a suggestive but cryptic remark:

> By my life, the argument he makes demonstrates how limited is his knowledge and how narrow the extent of his understanding, *with which I had some previous familiarity* [emphasis mine].[89]

[85] Wasserstein, 1985, p. 200, has noted that the substance of the religious polemic against the Torah in "The Refutation" (as opposed to its introduction and conclusion) is virtually the same as that in *Al-Fiṣal fī l-milal*. He further observes, p. 202, that "The form of the *Radd* is not dissimilar to that of a number of epistles [*risāla*s] written by Ibn Ḥazm. In these, the author, addressing himself to an imaginary correspondent, answers theoretical questions on various matters in the form of a letter."

[86] Ibid., p. 205. See the comments of Garcia Gomez, 1936–39, pp. 3–5. Yet Adang, 1995, pp. 1–2, has shown that Ibn Ḥazm sometimes espoused liberal legal opinions in his treatment of non-Muslims as compared to the views of the other legal schools.

[87] Ibn Ḥazm, 1981, 3:42 ("*Al-Radd*," no. 2). Aḥmad ibn Qāsim al-Ḥajarī, pp. 244–45, relates the pious counsel he was given by ʿĪsā b. ʿAbd al-Raḥmān al-Suktānī, the *qāḍī l-jamāʿa* of Marrakesh: "that refuting the falsehoods spoken by the Infidels concerning the religions is part of the jihād."

[88] Ibn Ḥazm, 1981, 3:42 ("*Al-Radd*," no. 2). Fierro, 1992a, p. 85, posits, as Sroumsa has shown, that the Muʿtazilite al-Jubbā'ī served as Ibn Ḥazm's Muslim source for refuting the anti-Quranic arguments.

[89] Ibn Ḥazm, 1981, 3:43 ("*Al-Radd*," no. 2): "*Wa-la-ʿumrī inna iʿtirāḍahu al-ladhī iʿtaraḍa bihi la-yadullu ʿalā diqqi baʿihi fī l-ʿilm wa-qillat ittisāʿihi fī l-fahm ʿalā mā ʿahadnāhu ʿalayhi qadīm[an]*." The translation is not without difficulty owing in part to the apparently deliberate ambiguity of the Arabic. Perlmann, 1948–49, p. 282, inserts a few additional words missing in the Arabic original, and translates: "By God, his argumentation proves how poor is his knowledge, how narrow his mind, about which I already knew something. For I used to know him when he was naked, except for charlatanry, serene, except for anxiety, void except of lies." Clearly, the text does not want to identify the alleged Jewish culprit by name, but only to suggest his identity.

Ibn Ḥazm's account of the text's genesis and his unelaborated enigmatic comment notwithstanding, there is much to suggest that *The Refutation* was undertaken as a sociopolitically motivated literary exercise rather than as a response to a contemporary anti-Quranic work supposedly authored by a prominent Andalusi Jew.

The Refutation may be outlined as follows: the "Introduction" assails the Jewish culprit and the party-kings who permit such and other offenses against Islam and Muslims (pp. 41–43); Part 1, in the form of eight chapters, represents the body of the work (pp. 43–60) as defined in the Introduction. This is where *The Refutation* undertakes a point-by-point defense of the problematic Quranic passages followed by a counterattack on passages in the Torah more objectionable than the ones questioned in the Qur'ān. Part 2, an epilogue (pp. 60–67), abandons the framework of a response to the Jew's anti-Quranic treatise in order to mount a full-blown assault on the theological absurdities in the Hebrew Bible and the classical rabbinic homiletic tradition. The Conclusion (pp. 67–70) restates the reasons for which the treatise was composed and reiterates the shrill diatribe against the Jewish author, the Jews in general, and the misguided Andalusi Muslim "party-kings" who grant the Jews political license. *The Refutation*'s puzzling structure thus appears to offer a means of grappling with the text's contradictions and provides a key to its significance.[90]

Here is how Ibn Ḥazm acquaints the reader with his literary and religious adversary and introduces the subject of the treatise:

> Now then, a man whose heart seethes with malice toward Islam and its community of believers and whose liver is molten with hostility for the Messenger, may God bless him and grant him peace, a man who belongs to the "materialist" [*al-mutadahhira*] heretics who conceal themselves among the most abject of religions and most detestable of religious doctrines, namely Judaism, upon whose adherents God's curse falls constantly and upon whose followers God's wrath, may He be exalted and magnified, resides permanently. Insolence has loosened this man's tongue and hubris has released his reins. His contemptuous soul has become arrogant because of his abounding wealth, and the abundance of gold and silver in his possession has inflated his detestable ambition, such that he composed a book in which he expressly intended to expose alleged contradictions in the Word of God, may He be exalted and magnified, in the Qur'ān . . . treating men of

[90] Perlmann, 1948–49, p. 281, already noted the difference between the tone and content of introduction and conclusion and the so-called body of the work. Wasserstein, Stroumsa, Fierro, and others also note this difference.

> religion with disdain on the one hand and the political leadership with impudence on the other.[91]

Apart from its clear repudiation of the *dahriyya* ("materialist heresy"),[92] the manifestly *political* discourse of the introduction is grounded entirely in the sociopolitical scene of eleventh-century al-Andalus. It makes no pretense of contributing to the world of religious ideas but instead harshly denounces the depraved Muslim ruler in whose realm the offending Jew resides, assails the wealth and influence of the Jews in general, and decries the insolence, baseness, and idiocy of the unnamed Jewish author. By contrast, Part 1 deals with essential scriptural/theological differences between Judaism and Islam such as those explored at length in *Al-Fiṣal fi l-milal* and in other prominent heresiographical works from the Muslim East. Unlike Ibn Ḥazm's unabashedly polemical treatment of Judaism, works such as *Al-Milal wal-niḥal* by al-Shahrastānī (d. 1153) are attempts at writing comparative religion with scholarly detachment from the perspective of a believing, committed Muslim.[93] As a reader of *Al-Milal wal-niḥal*, S. D. Goitein thus asserted that "when we compare Shahrastānī's detailed, well informed and remarkably unbiased accounts with the Greek and Latin texts relative to Judaism, we have to confess that between Tacitus and Shahrastānī, humanity has made a great step forward."[94]

The Conclusion of *The Refutation* returns to the universe of politically minded discourse, issuing an ominous warning to the Muslim "party kings" of al-Andalus regarding their association with Jews:

> It is my firm hope that God will treat those who befriend the Jews and take them into their confidence as He treated the Jews themselves. . . . For whosoever amongst Muslim princes has listened to all this and still continues to befriend the Jews, holding

[91] Ibn Ḥazm, 1981, 3:42–43 ("*Al-Radd*," no. 2).

[92] Ibid., p. 42 ("*Al-Radd*," no. 2): ("a man who belongs to the 'materialist heretics' who conceal themselves among the most abject of religions and most detestable of religious doctrines, namely Judaism"]; and "this despicable heretic who in his innermost faith adheres to the views of the materialists but outwardly seeks refuge in the Jewish ark" *("hādhā l-khasīs al-zindīq al-mustabṭin madhhab al-dahriyya fī bāṭinihi al-mutakaffin bi-tābūt al-yahūdiyya fī ẓāhirihi")*, trans. Stroumsa, 1987, p. 771.

"The Refutation" returns briefly to the motif of the *dahriyya* in the body of the text. It refers derisively to the Jew five times as *mutadahhir* (materialist) (nos. 7, 19, 25, 26, 32).

[93] Al-Shahrastānī, 2:13–24, discusses Judaism along with Christianity as a scriptural religion, then (rabbinic) Judaism in general and various other offshoots including Karaite Judaism.

[94] Goitein, 1996, pp. 229–30.

> intercourse with them, well deserves to be overtaken by the same humiliation and to suffer in this world the same griefs meted out to the Jews.[95]

Anticipating the rhetorical strategy and flagrant political goal of Abū Isḥāq al-Ilbīrī's notorious diatribe against Yūsuf ibn Naghrīla and the Jews of Granada, the text neither marginalizes nor denudes the Jew of cultural otherness but passes the sternest of judgments upon the Jewish author of the contemptible and blasphemous text. *The Refutation* indicts this author for violating the essential regulations of the social contract Islam stipulated for non-Muslims going back to the so-called Pact of ʿUmar. The legal authority al-Shāfiʿī detailed these stipulations and the consequences for violating them in the third Islamic century (eighth to ninth century):

> If any one of you speaks improperly of Muhammad, may God bless and save him, the Book of God or of His religion, he forfeits the protection [*dhimma*] of God, of the Commander of the Faithful, and of all Muslims; he has contravened the conditions upon which he was given his safe-conduct; his property and his life are at the disposal of the Commander of the Faithful.[96]

Here is how Abū Isḥāq invokes the transgression and prescribed punishment in his poem:

> Do not consider it a breach of faith to kill them
> the breach of faith would be to let them carry on.

[95] Ibn Ḥazm, 1981, 3:67 ("*Al-Radd*," no. 61); trans. Perlmann, 1948–49, pp. 281–83. Ibn Ḥazm, 1981, 3:68–69 ("*Al-Radd*," no. 62), envisions for the culpable Andalusi elite the wretched and accursed fate reserved for the Jews (i.e., Israelites) in the ultimate *biblical* proof-text (Deut. 28). What first appears to be an ironic application of an important biblical text in the service of Islam actually cements the association of the offending Muslims with the Jews. Ibn Ḥazm's critique of the authenticity of the Hebrew Bible to the contrary, Lazarus-Yafeh observes, 1992, pp. 43–44, n. 66, that Muslim writers sometimes found it useful to employ biblical prophetic passages rebuking the Israelites.

[96] Trans. Lewis, 1974a, 2:220. The final provision of al-Ṭurṭūshī's version of the Pact of ʿUmar, *Sirāj al-mulūk*, (Ṭurṭūshī, 1994, 2:542; trans. Lewis, 1974a, 2:219), indicates that the Jew's discourse invalidates the contract of protection guaranteed him by Islam. Islam holds him liable for a most serious offense against it, as follows: "If we in any way violate these undertakings for which we ourselves stand as surety, we forfeit our covenant (of protection [*dhimma*]), and we become liable for the penalties for contumacy and sedition." On the place of the "forfeiture clause" in the various recensions of The Pact, see Mark R. Cohen, 1999. For comments on the circumstances under which the protection guaranteed non-Muslims must be withdrawn, see Lewis, 1984, pp. 39–40.

They have violated our covenant with them so
how can you be held guilty against the violators?[97]

And in the words of *The Refutation* itself, the Jew must receive

> what he deserves by law, that is to say, the shedding of his blood, and the confiscation of his property and captivity of his women and children. [This is] because he promoted himself, threw off the mark of humility from his neck, and violated the contract of protection over his life, his property and his family.[98]

An interpersonal dimension may well indirectly inform some of *The Refutation*'s anti-Jewish rhetoric and animus. ʿAlī ibn Ḥazm's education and the social conditions in which he grew to maturity could not have been more favorable. He had the opportunity to study with great Andalusi religious intellectuals of the early eleventh century such as Ibn al-Faraḍī (d.1012/13),[99] author of *Ta'rīkh ʿulamā' l-Andalus* ([*A Biographical Dictionary on the*] *History of the ʿUlamā' of al-Andalus*). And through his father's position as *wazīr* at the ʿĀmirid court in Cordoba before the collapse of the unified caliphal state, ʿAlī tasted the life of position and power awaiting him as well as the world of learning.[100] Whenever the literary account of Ibn Ḥazm's early encounter with Ibn Naghrīla was drafted, it seems likely that the issue of the exercise of Jewish temporal power within the Andalusi sector of *Dār al-Islām* had unexpectedly become entangled in the personal histories of Samuel and ʿAlī. Both lives were profoundly touched by the social and political upheaval connected with the Berber sacking of Cordoba and the collapse of the Umayyad caliphate.

While Samuel's fortunes rose dramatically as a result of changes in the administration of al-Andalus and the opportunities presented to ambitious and talented Jews, Ibn Ḥazm's waned, and his once promising prospects for following in his father's political footsteps were effectively scuttled. Ibn Naghrīla was already entrenched in the fiscal bureaucracy of the Zirid regime, a position from which he would eventually enter

[97] Text in Ibn al-Khaṭīb, 1956, pp. 221–23; trans. Lewis, 1993, 167–74, with a detailed study of this poem in its historical context. The text and a translation also appear in Monroe, pp. 206–213. Bādīs even may have exiled Abū Isḥāq at Yūsuf's behest. Adang, 1995, p. 1, notes that "The Refutation" marks a culmination in Ibn Ḥazm's complaints about Jewish influence in al-Andalus and that he "apparently seeks to bring about the downfall of the Jewish vizier of Granada."

[98] Ibn Ḥazm, 1981, 3:42–43 ("*Al-Radd*," no. 2); partial trans. Stroumsa, 1987, p. 772.

[99] Ibn Ḥazm, 1986, p. 219, credits Ibn al-Faraḍī with having taught him Islamic traditions.

[100] Ibid., p. 49.

the confidences of the next *amīr* Bādīs. He also acquired the title and attained prestige as the Nagid of the Jews of al-Andalus (c. 1027), a station in which Samuel apparently came to imagine himself as the complementary fulfillment of the biblical prophecy he reportedly debated with Ibn Ḥazm. This seems to be a plausible interpretation of a line in a poem the Nagid dispatched in 1055 to the Exilarch Ḥezekiah in Baghdad invoking the *Ro'sh golah*'s political authority: "To you royalty and to me prophecy are vouchsafed; you and I alone are divine signs upon this earth."[101] By contrast, Ibn Ḥazm's political fortunes declined precipitously.

The privileged son of a once-influential *wazīr* of the ʿĀmirids in Cordoba during the waning days of the Umayyad caliphate, ʿAlī ibn Ḥazm was set to flight, then elevated to office again, including a very brief stint as *wazīr* of the ill-fated Caliph al-Mustaẓhir (c. 1024). According to Ibn ʿIdhārī, Ibn Ḥazm also served in the army of Zuhayr's Almeria in 1038, just around the time in which the neighboring Slavic kingdom came into conflict with Zirid Granada.[102] By Ibn al-Khaṭīb's reckoning, Ibn Ḥazm was appointed *wazīr* on three separate occasions and was imprisoned at least three times.[103] When attempts at reviving his political career a final time failed at provincial centers, Ibn Ḥazm eschewed his previous ambitions and turned his boundless intellectual energy exclusively to research and to a stricter piety.[104] Accordingly, some students of Ibn Ḥazm have imagined an embittered and disillusioned ʿAlī reflecting upon the ascent, position, and authority within a Muslim state of Ibn Naghrīla, the Jewish interlocutor of his youth. Ismāʿīl's success supposedly reminded Ibn Ḥazm of his own failures as much as of the collapse of an orthodox Islamic polity in al-Andalus and its replacement by the party-kings.[105] From the perspective of a pious Muslim scholar, it is also possible to appreciate how Ibn Ḥazm's declining influence and position and Ibn Naghrīla's contrasting fortunes might appear symptomatic of all that was wrong with Andalusi society.

Setting aside whatever social-psychological factors may have contributed to Ibn Ḥazm's attitude toward the Jews in general and Ibn Naghrīla in particular, what historical factors might have contributed to the twofold iteration of anti-Jewish rhetoric? In other words, what had happened after their original encounter in 1013 to prompt the drafting of *Al-Fiṣal fī l-milal* (and its incorporation of materials from the *Iẓhār*)

[101] Samuel ha-Nagid, 1988, 1:197 ("*Nigleit yᵉshara bᵉli ṣanif u-miṣnefet*," [l.44]).

[102] Ibn ʿIdhārī, 3:171.

[103] Ibn al-Khaṭīb, 1973, 4:115.

[104] In *Al-Akhlāq wal-siyār*, p. 131ff., Ibn Ḥazm dresses this decision in his personal piety.

[105] See Adang, 1996, pp. 43–44; Stroumsa, 1987, p. 769.

and the composition of *The Refutation*? From the standpoint of a pious and ideologically minded Muslim intellectual, the events of the eleventh century were altogether lamentable. Dispirited scholars such as Ibn Ḥazm were all too aware of the progressive social and political disintegration of al-Andalus and the resultant evaporation of its influence as a Mediterranean power.[106] Troublesome rumblings of a revitalized Castile under Ferdinand I (1035–1065) certainly reached al-Andalus, further contributing to an abiding sense of unease. Consider the following remarkable passage transmitted by Ibn ʿIdhārī preserving remarks attributed to King Ferdinand I of Castile addressed to a delegation of Muslims from Toledo:

> We seek only our lands which you conquered from us in times past at the beginning of your history. Now you have dwelled in them for the time allotted to you and we have become victorious over you as a result of your own wickedness. So go to your own side of the straits [of Gibraltar] and leave our lands to us, for no good will come to you from dwelling here with us after today. For we shall not hold back from you till God decides between us.[107]

This address, a construction of the thirteenth rather than the eleventh century and a reflection of Muslim rather than Christian historical sensibilities, captures a sense of the shifting political fortunes of Islam and Christendom in Iberia, ostensibly from the perspective of a Christian Spanish monarch. But the discourse must have struck a chord among Muslim scholars in the Maghrib who preserved and transmitted it on account of its particular reading of the Andalusis' failure and collapse.

Piety-minded Muslims viewed the disintegration of the unified state and the resultant civil strife over conflicting claims to political authority in al-Andalus. Another visible sign of internal weakness directly related to the proliferation of competing principalities in al-Andalus was the elevation of Jewish, and to a lesser extent Christian, officials to positions of power under the *mulūk al-ṭawāʾif*. Naturally, resentful Muslim intellectuals viewed this practice as violating the proper Islamic character of al-Andalus. They experienced such appointments as sabotage—undermining the social and political conditions necessary for the perfect practice of Islam. Ibn Ḥazm's comments on the state of al-Andalus after the *fitna* of 1009 recorded in *Talkhīṣ li-wujūh al-talkhīs* (*Abridgement of the Various Aspects of Salvation*) speak to these issues:

[106] Ibn Ḥazm's highly evocative and personal comments on the state of Cordoba after the *fitna* of 1009 are recorded in *Ṭawq al-ḥamāma*, 1986, pp. 182–83 (no. 88).

[107] Ibn ʿIdhārī, 3:282, trans. Wasserstein, 1985, p. 250.

> As for the question regarding this revolt (*fitnah*) and regarding the people involved in it and what happened to them, it is a question we have pondered on for a long time. We beseech God for well-being. Except for those who sought the protection of God, the revolt was an evil that will require detailed elaboration. For one thing, it ruined the religious beliefs in many respects. In brief, every ruler of a city or a fortress throughout the width and breadth of al-Andalus was the enemy of God and His Messenger. These rulers pursued corruption on earth. . . . they exact excise tax (*mukus*) and poll tax on Muslims; they made the Jews lords for collecting land tax and levy (*daribah*) from Muslims; they give reasons for the necessity of such taxes, which are forbidden by God—thus replacing His commands and prohibitions with their own.[108]

Influential Jews could already be found at the Umayyad and ʿĀmirid courts of the tenth century—a development, which, we have seen, apparently did not go uncriticized in some quarters—as noted in the previous chapter in connection with Ḥasdai ibn Shapruṭ. Although the evidence seems very scant, Samuel Stern and Nehemia Allony contend that popular anti-Jewish sentiment had already emerged during the tenth century. In their view, the vilification of Samuel and Joseph ibn Naghrīla in the eleventh century was simply a continuation of a predominant "anti-Jewish" vein in Andalusi society.[109] What can be said with greater certainty is that the loss of unified Muslim authority catalyzed Muslim anxiety over Jewish empowerment. That anxiety surfaced more sharply and openly during the eleventh century.

Heightened concern about the proper place of non-Muslims in Andalusi society articulated in the introduction and conclusion of *The Refutation* found an echo in an admonitory and programmatic *ḥisba*-manual by Muḥammad b. Aḥmad ibn ʿAbdūn, a *qāḍī* or *muḥtasib* living in the religiously strict atmosphere of twelfth-century Almoravid Seville. The document prescribes, among other things, strict regulations on the behavior of Jews and Christians in the marketplace in hope of restoring the proper relationship between Islam and its *dhimmī* subjects as delineated in Islamic law.[110] Indeed, in drawing a typology of the persecution of minorities in premodern Islam, Bernard Lewis identifies *dhimmī* arrogance and high public rank as primary causes in moving Islam to strike

[108] *Talkhīṣ li-wujūh al-talkhīs*, in Ibn Ḥazm, 1981, 3:173–74; trans. Chejne, pp. 32–33.

[109] Stern, 1946b, pp. 141–43; Allony, pp. 212–15.

[110] Lévi Provençal, 1934, pp. 238–48; trans. Lewis, 1974a, 2:157–65.

an aggressively defensive posture vis-à-vis its "protected peoples," Jews and Christians.[111]

Ibn Ḥazm's penchant for conferring with Jewish scholars was a habit he shared with other Andalusi intellectuals such as Ṣāʿid b. Aḥmad and with al-Masʿūdī (d. 956) in the Muslim East.[112] This practice suggests that neither the presence of Jews in Andalusi Muslim society nor even their prosperity relative to the Muslim population were cause for concern as such. Rather, the appearance and exercise of Jewish power and the Jews' visible trespass into the affairs of a Muslim state seemed threatening, never more so than while Andalusi Islam was fragmenting and in retreat. Ibn Ḥazm's reports of his own experiences with Jewish intellectuals only appear to contradict what he has to say about the Jews as a group in both *Al-Fiṣal* and *The Refutation*. An anecdote preserved in the biographical dictionary of the pietist Abū ʿAbd Allāh Muḥammad al-Ḥumaydī (b.c. 1029), one of Ibn Ḥazm's Andalusi disciples who later went to Baghdad, relates the experience of a devout tenth-century Andalusi scholar. The traveler (Abū ʿUmar ibn Saʿdī) was horrified and incensed by the extent to which Jews and Christians were accorded religious respect and intellectual freedom in the famous public symposiums reportedly conducted among rational theologians in Baghdad.[113] The supposed contradiction between Ibn Ḥazm's discursive presentations and his personal conduct suggests that the position Ibn Ḥazm takes in these works is adopted for polemical purposes. *The Refutation* explicitly calls upon informed and concerned Muslims to reject the untenable sociopolitical and socioreligious situation of eleventh-century al-Andalus, a position Ibn Ḥazm certainly actually held. But what can we say about his personal relations with Andalusi-Jewish intellectuals? Why else would Ibn Ḥazm bother so frequently to engage members of a community of liars, scoundrels, miscreants, and unbelievers in open intellectual debate, other than because he hoped he might convince even one of them to embrace Islam?

Recent research on *The Refutation* has focused on source-critical exposition of Ibn Ḥazm's polemic and on determining the identity of his literary adversary.[114] For our purposes of reading *The Refutation* as an artifact of Andalusi-Muslim culture in a moment of crisis, we may set aside a definitive solution to the problem of whether or not Samuel the

[111] Lewis, 1984, p. 53.

[112] Al-Masʿūdī (*Kitāb al-tanbīh wal-ishrāf*, pp. 112–14) remarks that he met many of the scholars listed in his roster of eleventh-century Jewish intellectuals. See Kraemer, 1986, pp. 83–84.

[113] Al-Ḥumaydī, pp. 101–102.

[114] See Perlmann, 1974, pp. 108ff.

Nagid actually composed a treatise against the Qur'ān.[115] Suffice it to say that Sarah Stroumsa argues that the *Al-Radd ʿalā ibn al-naghrīla al-yahūdī* actually refutes *Kitāb al-Dāmigh*, a ninth-century heterodox Muslim source by the well-known heretic Ibn al-Rāwandī (whose Jewish confidant also happens to be called Ibn Lāwī), rather than an eleventh-century Jewish polemical text.[116] In her view and in the opinion of Camilla Adang, Ibn Ḥazm hoped to pin a capital offense upon Ibn Naghrīla by ascribing to him the anti-Quranic arguments.[117] Maribel Fierro, by contrast, identifies the two "free-thinking" materialist/agnostic Jewish physicians named Ismāʿīl (b. Yūnus al-Aʿwar and b. al-Qarrad) living in Almeria with whom Ibn Ḥazm was acquainted. She notes Ibn Ḥazm's references in *Al-Fiṣal* (and Ismāʿīl b. Yūnus al-Aʿwar again in *Ṭawq al-Ḥamāma*) to his acquaintance with the two Jewish physicians who were allegedly adherents of the *dahriyya*. Fierro suggests that one of them could well have written such an anti-Quranic polemical work in the unusual intellectual and social climate of eleventh-century al-Andalus, perhaps by drawing upon existing heterodox Muslim texts such as *Kitāb al-Dāmigh* identified by Stroumsa.[118]

In any case, it appears more likely that Ibn Ḥazm believed that the author of the unavailable text was a Jewish contemporary in al-Andalus. Or, alternatively, he found it useful to attribute the arguments of an offensive anti-Quranic tract to a highly conspicuous Andalusi Jew such as Ibn Naghrīla without actually identifying him. Reading *The Refutation* as an artifact of Andalusi-Arabic culture in a moment of crisis, we need not feel obliged (in the absence of compelling textual evidence) to identify the particular Jew who meets all of the various conditions set forth in the text. That figure is (1) a free-thinking Jewish heretic associated with the views of the *dahriyya*; (2) an Andalusi Jewish dignitary supposedly known to Ibn Ḥazm; (3) a Jew of such substantial means, influence, and bravado that he was unafraid to openly voice criticism of the Qur'ān and Islam in the form of a religious polemic written in Arabic. Like the textual strategy of Ibn Bassām's *Dhakhīra* (studied in the next chapter), there is a clear sense in which *The Refutation* accumulates offenses against Islam in general and Muslims in al-Andalus in particu-

[115] Wasserstein, 1985, pp. 199–205, carefully discusses the rationale for and against the existence of such a pamphlet. Ibn Bassām, 2:766, claims that Ibn Naghrīla composed a book in response to something Ibn Ḥazm had written. Perhaps he has in mind *Al-Fiṣal fī l-milal*'s critique of the Hebrew Bible: "He [Ibn Naghrīla] composed a book in response to the jurist Abū Muḥammad ibn Ḥazm, mentioned above, in which he expressed open enmity in defaming Islam."

[116] Stroumsa, 1987 and 1994.

[117] Stroumsa, 1987, p. 772.

[118] Fierro, 1992a, p. 82.

lar, bundling religious affronts with social and political malfeasance and attributing the entire list of outrages to a common source who is identified only as a well-placed Andalusi-Jew.

The Refutation itself is silent on the identity of the alleged Jewish polemicist. Accordingly, why did later literary historians, beginning apparently with Ibn Bassām and continuing down to Ibn Saʿīd al-Maghribī (d. 1286), all take it for granted that Ibn Naghrīla was the object of the *The Refutation*'s invective? Or why did the editor, perhaps Ibn Ḥazm himself, or editors responsible for supplying the title of the treatise in the manuscript (used by Iḥsan ʿAbbās) identify the Jewish offender in the title but not in the work itself? "Free-thinking materialism" cannot reasonably be attributed to the rabbinic scholar Samuel the Nagid.[119] Other high-ranking Jews could certainly be found during the eleventh century in Saragossa (Abū l-Faḍl ibn Ḥasdai; Yequtiel ibn Ḥasan), Almeria, Seville (Abraham ibn Muhājir; Isaac ibn al-Baliʿa), and Toledo.[120] The answer to the problem, I believe, is that Samuel the Nagid was the most visible and important member of this group of Andalusi Jewish notables. The Nagid was the only one to attain ecumenical status among the Jews of al-Andalus and, as far we know, the only Andalusi Jew to actually pass on political authority to his son. Imagine what Muslim scholars would have thought had they access to the Nagid's Hebrew poetry produced for Jewish consumption or if a hint of the Jewish hubris he expresses in that verse were evident in Ismāʿīl's public demeanor that Ibn Ḥayyān and ʿAbd Allāh represent as unimpeachable.[121]

Ismāʿīl appeared to some of his Muslim counterparts as the incarnation of Jewish empowerment and arrogance. Similarly, the city-state of Granada under the administration of successive Ibn Naghrīlas, referred

[119] Ibn Bassām, 2:766; Ibn Saʿīd al-Maghribī, 1955, 2:114–15 ("He mocked the Muslims and vowed to set the Qur'ān to verse for singing aloud").

[120] See Ashtor, 1992, 2:197, 217–21, 225, 238, 253–64; and Wasserstein, 1985, pp. 190–222.

[121] I am thinking specifically of the Nagid's preoccupation with his aristocratic (Levitic) lineage, his concerted effort to bring his public image into line with the typology of King David, and his pretensions to higher authority. See Brann, 1991, 47–58. As Gerson Cohen noted in his edition of Abraham ibn Daud, p. 277:

> The hope for the fulfillment of the messianic dream in Andalus, through the class of Jewish courtiers, was not a secret of the Jewish underground. The Jewish pride, which the Muslims construed as Hubris and defiance of Islam, drew its nourishment from the assumption that the age of the Bible was again come to life and that the exiles of Judea in Sefarad would soon assume their rightful station.

Open, public defiance toward Islam is another matter even if the Nagid never uttered an Arabic word on the subject.

to in Arabic texts as *gharnāṭat al-yahūd* ("Jewish Granada"),[122] is a perfect locus for various grievances against Jewish power and influence within the Islamic polity of al-Andalus.[123] Indeed, Ibn ʿIdhārī charges that Yūsuf ibn Naghrīla sought to establish an independent Jewish kingdom in Almeria, giving the impression that under successive Ibn Naghrīlas the Jewish community functioned as a quasi-independent polity and aspired to complete independence.[124] Ismāʿīl and Yūsuf's unusual powers as well as the number of ranking Jewish officials serving at the courts of other party-kings meant that the situation in eleventh-century al-Andalus did not exist elsewhere in Islam. Even Fatimid Egypt, where Jews and Jewish converts such as Jacob ibn Killis served in important positions of government and where the perception of Jewish power was sometimes exaggerated, did not rise to the level of the Andalusi matrix.[125]

In contrast with the Jews of eleventh-century al-Andalus, far fewer Christians were appointed to government posts partly because of their more significant numbers in the general population. In particular not a single Christian courtier in the service of one of the party-kings can be identified who was invested with quite the degree of authority Ibn Naghrīla attained in Granada. It is true that a Christian *wazīr* was appointed in Saragossa and another in Zirid Granada shortly after the murder of Yūsuf ibn Naghrīla.[126] In the latter case, the appointment of Abū l-Rabīʿ al-Naṣrānī, previously an associate of Yūsuf's, scarcely reversed the Zirid policy of entrusting their administration to non-Muslims. It merely replaced successive Jews with another non-Muslim.[127] The practice of appointing *dhimmī*s to high office was by no means unique to eleventh-century al-Andalus. On the contrary, Jewish courtiers functioned as tax collectors in both Marinid Morocco and fourteenth-century Castile. In each domain they not only served the interests of the state; they also acted as guardians of the welfare of the Jews of

Christians

[122] ʿAbd Allāh bin Buluggīn, 1986, pp. 206–207, citing al-Ḥimyarī, *Kitāb al-Rawḍ al-Miʿṭār*, ed. and trans. Lévi-Provençal, p. 23.

[123] During the Zirid era, the Jews of Granada represented a very significant segment of the population. Appointment of two successive *dhimmīs* to high office appears to have been part of a system of checks and balances specific to Berber rule in eleventh-century Granada. See Handler, pp. 26, 45; and the discussion below in chapter 4. For an estimate of the Jewish population in al-Andalus, see Ashtor, 1963; and on their distribution, Ashtor, 1992, 2:201–300.

[124] Ibn ʿIdhārī, 3:266, and Ibn Bassām, 2:766.

[125] Goitein, 1967–93, 2:375.

[126] Wasserstein, 1985, pp. 244–45.

[127] ʿAbd Allāh bin Buluggīn, 1986, p. 84; (Ar.) ʿAbd Allāh bin Buluggīn, 1955, p. 66.

the land. And when they ultimately met their personal demise it invariably carried repercussions for the Jewish community as a whole.[128]

An arresting and vivid illustration of why the reader must always venture to historicize Muslim treatment of *dhimmīs* in al-Andalus and the other lands of Islam is available in an account of the so-called Cordoban martyrs' crisis around 850. As is well known, members of the Mozarabic community in and around Cordoba began to come forward to publicly denounce Islam and blaspheme the Prophet. They did so, it appears, with the full intention of forcing the *amīr* ʿAbd al-Raḥmān II and subsequently Muḥammad I, to execute them. Some prominent (and more politically accommodating) elders of the Mozarabic church decried these acts and sought to curtail them by citing the generally tolerant treatment of Andalusi Christians under Muslim rule. Other communal authorities such as the priest Eulogius and his lay associate Paulus Alvarus sought to encourage the martyrs in order to galvanize what they viewed as the moribund cultural, political, and religious existence of Christians under Andalusi Islam. Muhammad I finally ordered a purge of Christians working in the state bureaucracy in compliance with Islamic law. Eulogious wondered: "why . . . if the emir enjoyed such free exercise of power, did he not also force the Jews to be removed from his presence . . . ?"[129]

In ninth-century Cordoba Andalusi Muslims thus perceived a series of Christian insults to Muslim rule if not to Islam itself. Accordingly, oppressive measures were enforced over that particular community, but not over the Jews, who played no role in the "crisis." In eleventh-century Granada some Muslims experienced a threat to Muslim prerogatives, perhaps even to Muslim rule, from the highly visible and powerful Jewish courtiers Ismāʿīl and Yūsuf, as well as the well-placed Jewish subordinates they brought into office and influence. Andalusi Christians were spared in the anti-Jewish uprising of 1066. One was even elevated to *wazīr* in place of Yūsuf. The two crises were, of course, different in kind. But reading them together as Muslim responses to real or perceived threats and insults to Andalusi Islam reveals just how misplaced Eulogius' question is. Andalusi Muslim "policy" toward Jews and Christians nearly always varied according to time and place, and the flexibility or rigidity with which political authority enforced the disabilities provided for *dhimmī* subjects in Islam. The outlines of these two crises and their textual tracks seem to validate Abraham Udovitch's

[128] Shatzmiller, 1983.

[129] Wolf, p. 17. Logic is not always the most useful tool in evaluating such policies. The Fatimid caliph al-Ḥākim first turned against the Christians of Egypt alone before mounting a murderous campaign against the Jews of that land.

thesis that "Islamic attitudes, practices and policies toward Jews and non-Muslims . . . was [*sic*] determined in the first instance by political and social considerations and were not primarily motivated by religious-ideological considerations."[130]

To return to *The Refutation.* Ibn Ḥazm, subsequent Muslim literary intellectuals, or the editor of *The Refutation* might have identified Ibn Naghrīla as the source of the subversive discourse or thought it natural to cast him in this menacing role on account of his singularly conspicuous position, prominence, and political agency in Zirid Granada. A pious Muslim could easily identify Ibn Naghrīla's figure and his intrusion into the affairs of Muslims as contributing to the progressive social and political disintegration of al-Andalus during the eleventh century. Arabic historiography labeled this period *fitna*, by which it meant the sort of civil war that "breeds schism and in which the believer's purity is placed in grave danger."[131] *Al-Fiṣal fī l-milal* and *The Refutation* testify that Ibn Ḥazm was preoccupied with the problem of *fitna* in al-Andalus.[132] He even refers to this religious and political problem in *Ṭawq al-ḥamāma* and *Al-Akhlāq wal-siyār* where the reader does not necessarily expect to find it.[133] Later sources such as Ibn ʿIdhārī and Ibn al-Khaṭīb, it will be recalled, cite the Jews of eleventh-century Granada in general and the Ibn Naghrīlas in particular for their accumulation of wealth.[134] Yūsuf is further singled out for his partiality toward Jewish secretaries in filling lower-level administrative and financial offices.[135] The episode involving Ismāʿīl Ibn Naghrīla and Aḥmad ibn ʿAbbās, *wazīr* of neighboring Almeria, is also indicative of Ismāʿīl's disrepute among some Andalusi Muslims and instructive as a failed rehearsal of what eventually befell Yūsuf in 1066. Unremittingly hostile to the Zirid's Jewish *wazīr*, Ibn ʿAbbās is said to have circulated letters among influential Muslims of Granada and petitioned Ḥabbūs and Bādīs successively in a concerted effort to depose Samuel from office. For good measure, Ibn ʿAbbās also enlisted his own master Zuhayr, the "Slav" prince of Almeria, in a plan to isolate Granada, intervene in its administration, and bring down the Jew and his supporters.[136] Ibn Ḥazm himself must have been aware of the opposition to Ibn Naghrīla because

[130] Udovitch, p. 664.
[131] Gardet, *EI*², 2:930.
[132] Ibn Ḥazm, n.d. (*Al-Fiṣal fī l-milal*), 5:193.
[133] Ibid,. 1981a, p. 127; 1986, p. 147.
[134] Ibn ʿIdhārī, 3:264–65.
[135] Ibid., 3:265.
[136] This is taken up in chapter 4. See Ashtor, 1991, 2:71–79.

these events coincided with his term of service in Almeria's army at least as reported by Ibn ʿIdhārī.[137]

The Refutation's fuzzy but suggestive testimony on the identity of the Jewish polemicist as well as the Andalusi-Maghribi traditional identification of the treatise's author with Ibn Naghrīla permit us to think of Ibn Ḥazm's literary adversary as a composite Andalusi Jew. The Jew in the text is a notable, an official, and a religious intellectual reminiscent of Samuel—a construct of the social imagination of a deeply troubled eleventh-century Muslim intellectual. The Jew in the text, uniformly assumed by subsequent Islamic tradition to be Ibn Naghrīla, is thus a typological figure comparable in function to Almanzor (i.e., al-Manṣūr) in Latin and Romance texts,[138] and Ibn al-Rāwandī in Muslim heresiography. The Jew in the text here is a linguistic trope: He embodies a spectrum of offensive beliefs, attitudes, and conduct considered dangerous to Islam and threatening to the well-being of Muslims in al-Andalus.[139] A typological approach to the cast of characters presented in *The Refutation* helps explains how Ibn Bassām (and subsequently Ibn Saʿīd al-Maghribī following *Al-Dhakhīra*) confuses and conflates Ismāʿīl and Yūsuf ibn Naghrīla apparently unwittingly, while relying on the "testimony" of *Al-Fiṣal* and *Al-Radd*. Whatever Ibn Ḥazm's intention in drafting the latter work and whomever its real target, *The Refutation*, as texts invariably do, took on a life of its own in subsequent Andalusi and Maghribi-Muslim tradition and for its readers.[140]

[137] Ibn ʿIdhārī, 3:171.

[138] For example, see the Latin account (preserved as an appendix to the *Historia Turpini*) of al-Manṣūr's affliction with dysentery in Colin Smith, 1988–89, 1:76–79.

[139] Fierro, 1992b, pp. 21–22, cites an Andalusi anecdote related in *Kitab al-ʿāqiba*, an unpublished treatise on eschatology by Ibn al-Kharrāṭ (d. 1186). It indicates that a person is described as a Jew so as to disqualify him. Fierro writes: "It is worth noting that the anonymous person who liked to discuss God and the Qur'ān is described as a Jew by Abū Marwān. . . . As he tried to introduce young Muḥammad to certain theological doctrines considered suspect, he resembled more a Jew than a Muslim, in the same way that his doctrines were not Islamic."

[140] Dagenais's recent study argues that scholars frequently place too much emphasis on the establishment of a single authoritative text in order to recover the "author's intention." In so doing they commit themselves to a process that deprives us of the possible readings supplied by variant traditions, that is, the scribal notations found on the margins of the manuscripts. This instructive argument can be extended to the dialectical relationship between the author's text, in this case Ibn Ḥazm's, and the place, reception, and use of the text within the broader literary-cultural and religious tradition.

CHAPTER THREE

Textualizing Ambivalence*

Ibn Bassām's Literary Miscellany, *The Treasury concerning the Merits of the People of Iberia (Al-Dhakhīra fī maḥāsin ahl al-jazīra)*

Let us now turn to the extended passage in Abū l-Ḥasan ʿAlī Ibn Bassām al-Shantarīnī's (d. 1147) monumental Andalusi-Arabic literary miscellany, *Al-Dhakhīra fī maḥāsin ahl al-jazīra* (*The Treasure Concerning the Merits of the People of the [Iberian] Peninsula*). This text initially presents Ismāʿīl ibn Naghrīla as a Jew worthy of admiration, respect, and tribute. Then conversely, the text demonizes Ibn Naghrīla as a scoundrel who utilized his office to undermine Islam and attempt to establish a Jewish polity in its place while denying Muslims their rights and depriving them of their wealth. We can think of this textual maneuver as a variation of the doubly iconic way (positive and negative) in which Ismāʿīl is depicted in Ibn al-Khaṭīb's history of Granada (the contrasting approaches in the citations of Ibn Ḥayyān and Ibn ʿIdhārī examined in the first chapter) and in which successive Ibn Naghrīlas inhabit the text of *The Tibyān*—the father an honorable figure, the son a more sordid and disreputable character.

The first passage of *Al-Dhakhīra*'s two chapters devoted to Ibn Naghrīla transmits a highly ornate rhymed-prose epistle interspersed with lines of panegyric ascribed to the Andalusi-Arabic poet Abū Aḥmad ʿAbd al-ʿAzīz ibn Khayra al-Qurṭubī. The epistle and its lines of verse are addressed to Ismāʿīl, the poet's apparent patron.[1] The poet is identified here as al-Munfatil ("the one who turns away"),[2] presumably on account of his singularly unctuous literary tribute for the Zirids'

*My thanks to Everett Rowson, Raymond Scheindlin, and Esperanza Alfonso for their helpful comments on an oral precis of this chapter presented at a seminar held the University of Pennsylvania Center for Advanced Judaic Studies.

[1] Ibn Bassām, 2:761–65.

[2] On the poet, see Ortega and del Moral, pp. 163–64; and on the first section of the passages in *Al-Dhakhīra* studied here, Stern, pp. 138–39. Apart from the sources discussed or mentioned in this chapter, al-Munfatil is represented in Ibn Saʿīd al-Maghribī [al-Andalusī], 1973, pp. 89–90 (n. 78). My thanks to Maribel Fierro for sharing with me the bibliographic entry on al-Munfatil from her forthcoming *Historia de los Autores y Transmisores Andalusíes*.

Jewish dignitary. The second and much briefer section of the first chapter of *Al-Dhakhīra*'s report more closely follows other texts of Andalusi-Arabic tradition in its attitude toward the Jewish *wazīr* of Granada. This second passage is transmitted in Ibn Bassām's own name and represents a biting editorial critique of the content (but not the form, as we shall see) of al-Munfatil's epistle and poems acclaiming Ibn Naghrīla.[3] The next chapter of *Al-Dhakhīra* then recounts the events leading up to December 1066. It highlights the critical role the Jewish *wazīr* named Ibn Naghrīla played in setting in motion his political downfall, his assassination, and the resultant brutal onslaught of the Muslim populace against the Jews of Granada.[4] Let us first examine al-Munfatil's rhymed-prose letter and lyrics apart from the larger text in which they are situated, then comment on Ibn Bassām's censure of al-Munfatil's unrestrained and uninhibited praise of Ismāʿīl ibn Naghrīla. Finally, we will reflect upon the significance of the entire sequence of passages in the first chapter as a single text made up of contradictory sources and then proceed to discuss the second chapter devoted to Ibn Naghrīla and the construction of his role in the political circumstances culminating in the violent events of 1066.

At first blush, there is nothing exceptional about the fawning manner and obsequious tenor of al-Munfatil's epistle and poems glorifying the Zirid *wazīr* and touting his magnanimous generosity. Ibn Naghrīla's position and wealth in a Muslim society would have made him a natural subject for such transparent flattery and appeals for financial support. Other Andalusi Muslims also composed Arabic verses in honor of Ismāʿīl.[5] In particular, the poet al-Akhfash b. Maimūn al-Qabdhākī, otherwise known as Ibn al-Farrā', is said to "have applied himself religiously in Granada to eulogizing its Jewish *wazīr*" (Ar. *wa-ʿtakafa bihā ʿalā madḥi wazirīhā l-yahūdī*).[6] The only problem with such obsequious poetic adulation is Ibn Naghrīla's identity as a Jew, indeed a powerful Jew in a Muslim society.[7] Yet for purposes of reading al-Munfatil's

[3] Ibn Bassām, 2:765.

[4] Ibn Bassām, 2:766–69, mistakenly identifies the murdered Jewish *wazīr* of Granada as Ismāʿīl rather than Yūsuf, a tradition frequently transmitted in the Arabic historiography of al-Andalus. Clearly, the historiographers knew nothing of *The Tibyān*'s account of 1066 and seem to have followed Ibn Bassām in confusing or conflating Ismāʿīl and Yūsuf. Stern, 1963, p. 257, attempts to give some plausible explanations for the confusion in Ibn Bassām.

[5] See Pérès, pp. 268–73.

[6] Al-Maqqarī, 4:358. See also Ibn Khallikān, 7:119.

[7] According to al-Maqqarī, 4:358, Ibn al-Farrā' left Granada for Almeria after Ibn Naghrīla's death. Denounced for his praise of the Jewish courtier, Ibn al-Farrā' is said to have apologized. Ironically, al-Maqqarī preserves a few verses in which Ibn al-Farrā' himself is satirized by al-Munfatil, a rival poet.

rhymed-prose letter and its accompanying poem, it is important to note that the patron's sole attribute that matters at all to the text—his credentials as a patron, so to speak—is his gracious munificence, potential or realized, toward the poet.

The epistle al-Munfatil addresses to Ibn Naghrīla begins with an extended lyrical prelude in rhymed prose. Employing conventional language and highly stylized imagery, the poet laments his grievous predicament owing to Fate's vicissitudes. He goes on to anticipate that his many days of want, wandering, and deprivation have come to an end thanks to Ismāʿīl's generous patronage:

> You will forget this [dire] situation when you come upon Ismāʿīl bin Yūsuf, a youth of noble lineage on both his mother's and father's side, who enlightens the splendor that was obscure. He is like Quss in eloquence, Kaʿb in generosity, Luqmān in his knowledge, and al-Aḥnaf in moderation. He is nobler in high-mindedness than Hammām and more unstinting than Basṭām.[8] When he speaks he is to the point; in competition he incapacitates; when he bestows he confers excellently; when he makes a promise he keeps it; he commands and provides, rewards and shelters, he is a harbor of generosity and hospitality and a haven in summer and winter; a guardian of honor, bold on the field of action, he does not oppress the weak or disappoint the poor. One watches out for his largesse as one attends to one's prayers; and he yearns to give generously, as an exile longs for his family.

> He combines distinction and virtues,
> exceeds his contemporaries and predecessors.
> They sink in stature in relation to his distinction
> as the sun behind the mountains.
> This is the son of Joseph
> who inherited distinction from gracious ancestors.
> Time itself is honored by his distinction
> as spearheads are distinguished by their tips.
> Whosoever does not take refuge in his protection
> will not be safe from Fate's deceptions.
> He girds himself with the sword of excellence
> and nobility of character his belt.
> I am remiss in describing him justly
> although I am like Saḥbān Wā'il![9]

[8] I was unable to locate references to these last two proverbial figures. They are not mentioned in sources where one might expect to find them, such as Ibn Rashīq and al-Thaʿālibī.

[9] A legendary pre-Islamic Arab poet. See Fahd.

How weak is the yearning for perfection
 in one whose ancestors were not perfect.
The dew of generosity rests in his palms
 as joints next to the fingertips.
Modesty follows his presence
 as an exquisite sword follows the blade.[10]

What, exactly, are the contours of the figure of Ismāʿīl presented in al-Munfatil's epistle and its accompanying poem? Chiefly, the text ascribes to Ibn Naghrīla all of the meritorious characteristics and virtues of nobility widely appreciated in Andalusi aristocratic circles: noble lineage, eloquence, generosity, kindness, wisdom of both the theoretical and practical varieties, and mastery of the requisite social graces. Despite reference to the nobility of the patron's lineage, no mention is made of Ibn Naghrīla's origins, associations, or even his religious affiliation. It is as if the text consciously and conveniently avoids mention of this background—we might say it *erases* Ismāʿil's background even more than Ibn Ḥayyān—in order to cast the patron in the best possible light. This is, of course, precisely the poet's mandate. By representing the patron as one who is essentially undifferentiated from the consummate benefactor depicted in all of Arabic *madīḥ* (panegyric), al-Munfatil's epistle and its accompanying poem are simply composed according to the requirements of the genre.

The highly stylized rhetoric of the epistle's encomium for Ibn Naghrīla thus proceeds according to its own "poetic logic," as panegyrics of professional poets are wont to do. Here, epistle and verse are designed to impress the patron with the poet's abundant literary skills as much as to perform a professional service and flatter him. Read today, the endlessly compounded generalities of the rhetoric of praise might seem overwrought, tiresome, or trite to our sensibility as readers. But dignitaries such as Ibn Naghrīla would never weary of receiving such praises or hearing them recited. On the contrary, the insatiable literary taste of rulers and notables for honorable literary acclaim is evident in the myriad poems establishing the panegyric *qaṣīda* as a central art form of the Arabo-Islamic world.[11] The Arabic panegyrical ode in essence ritualizes the relationship of poet and patron that is implicit in the production and consumption of such verse. This ritual function was arguably nowhere more significant than in verses addressed to political and religious figures ensconced in the Umayyad, ʿĀmirid, and

[10] Ibn Bassām, 2:762.
[11] Sperl and Shackle.

ṭā'ifa courts of al-Andalus as in the better known Arabic panegyrics of the Muslim East.[12]

In any case, typological points of reference to legendary figures of the past are all drawn from the Qur'ān and Islamic tradition, further identifying the subject of the epistle and poem's praise with the Arabic poet's and readers' cultural background rather than with the patron's unrevealed religious roots. For example, Ismāʿīl's eloquence corresponds to that of the semilegendary pre-Islamic orator Quss b. Sāʿida;[13] his temperament is comparable to the proverbial forbearance of al-Aḥnaf, of the first generation of Muslims;[14] his wisdom is likened to that of Luqmān, a celebrated pre-Islamic sage of Quranic lore ("Indeed, We gave Luqmān wisdom").[15] The text even draws a parallel between the fidelity and ardor with which a Muslim attends to (the five) daily canonical prayers and the steadfast devotion with which the poet anticipates Ismāʿīl's magnanimity. The patron Ismāʿīl ibn Naghrīla, however, is not a Muslim but a Jew—Samuel the Nagid—as both the poet al-Munfatil and the editor Ibn Bassām ultimately remind us.

The tone as well as the overparticularized representation of the figure of Ismāʿīl in the second of three additional poems (of al-Munfatil) transmitted by Ibn Bassām differ sharply from the thematic material and tenor of the epistle and its lyric:

A clan from whom Moses and company sprang:
  Say of them what you will; you can never describe even a tenth of them.
How numerous are their signs on earth;
  How great are their generous deeds among men.
True, you collect the scattered elements of praise
  and release incarcerated generosity.
You exceed in generosity the people of east and west
  as pure gold exceeds the value of bronze.
If people could distinguish error from truth
  they'd kiss naught but your ten fingertips!
They'd embrace your hands like the (Kaʿba's) Black Cornerstone,
  your right to theirs, your left to theirs.

[12] The poetics of ritual ceremony in three Andalusi panegyrics are studied by Stetkevych, 1997. For this aspect of the poetry of the Muslim East, see Sperl; and Stetkevych, 1991.

[13] Pellat, *EI*^{2}, 5:528–29.

[14] Pellat, *EI*^{2}, 1:303–304.

[15] Qur'ān (Sūrat Luqmān) 31:12–13.

I've succeeded in this world and obtained my desire through you;
  and through you I hope to attain my aspiration in the Hereafter.
I obey the law of the Sabbath [openly] among you;
  among my own people I observe it in secret.
Even Moses was afraid, kept a cautious lookout,
  and was in want. But you safeguard from fear and deprivation.[16]

Here, the poet al-Munfatil avails himself of a very mixed bag of religious idioms and symbols. He pays tribute to Ismāʿīl's Levitic heritage ("A clan from whom Moses and company sprang")[17] and boldly likens Ibn Naghrīla's power to bestow favor to the Stone within the sacred shrine of Mecca, the very locus of holiness in Islam. It is as though the patron's support of the poet establishes a religious bond between them that the well-compensated al-Munfatil will take with him to the peace and reward of the next world. And so finally, al-Munfatil "avows" that he secretly "professes" the law of Ismāʿīl's religious community (Ar. *Adīnu bi-dīni l-sabt ladaykum wa-in kuntu fī qawmī adīnu bihi sirr[an]*), protected by Ismāʿīl, as it were, from any harm that might come to him on account of his new "faith."

The declaration of such a seemingly strange manner of loyalty as we read in al-Munfatil's poem—feigned religious affiliation with one's patron's religious community—is in fact related closely to more conventional conceits found in Arabic panegyric and love poetry. In a panegyric, the object of the poet's attention is naturally presumed to be a Muslim. But in the Arabic lyrics of some poets it is not unusual for the object of the poet's amorous affections to be a non-Muslim. Abū Nuwās's (ninth-century Muslim East) transgressive exercises on this theme (in this case, love for a Christian boy) earned the poet widespread notoriety.[18] As for comparable Andalusi lyrics, there are Abū ʿAbd Allāh b. Ḥaddād's (eleventh century) poem of love for a Christian girl of Guidix whom he calls Nuwaira (aka Jamīla),[19] famous idiosyncratic exercises on the theme by Ibn al-Zaqqāq of Valencia (d.c. 1133),[20] or by Ibrāhīm ibn Sahl of Seville, the thirteenth-century Jewish courtier and convert to Islam, in which the poet speaks tongue-in-cheek of exchanging the love of a certain lad called Mūsā (Moses) for the love of another youth named Muḥammad.[21]

[16] Ibn Bassām, 2:765.

[17] The very *ḥasab* and *nasab* Samuel celebrates in his own Hebrew verse. See Brann, 1991, pp. 52–54, 57.

[18] For example, "*Al-jismu minni saqīm[un]*," by Abū Nuwās, p. 333.

[19] "Qalbiya fī dhāti l-uthaylāti," in Melville and Ubaydli, pp. 74–77.

[20] "*Wa-ḥabbab yawma l-sabti*," by Ibn al-Zaqqāq, p. 113 (no. 15). Pérès, p. 268, drew my attention to Ibn al-Zaqqāq.

[21] "*Tasallaytu ʿan mūsā*," by Abū Isḥāq Ibrāhīm ibn Sahl, p. 32 (no. 24).

The motif turns up in Andalusi prose sources as well. In *Ṭawq al-ḥamāma*, Ibn Ḥazm relates an anecdote (with very obvious polemical overtones) concerning a distinguished Muslim scholar falling so in love with a young Christian lad as to gravely compromise his Islam: "Abū 'l-Ḥusayn Aḥmad ibn Yaḥya ibn Isḥāq al-Rāwandī . . . mentions that Ibrāhīm ibn Saiyar al-Naẓẓām, the head of the Muʿtazilī sect, for all his eminence in scholastic theology and his supreme mastery of the higher knowledge, in order to enjoy forbidden relations with a certain Christian boy whom he loved to madness went so far as to compose a treatise extolling the merits of the Trinity over monotheism."[22] Another illustrative story preserved in a different source concerns the famous tenth-century Andalusi poet al-Ramaḍī (Abū ʿUmar Yūsuf ibn Hārūn al-Qurṭubī) who supposedly became so "infatuated with a Christian youth" that he wore the distinctive belt (*zunnār*) that Christians had to wear and made "the sign of the Cross on the cup before drinking wine."[23]

Al-Munfatil's poetic declaration of clandestine Jewish faith and allegiance has nevertheless persuaded some scholars to believe that the poet actually embraced his patron's religion. For instance, A. R. Nykl deems the poet the literary opposite of Abū Isḥāq al-Ilbīrī whose *qaṣīda* reviling Yūsuf ibn Naghrīla and the Jews of Granada was noted in the previous chapter. And relying upon Henri Pérès's reading of al-Munfatil, Nykl asserts that the poet "*was secretly converted to Judaism* and praised the Jews in a very servile manner [emphasis mine]."[24] So, too, and more recently, Otto Zwartjes follows Nykl in observing "the poet al-Munfatil, who wrote in the Taifa Granada, converted to the Jewish religion and praised the Jews and their religion in his poems."[25] The poet's genuine acceptance of Judaism would have represented a truly peculiar and manifestly dangerous instance of what Muslims, especially the Shīʿa, call *taqiyya*: religious dissimulation, usually for the purpose of accommodating political and religious authority.[26] If discovered, such a practice would have required al-Munfatil's swift execution. But the reader should not make the mistake of confusing religious dissimulation

[22] Ibn Ḥazm, 1986, p. 234; trans. Arberry, 1953, p. 243.

[23] Nykl, pp. 58–59. The prescription in Islamic law for the *zunnār* goes back to the Pact of ʿUmar as transmitted by Muḥammad ibn al-Walīd al-Ṭurtūshī, 1994, 2:542, "*wa-an nashudda l-zanānīr ʿalā awsāṭinā*"; trans. of Cairo, 1872, edition in Lewis, 1987, 2:218: "We shall dress in our traditional fashion wherever we may be, and we shall bind the *zunnār* (a distinctive belt) around our waists."

[24] Pérès, pp. 269–73; Nykl, p. 200.

[25] Zwartjes, p. 71.

[26] R. Strothman-(Moktar Djebli).

with literary pretence; the poet is toying in verse with a religiously inflammatory hyperbolic poetic conceit.[27]

S. M. Stern cites the following Arabic *kharja* (envoi) preserved in a panegyrical Hebrew *muwashshaḥa* (strophic poem) attributed to Isaac ibn ʿEzra' (twelfth century) but of uncertain authorship: "The Sabbath is my festival on account of this Jewish noble!" (Ar. *al-sabt ʿīdi min ajli hādhā l-rūsi l-yahūdī*).[28] Noting the widespread practice of contrafaction (*muʿāraḍa*) in the production of Arabic and Hebrew strophic songs, Stern suggests that this *kharja* may have been appropriated from a popular Arabic composition. The oft-cited lines of satirical verse by an Egyptian poet referring to the political rise and weighty influence in the Fatimid government of the Jewish functionary Abū Saʿd Ibrāhīm al-Tustarī (d. 1047) further indicate that allusion to the poet's feigned "Jewishness" in al-Munfatil's text was simply an extension of a well-known Arabic rhetorical trope:

> The Jews of our time have attained the goal of their aspirations;
> The honors are theirs and so are the riches. Counselors and kings are taken from their midst.
> Egyptians! I advise you, become Jews, for Heaven itself has turned Jewish![29]

In any case, it is clear that in al-Munfatil's lyric we are dealing with a conventional literary topos and an instance of praise for a patron wherein the poet presses a rhetorical conceit to its extreme—an effective yet unsettling literary gambit in a society where identity is determined and status conferred according to one's affiliation with a particular religious community.

Viewed from the more narrow perspective of Arabic poetics, al-Munfatil's conceit is an acceptable, even bewitching and commendable poetic artifice. It falls under the rhetorical license given to poets who, according to familiar Quranic topos, are well known for devising overly

[27] For very different interpretations of al-Munfatil's "intent," see Dozy, 1972, p. 609; Baron, 3:157; and Roth, 2:198–99.

[28] Stern, 1950, p. 140; Isaac ibn ʿEzra', p. 145. Isaac ibn ʿEzra', the son of the Andalusi-Jewish polymath Abraham ibn ʿEzra', is known to have traveled to the Muslim East where he studied with the famous philosopher and convert Abū l-Barakāt al-Baghdādī. It was once believed that Isaac ibn ʿEzra' converted to Islam but this alleged "conversion" as well as a reputed "deconversion" are by no means certain and are still matters of controversy among scholars.

[29] Goitein, 1967–93, 2:374, surmises that the lines of verse transmitted by Ibn Muyassar, a thirteenth-century Egyptian historian of the Fatimid and Ayyubid periods, pp. 61–62, as well as by al-Suyūṭī, 2:201, cited by Stillman, 1979b, p. 51, were based on an earlier poem. See Cahen, *EI*^{2}, 3:894. On the Tustarī family and its importance in the history of the Jews in Palestine and Egypt, see Gil, 1981.

imaginative utterance at variance with their own behavior, beliefs, and commitments.[30] Indeed, Ibn Bassām's literary-critical comments (inserted after the illustrations of al-Munfatil's verse) make a point of speaking of acceptable and unacceptable hyperbole (the Arabic trope *ghulūw*) in al-Munfatil's lyrics:

> In this ode the poet included hyperbolic praises of him [Ismāʿīl] that I will neither record nor cite. May God's curse be upon al-Munfatil on account of the poem and prose he composed in his [Ismāʿīl's] honor. . . . He [al-Munfatil] does have in the ode instances of exaggerated rhetoric that we can deem acceptable.[31]

This trope could, by turns, function as an easily recognized hyperbolic metaphor for the poet's devotion to his patron or as a caustic critique of a state policy that appointed Jews to high office and placed them in positions of political power over Muslims.

Rhetorical convention and poetic accomplishment aside, Ibn Bassām and other Andalusi literary intellectuals of the twelfth century surely found it an embarrassing affront to the dignity of all Muslims for al-Munfatil to demean himself by addressing a Jew in such a seemingly deferential manner. What some Muslims might have tolerated or been helpess to prevent during the exceptional circumstances of eleventh-century *mulūk al-ṭawā'if* al-Andalus could have no place in the twelfth, a period ostensibly dominated by Islamic religious reform and the strict orthodoxy of Almoravid and Almohad piety and policy.[32] In al-Munfatil, Ibn Bassām therefore finds an Andalusi-Arabic poet "validating" Ibn Naghrīla's appointment to high executive office by the Zirids and its implicit violation of the rights of Muslim and Islamic law. The poet compounds his own "transgression" and further compromises Muslim sensibilities by heaping praise upon the Jewish culprit and celebrating or pretending to embrace his religious tradition. Ibn Bassām thus vehemently castigates al-Munfatil:

> May God's curse be upon him because of the compensation he received and may He remove him from belief in that religion he embraced on account of money. I do not know what is more incredible in the affairs of this admitted sinner who was insolent

[30] Qur'ān 26:227

> And the poets—the perverse follow them;
> Hast thou not seen how they wander in every valley
> And how they say which they do not?

On the license given to poets, see Ibn Rashīq al-Qayrawānī, 2:61.

[31] Ibn Bassām, 2:765.

[32] Abun-Nasr, pp. 98–99, 103, 108–109.

> toward his Lord: that he preferred this accursed Jew over the prophets and messengers or that he attributed to him such success in this world and the next. On the Day of Judgement, may God raise him by the Jew's standard and forbid him entry to Paradise but by His mercy.[33]

It should be recalled that Ibn Bassām al-Shantarīnī himself was forced to abandon his native town (Santarem) when the Christians conquered it in 1092.[34]

To put al-Munfatil's praise of Ibn Naghrīla, and Ibn Bassām's denunciation of the poet and his professional conduct, in the perspective of the norms of Muslim behavior toward *dhimmī* subjects, it will be useful to cite a relevant *fatwā* (religiously binding legal opinion) by Abū l-Ḥasan al-Qābisī, one of the leading Mālikī thinkers of tenth-century al-Andalus.[35] As preserved in al-Wansharīsī's fifteenth-century *fatwā* compendium, the text speaks of strictly regulating social contact between Muslims and *dhimmīs*. The relations in question are those of the precise type embodied in al-Munfatil's poetry and in his dependence on his Jewish patron (emphasis mine):

> Do not associate with someone whose religion is different from yours; that is the safer for you. There is no harm in doing your neighbor a favor if he asks you and if what he asks for is not sinful. *There is no harm either if you were to respond to him with kind words providing that this does not unduly magnify him or place him in a rank of honour higher than his own, nor should it make him pleased with his religion.*[36]

So much for al-Munfatil's subversive verse and rhymed prose.

What of Ibn Bassām, the editor of the text who preserves and transmits al-Munfatil's offensive verse and shocking literary prose in praise

[33] Ibn Bassām, 2:765.

[34] Ibn Bassām, cited by Wasserstein, 1985, p. 280 (from Ibn Bassām *al-Dhakhira*, Cairo 1942 ed., 1 part 2, p. 430), quotes a line of verse describing the Andalusi nobility as follows: "Their minds were occupied with wine and song and listening to music." In the introduction to *Al-Dhakhīra* (ed. Iḥsān ʿAbbās), 1:14, cited and translated by Kassis, 1990, p. 153, Ibn Bassām observes:

> On account of their location in this clime, close to the Christians in a land which is at the extremity of those conquered by Islam and quite removed from the influence of Arab traditions, surrounded by the vast sea, by the Christians and the Goths—they [the people of al-Andalus] reap nothing but perdition and drink of a torrential sea.

[35] Ibn Khallikān, 3:320–22.

[36] Abū l-Ḥasan al-Qābisī, *apud* Aḥmad ibn Yaḥyā al-Wansharīsī, 11:300–301, cited by Kassis, 1994, pp. 405–406.

of Ibn Naghrīla? The reader cannot help but wonder what purpose is served when an editor transmits that which he deems utterly objectionable and religiously offensive. Do al-Munfatil's epistle and poems simply serve as a pretext, an anti-text for Ibn Bassām's cautionary editorial? Such expressions of socioreligious indignation as we read in Ibn Bassām's remarks castigating al-Munfatil cannot be explained solely as the pious literary posture of a writer (living in an age of zealous religious reform) reporting the distant events of the previous century. As we have seen in the previous chapter, such reports preserve and reproduce accurately Muslim hostility toward Jewish courtiers of Ibn Naghrīla's own time—hostility of a religious, political, and social nature. However, they also reflect the genuine bewilderment of twelfth-century literary intellectuals reflecting on the tumultuous affairs and events of the eleventh century. They saw in traditions and reports of the kind preserved in *Al-Dhakhīra* evidence of the egregious missteps of the Muslim rulers of al-Andalus whose policy blunders seemed to lead directly to the even more unfavorable situation (vis-à-vis the Christian kingdoms of northern Iberia) of the twelfth century.

At the same time, the portrait of Ibn Naghrīla preserved in the first of *Al-Dhakhīra*'s two chapters is by no means uniformly hostile to the Jewish dignitary. Just as Ibn Bassām can denounce the contents of verse he considers rhetorically accomplished, we can ascribe *Al-Dhakhīra*'s balancing of positive and negative representations of Ibn Naghrīla to a stylistic requirement of the literary genre in which we find them. This Arabic discursive style has been said to reflect the skepticism and relativism frequently prevalent in the intellectual outlook of literary circles.[37] Indeed, *adab* places a premium on artful juxtaposition of widely divergent if not perfectly contradictory points of view.[38] For our purposes, the contrasting images of the Ibn Naghrīlas embedded in the *structure* as well as evident in the discursive content of this chapter of *Al-Dhakhīra* recall similar strategies we found in Ibn al-Khaṭīb's history of Granada and ʿAbd Allāh b. Buluggīn's apologetic memoir *Al-Tibyān*, each of which can be read as a textualization of Muslim ambivalence toward the Jews of al-Andalus.

Ibn Bassām introduces the next chapter of *Al-Dhakhīra*, which is devoted to the events of December 1066 ("[a] chapter summarizing what is known of the murder of that Jew"), with an extended and at times lyrical tirade against Ibn Naghrīla. This second of two chapters devoted to Ibn Naghrīla may be outlined as follows:

[37] As noted in the previous chapter, this inflection of Arabic style goes back to alJāḥiẓ in ʿAbbasid Islam. See Pellat, 1990, p. 92; and 1956.

[38] See the comments of Scheindlin, 1999b, p. 43, as they apply to poems that present "arguments for and against a given proposition."

1. Introduction of Ibn Naghrīla on a cautionary note
   a. contrast with father who worked for Ḥabbūs and Bādīs in the state financial administration
2. Ibn Naghrīla, the son, a perverse unbeliever with extensive authority
   a. author of blasphemous treatise against Islam in refutation of Ibn Ḥazm
3. Ibn Naghrīla's complex relations with the Jews of Granada
4. Comments (about Ibn Naghrīla's Jewishness) and anecdote (about Ibn Naghrīla's authority)
5. Ibn Naghrila's conspiracy to depose the Zirids of Granada with al-Muʿtasim ibn Ṣumādiḥ of Almeria
   a. anecdote (parallel) of Umayyad Caliph ʿAbd al-Malik with whose adversary Ibn Naghrīla compares unfavorably
   b. conspiracy fails
   c. Ibn Naghrīla killed, Jews of Granada attacked; Ibn Ṣumādiḥ

As though Ismāʿīl did not die of natural causes in 1055/1056 but continued to serve the *amīr* Bādīs for another ten years, the text continues to speak of Ismāʿīl, conflating, as it were, the careers of father and son surnamed Ibn Naghrīla.[39] The entire Granadan political crisis is framed as a radical departure from the commonplace (Ar. *wa-kāna min ʿajā'iba dhālika l-zamān*) and the text reviles Ibn Naghrīla's haughty character, his effrontery and impudence in ruling Muslims and lording it over them, and his accumulation of extraordinary wealth at the Muslims' expense. *Al-Dhakhīra* goes on to assail Ibn Naghrīla's insolent literary-religious polemic with Ibn Ḥazm in which he is said to have attacked Islam and slandered the Prophet.

Ibn Bassām also reports that Ibn Naghrīla's Muslim enemies accused the Zirid *wazīr* of outwardly following Judaism while privately (actually not so privately) holding the views of a nonbeliever. Even the Jews of Granada are said to have joined their Muslim neighbors in repudiating Ibn Naghrīla, supposedly on account of his brazen renunciation of Judaism. Accordingly, *Al-Dhakhīra* indicts Ibn Naghrīla on two counts, much as Ibn Ḥazm's *Refutation* prefers twin charges against its unnamed Jewish addressee. In both texts "Ibn Naghrīla" is accused of compounding very serious sociopolitical offenses against Islam and the community of Muslims by committing a capital religious transgression against Islam and God.[40]

[39] In this account, Ibn Naghrīla's son Yūsuf is said to have fled to North Africa and escaped the fate of his father and the Jewish community of Granada.

[40] Lewis, 1984a, p. 68, asserts that in the intra-Islamic context, "heresy" is persecuted primarily when it comes to represent some kind of political threat.

Here is how *Al-Dhakhīra* puts it:

Among the extraordinary events of that period of fractious order and tribulations was the elevation of that Jewish scoundrel who upbraided all who ascribed to a revealed religion. Even the Jews, with their accursed religion, did not heed him nor did they trust him regarding esoteric matters. His father Yūsuf, a man from the common folk of Jews, had fine manners for one of them and a favorable character for their like. He was enlisted in Granada by Bādīs and his father Ḥabbūs before him to work in the state treasury and the administration of most of its operations.

His son succeeded him while only a youth and, as people maintained, just a tender colt. He spellbound those responsible for young men such that it was said of him: "He's the one; he's the one!" Before long he assumed the reins of administration and had a free hand with the better part of the state funds. A mass of people followed in his footsteps with whom he ran a perverse footrace, making light of the most serious of ugly deeds, he strayed too far and was not mindful of the consequences, such that his hands were awash in kisses and he boasted of his refutation of religion. He composed a treatise in refutation of the aforementioned scholar of religious law Abū Muḥammad b. Ḥazm in which he openly expressed calumny against Islam. He was not deterred from [writing] this [treatise] by rebuke nor was anyone able to excise it except from one's own mind.

The position in which the government installed him was a source of rage for the Muslims day and night. For that matter the Jews sensed there would be disaster on his account and complained of his tyrannical rule even though he had pulverized rubble for them and paved the way for them in the most difficult matters. Nevertheless, he remained steadfast in his extremist views and turned away from the path of God in his relations with others. He forced his judgements upon the Jews, deposed their leaders, and in accordance with their religious law was named "Nagid," which means "administrator" to them, a position their ancients had regarded with suspicion. Their communal leaders initially treated it (the office) with deference [but] he behaved audaciously with his weak foundation and without regard for his soul.[41]

The reader need not be troubled by *Al-Dhakhīra*'s conflation of the terms of office of father (Ismāʿīl) and son (Yūsuf), or alternately, by the

[41] Ibn Bassām, 2:766.

simple confusion of the names Yūsuf and Ismāʿīl in this second chapter devoted to Ibn Naghrīla. Such an obvious historical inaccuracy indicates that *The Tibyān*'s account of these events did not survive as an accessible source for twelfth-century authors. The errors in reporting also may reflect the tendency of Arabic literary historians such as Ibn Bassām to privilege reporting anecdotes and transmitting poetry and elevated prose in their *adab* anthologies over attending carefully to the sorts of historical concerns, exacting detail, and precision characteristic of much of Muslim historiography. If this supposition is correct, it would appear that Ibn Bassām was himself the primary source of the aforementioned confusion of Ibn Naghrīlas also evident in the Muslim historiography of thirteenth-century North Africa.[42] For our purposes, it is doubtless more significant that this passage of *Al-Dhakhīra* goes out of its way to avoid mentioning Ibn Naghrīla by name or even by derogatory epithet except for the sole conventional gesture of the phrase "that Jewish scoundrel" (*dhālika l-yahūdī l-ma'būn*). The Jew in the text is essentially stripped of individuality apart from his belonging to a *dhimmī* religious community. Instead the text emphasizes the Jewish miscreant's perverted unbelief and its ruinous effects on his behavior. The next section describes his tyrannical abuse of the powers of his office against Muslim and Jew alike.

Here, too, as in Ibn Ḥayyān (*apud* Ibn al-Khaṭīb) and ʿAbd Allāh b. Buluggīn, care is taken to distinguish the noble father from the contemptible son. The former plays an important but circumscribed role in the Zirid administration according to Ibn Bassām ("fine manners for one of them and favorable character for their like," "enlisted . . . to work in the state treasury and the administration of most of its operations"), reminiscent of *The Tibyān*'s carefully drawn picture of a skilled yet cautious Ismāʿīl who knows his proper subordinate place in Muslim society. But the son's unbridled ambition, hubris, and extensive authority posed a danger to the Jews of Granada and placed him in harm's way. In this passage of *Al-Dhakhīra*, perhaps inspired by a reading of Ibn Ḥazm, Ibn Naghrīla is demonized as much for his religious perfidy as for his violation of Muslim rights, political sensibilities, and Islamic law.

The passage begins and ends with observations of Ibn Naghrīla's disdain for correct monotheistic belief ("that Jewish scoundrel who upbraided anyone who ascribed to a revealed religion" [Ar. "*al-zārī ʿalā kulli dhī dīn*"]). And it suggests that Ibn Naghrīla's insolence before God led directly to his downfall ("he behaved audaciously with his weak foundation and without regard for his soul" [Ar. "*ijtara'a huwa*

[42] On which, see below.

ʿalayhā bi-wahī ussihi wa-qillati naẓarihi li-nafsihi"]). These initial and closing accusations against Ibn Naghrīla are reiterated in the middle of the passage ("making light of the most serious of ugly deeds, *he strayed too far and was not mindful of the consequences*, such that his hands were awash in kisses and he boasted of his refutation of religion" [Ar. "*wa-yatamaddaḥu bil-ṭaʿni ʿalā l-milal*"]), further drawing the reader's attention to the perverse religious nature of his offense. As expressed here, Ibn Naghrīla's unbelief as a Jew could serve as a proof-text for the Quranic warnings and reassurances about the ultimate test by which God will judge every soul: "Surely those who believe and those Jews, Christians and Sabean who believe in God and the last day and do good deeds, their reward is with their Lord; they have nothing to fear nor shall they grieve" (2:63); "Believers, Jews, Sabeans, and Christians—whoever believes in God and the Last Day and does what is right—shall have nothing to fear or to regret" (5:70).

As for the *Al-Dhakhira*'s reference to Ibn Naghrila's supposed literary polemic with Ibn Hazm ("in which he openly expressed calumny against Islam" [Ar. "*wa-jāhara bi-kālami fī l-ṭaʿni ʿalā millati l-islām*"]), the Jew stands in clear contravention of al-Shāfiʿī's classical articulation of the limits of *dhimmī* discourse prescribed by Islamic law: "If any one of you speak improperly of Muḥammad, may God bless and save him, the Book of God, or of His religion, he forfeits the protection [*dhimma*] of God, the Commander of the Faithful and of all the Muslims; he has contravened the conditions upon which he was given safe-conduct; his property and life are at the disposal of the Commander of the Faithful, like the property and lives of the people of the House of War [*dār al-ḥarb*]."[43] Having encountered the conjunction of Islamic heresy and religious otherness in *Al-Fiṣal* and *The Refutation* along with repeated calls for its suppression and for the *sharīʿa*-sanctioned persecution of those who hold and embody it, the reader should not be surprised that the construction of Ibn Naghrīla's religious otherness in this passage of *Al-Dhakhīra* resembles that of a *munāfiq* (hypocrite) and *zindīq* (heretic) more than a Jewish *dhimmī*. That is, he appears as a Muslim heretic who makes it a habit of concealing his true beliefs so as to do his worst, without notice, restraint, or punishment.

Arguably the strongest impartial "evidence" *Al-Dhakhīra* presents of Ibn Naghrīla's villainous character is that the Jews of Granada themselves are said to have regarded him with suspicion ("Even the Jews, with their accursed religion, did not heed him nor did they trust him regarding esoteric matters"). The text does not condemn the Jews per se but only their religiously misguided "leader." *Al-Dhakhīra* in fact ap-

[43] Al-Shāfiʿī, 4:118–19; trans. Lewis, 1987, 2:220.

pears to contradict itself regarding Ibn Naghrīla's relationship with the Jews of Granada. The Jews are alternately distant and removed from him and worried about the consequences of his reckless behavior and depraved religious beliefs; yet they behave deferentially toward him and derive substantial benefit and protection from his position and power.[44] Whether this ambiguity represents actual divisions within the Jewish community of Granada or not, or the reservations some Jews may have harbored about the Nagid's activities, echoes of which may survive in Samuel's own poetry, we cannot know.[45] It seems likely that political disagreements among factions within the Jewish community of Granada such as are reported in *The Tibyān* appear in *Al-Dhakhīra* reformulated as religious misgivings and questions swirling about Ibn Naghrīla's alleged intellectual orientation and impious behavior.

As for opposition among some Jews to Samuel's or Joseph's political activities, schemes, and the intrigues in which they became enmeshed, it is instructive that Ibn Daud identifies three Granadan Jews who had endorsed Buluggīn's candidacy for *amīr* and opposed Samuel ibn Naghrīla in supporting Bādīs. Accordingly, the three were supposedly forced to seek refuge from Ibn Naghrīla and flee to Seville:

> Now the king had two sons, Badis the elder and Buluggin the younger. Although the Berber princes supported the election of the younger Buluggin as king, the people at large supported Badis. The Jews also took sides, with three of them, R. Joseph b. Megash, R. Isaac b. Leon, and R. Nehemiah surnamed Ishkafa, who were among the leading citizens of Granada, supporting Buluggin. R. Samuel ha-Levi, on the other hand, supported Badis. . . . Buluggin then died, and the kingdom was established in the hand of Badis. Thereupon, the three leading Jewish citizens mentioned above fled to the city of Seville.[46]

Against the backdrop of the strained relations, rivalry and outright hostilities between ʿAbbādid Seville and Zirid Granada during the eleventh century,[47] the defection of a Jewish party from Granada to Seville would have signaled very deep divisions in the Jewish community of Granada

[44] According to Ashtor, 1992, 2:167, Yūsuf's compatriots anticipated the communal consequences of his risky political intrigues. As for Samuel ha-Nagid, "*L*ᵉ*vavi tokh q*ᵉ*ravai*," Samuel ha-Nagid, 1966, 1:211–12; trans. Cole, pp. 31–32, and its superscription allude to unspecified intrigues against the poet.

[45] See Brann, 1991, pp. 52–58.

[46] Abraham ibn Daud, pp. 55–56 (trans. pp. 73–74).

[47] On which, see Wasserstein, 1985, pp. 127–33, who discusses the nature of this and other rivalries in eleventh-century al-Andalus.

at a time when Samuel the Nagid had already attained a kind of ecumenical status among the Jews of al-Andalus. If Jewish opposition in Granada could develop and be mounted against Samuel there certainly could have been widespread concern about the character and activities of his youthful, untested son and successor Joseph, as well as in response to his departures from his father's programs, strategies, and tactics.[48]

Ibn Bassām continues his account of the events leading to 1066 with an observation and an illustrative anecdote. The reader should note the continuing convergence of religiopolitical motifs in the danger Ibn Naghrīla poses as an enemy of the Muslim state and as a barely covert unbeliever:

> As for the [high] position he [Ibn Naghrīla] attained at his ruler's side, even surpassing him, there has simply never been anything like it.
>
> I have been told by someone who witnessed him [Ibn Naghrīla] strolling the streets of Cordoba with his master during one of his visits there on the occasion of [attending to] some unruly matters and alarming disturbances. My source reports: "I saw him with Bādīs and I could not tell apart the leader from the led. So I recited [the following half-verse]: 'The shoulders and heads are all the same!' "
>
> Ibn al-Saqqā', the governor of Cordoba in those days, further said to me: "There would be nothing objectionable about Ismāʿīl if he had not forgotten Judaism/[his] Jewishness!"
>
> Along these lines, he took up Arabic books and delved into the science of the Arabs. In the end, he concealed his master from the public, imprisoned him with the bottle and cup, and abandoning his religion settled on the means to betray him. He promised to install his ally Ibn Ṣumādiḥ of Almeria [as *amīr*] in his [Bādīs's] place and confer to him [Ibn Ṣumādiḥ] his [Bādis's] sovereign authority. Al-Muʿtasim ibn Ṣumādiḥ transmitted to him [Ibn Naghrīla] the core of the state treasury, exposing his deepest hopes. Indeed, he [Ibn Naghrīla] sought to topple Bādīs' throne

[48] A Jewish text can be cited to cast doubt on the reports of Ibn Naghrīla's Jewish opposition, notwithstanding *Sefer Ha-Qabbalah*'s comments on Joseph's character. It is a soulful strophic elegy R. Isaac ibn Ghiyāth (d. 1089) composed on the occasion of Joseph ha-Nagid's death, "*Heylili torah w^{e}-sh'agi kha-lavi'*." Schirmann, 1965, pp. 190–91 (no. 81). Schirmann posits that another elegy by Ibn Ghiyāth, "*Eikhah pit'om*," p. 191, (no. 82) is also devoted to Joseph.

> with Ibn Ṣumādiḥ's rule because he knew of his [Ibn Ṣumādiḥ's] feebleness.[49]

In the first of *Al-Dhakhīra's* two chapters devoted to Ibn Naghrīla, the Andalusi-Muslim poet al-Munfatil is the text's principal subject and the primary target for Ibn Bassām's sternest objections. The text before us that is the second and more narrative-minded chapter zeroes in on the figure of Ibn Naghrīla himself. His position of authority is described as extraordinary ("there simply has never been anything like it"), a conclusion justified by the casual observer of the street scene in Cordoba who reports that he could not distinguish the *amīr* from the government official ostensibly in his service (Ar. "*fa-lam afraq bayna l-ra'īs wal-mar'ūs*").

Ibn Naghrīla's empowerment within the Muslim state bureaucracy of Granada and his success in undermining the established political hierarchy would be sufficiently disconcerting for an Andalusi Muslim in any circumstances. But in this case, the nominal Muslim ruler is also rendered indistinguishable from the Jewish courtier supposedly serving him. The very purpose of Muslim society is overturned and its natural order upset to the Jew's advantage over the Muslim *amīr* as well as at the expense of the Muslims whose rights he is charged to protect. Muslim anxiety about the place of the Jew in Andalusi society thus goes beyond concern for the Jews' place in the unusual political circumstances of eleventh-century Granada during which Samuel and Joseph wielded extraordinary authority in Granada and supposedly played important roles in the very real internal intrigues involving Zirid succession (as reported in *The Tibyān*).[50] Rather, the expanded iconic language in which *Al-Dhakhīra* couches these concerns suggests that the construction of Ibn Naghrīla flows from and is deepened by longstanding Muslim anxieties about the proximity of Jew to Muslim, of Judaism to Islam such as we found in Ibn Ḥazm. That is, the figure of Ibn Naghrīla is shaped and informed by the paradigmatic ways in which some Muslims supposed that Jews insinuated themselves repeatedly into the very structures and administration of Muslim society and exerted their influence underhandedly on the articulation and practice of Islam going back to the time of the Prophet and the formative age of classical Islam. In turn, the figure of Ibn Naghrīla and the events of 1066 themselves became central components of the classical paradigm and, through Arabic historiography and Abū Isḥāq al-Ilbīrī's invective propaganda, came to inform the ways in which later *maghribī* Muslim activist-pietists

[49] Ibn Bassām, 2:767.

[50] As reported in *The Tibyān* and as represented in various allusions in Samuel the Nagid's Hebrew poetry. See Ashtor, 1992, 2:197, and the references cited there.

thought of their all-too-close Jewish neighbors.[51] For parallels to the sense of crisis enveloping Islam in the West, arising from our reading of texts authored during the eleventh and twelfth centuries, we can point to the discourse of uncompromising religious scholars of turn-of-the-sixteenth-century Maghrib, notably Muḥammad b. ʿAbd al-Karīm al-Maghīlī (b.c. 1440; d. 1503–1504) who seems to have vented his profound fear of and hostility toward Europe and Christianity by attacking the Jews of Morocco.[52] Al-Maghīlī's biographer Ibn ʿAskar summarizes the views al-Maghīlī expressed in a virulent anti-Jewish pamphlet: "that the Jews—may God curse them—had no bond [of protection (*dhimma*)], since they had broken it by their association with men of authority among the Muslims, [an action] which went contrary to the humiliation and abasement (*al-dhull wal-ṣaghar*) stipulated in the payment of the *jizya*. . . . He declared it licit to spill their blood and plunder their property."[53]

The figure of Ibn Naghrīla drawn in this chapter of *Al-Dhakhīra* violates one of the essential stipulations in the recension of the Pact of ʿUmar transmitted by the Andalusi Mālikī scholar al-Ṭurtūshī (d. 1126), that of *ghiyār*—being distinguishable from Muslims: "We shall not attempt to resemble the Muslims in any way with regard to their dress. . . . We shall not speak as they do, nor shall we adopt their *kunyas*" (Ar. "*wa-lā natashabbaha bihim fī shac'[in] min libāsihim . . . walā natakallama bi-kalāmihim wa-lā-natakanna bi-kunāhum*"].[54] Andalusi and Maghribi *fatāwā* demonstrate that the Pact of ʿUmar was not only an ideal legal abstraction but also a living document to which Muslim jurists turned in trying to regulate the alternately annoying and productive relations between Muslims and Jews.[55] One such *fatwā* studied by Matthias Lehmann relates a twelfth-century complaint from Fez brought against Ibn Qanbal, a Jewish physician who "wears a turban and ring, rides on a saddle on a beautiful riding animal and sits in his shop without a distinguishing mark [*ghiyār*] and without a belt [*zunnār*], and he also walks around in the market streets without a distin-

[51] Hunwick, 1985.

[52] Abun-Nasr, p. 158; Vajda, 1962; Hunwick, 1985; Alfonso, 1999, a longer version of which, "ʿAbd al-Karīm al-Maǧīlī (n.c. 1440): El contexto socio-literario de un poema contra los judios," will appear shortly.

[53] Trans. Hunwick, 1985, p. 161.

[54] Al-Ṭurtūshī, 2:543; trans. of Cairo, 1872, edition, Lewis, 1987, 2:217–19; on al-Ṭurtushī, see Ibn Khallikān, 4:462–63, and al-Ṭurtūshī (ed. Fierro), 1993, pp. 68–73.

[55] Lehmann, 1999a, an elaboration of his 1999b presentation, studies the important use of the Pact of ʿUmar in *fatāwā* from Al-Wansharīsī's collection *Al-Miʿyār al-mughrib ʿan fatāwī ʿulamāʾ ifrīqiyā wal-andalus wal-maghrib*. See also an earlier study on the contract between *dhimmīs* and Islam in the Muslim West, Idris, 1974.

guishing mark which would allow him to be recognized [as a *dhimmī*]. Rather he wears the most exquisite [garb], like the Muslim notables or even better." In reply the *muftī* advises the jurists of Fez, among other things, to remind the Jews of the stipulations of the Pact of ʿUmar.[56] The force of this *fatwā*, our passage from Ibn Bassām, and the anecdote about Abraham ibn ʿAṭā' related in the Introduction is clear: When permitted to function indistinct from Muslims, the Jew is seemingly free to undermine the established social and political hierarchy and overturn the natural order of Muslim society.

Ibn Bassām's next informant (Ibn al-Saqqā', the governor of Cordoba) introduces a brief and seemingly perplexing assessment of Ibn Naghrīla: "There would be nothing objectionable about Ismāʿīl if he had not forgotten [his] Jewishness/Judaism!" (Ar. *Lā ba'sa bi-'smāʿīl lawlā annahu nasiya l-yahūdiyya*). The reader may prefer to understand this statement as signifying Ismāʿīl's "Jewishness" (a likely meaning of the Arabic), that is, his proper sense of occupying a subordinate place as a Jewish *dhimmī* in Muslim society. Indeed, if we read this paragraph in light of *Al-Dhakhīra*'s previous report, the social and political context of the anecdote (the inability of the observer to differentiate Ibn Naghrīla's from the *amīr*) supports the reading of *yahūdiyya* as "Jewishness" in Ibn al-Saqqā's observation. Ibn Naghrīla would thus have managed to avoid the stipulations of Islamic law designed to restrict his behavior and limit his status in Muslim al-Andalus. And by *displacing* the Muslim *amīr* he manages in effect to overturn the stipulations of the *dhimma* and void them entirely. The supposedly debased and inferior Jew achieves a status equal to or surpassing that of the Muslim, undoing and inverting the social and religious boundaries and order imposed on him by Islam for the protection of Muslim society.

But if we read Ibn al-Saqqā's reported quip in the context of the next following paragraph beginning with the explicit connecting phrase "Along these lines . . . " it would seem to support an understanding of *yahūdiyya* as "Judaism," another possible meaning of the Arabic ("Along these lines he took up Arabic books . . . and abandoning his religion . . ."). In fact, the second paragraph expressly couples Ibn Naghrīla's social and political offenses against Islam (appropriating Arabic learning and usurping authority over Muslims) with his religious transgression of "abandoning his [revealed] religion [Ar. *mulḥid[an] fī amrihi*])," much as these offenses were interconnected in the previous and longer passage. Note that *Al-Dhakhīra* employs the identical term for the Jew's heretical orientation (*mulḥid[an]*) Ibn Ḥazm applied in *Al-Fiṣal* to the rabbis of classical Judaism and his unidentified Jewish here-

[56] Lehmann, 1999a, p. 31, citing al-Wansharīsī, 2:254.

tic. In this respect, *Al-Dhakhīra*'s presentation of Ibn Naghrīla as a religious renegade may owe its formulation to the impression created in Ibn Ḥazm's *Refutation* that the Jewish interlocutor identified as Ibn Naghrīla by Andalusi and *maghribī* historians was seduced by intellectual heresies Judaism shared with Islam (i.e., the identification of the Jews as *min ahl al-mutadahhira*, "the materialists").[57]

In any case, the report alleges that Ibn Naghrīla's extensive learning led him astray from the fractured scriptural confession of Judaism that was corrected and superseded by Islam. What sounds as if it were a condemnation of Ibn Naghrīla for his supposed failings as a Jew in fact represents him as lapsing into complete *kufr*, a misstep that would remove him altogether from what Muslims and Muslim society may tolerate in their midst. Ultimately, the aforementioned ambiguity of Ibn Naghrīla's forgetting of *yahūdiyya* set forth in the text proves highly constructive in the context of the entire chapter of *Al-Dhakhīra*: The Jew stands accused of holding religiously dangerous opinions and of conducting himself in countless ways completely proscribed for a *dhimmī* subject in Islam.

We have already noted in our reading of Ibn Ḥazm's *Al-Fiṣal* precisely what sort of learning and intellectual orientation a Muslim audience could imagine leading Ibn Naghrīla so far astray from monotheism. But which Arabic books does *Al-Dhakhīra* imagine the Jewish savant taking up? Ibn Bassām's report about Ibn Naghrīla's state-of-the-art Arabic library offers a skewed parallel of two passages in *Sefer Ha-Qabbalah*, a Hebrew text by Abraham ibn Daud written in 1160–61:

> Besides being a great scholar and highly cultured person, R. Samuel was highly versed in Arabic literature and style. . . . He also purchased many books—[copies] of the Holy Scriptures as well as of the Mishna and Talmud. . . . Moreover, he retained scribes who would make copies of the Mishna and Talmud.[58]

And regarding Joseph the Nagid, Ibn Daud reports:

> His son, R. Joseph ha-Levi the Nagid, succeeded to his post. Of all the fine qualities which his father possessed he lacked but one . . . his father's humility. Indeed, he grew haughty—to his destruction. The Berber princes became so jealous of him that he was killed on the Sabbath day, the ninth of Tebet [4]827, along with the community of Granada and all those who had come from distant

[57] See chapter 2, above.

[58] Abraham ibn Daud, p. 53 (trans. pp. 71–72), p. 56 (trans. pp. 74–75).

> lands to see his learning and power. After his death, his books and treasures were scattered all over the world.[59]

Ibn Bassām and Ibn Daud may or may not have shared a common source regarding the Ibn Naghrīlas' extensive libraries (as well as the matter of Joseph's flawed character). Following *Al-Dhakhīra* but with greater specificity, Ibn ʿIdhārī reports that Ibn Naghrīla amassed a library of Arabic books devoted to the Islamic sciences.[60] The differences between the reports of the Jewish and Muslim texts are critical in two respects: (1) the significance they assign to the Ibn Naghrīla's acquisition of Arabic lore and (2) the consequence of this acquisition for the programmatic refashioning of Jewish culture and society in al-Andalus, that is, for Andalusi-Jewish identity.

For Ibn Bassām, as opposed to our first reading of Ibn Ḥayyān *apud* Ibn al-Khaṭīb, Ibn Naghrīla's practices as a connoisseur of Arabica and as an Arabic bibliophile have all the quality of an appropriation from which no good can come to Islam and Muslims. Concern for the easy availability and accessibility of Islamic sacred texts to Arabic-speaking *dhimmī*s seems to inform another provision of al-Ṭurtūshī's recension of the Pact of ʿUmar: "We shall not teach our children the Qur'ān" (Ar. "*wa-lā nuʿallima awlādanā l-qur'ān*").[61] Having usurped the *amīr*'s mantle, Ibn Naghrīla thus proceeds to take up, or better yet, take hold of the Muslim ruler's culture and religion. This is precisely the sort of subversive appropriation Ibn ʿAbdūn's twelfth-century *ḥisba* manual for Seville treats as a kind of *dhimmī* seizure of Muslim intellectual property:

> Books of science ought not to be sold to Jews and Christians, except those that treat their own religion. Indeed, they translate books of science and attribute authorship to their co-religionists or their bishops, when they are the work of Muslims.[62]

Ibn Naghrīla's readings in Islam as imagined by Ibn Bassām, Ibn Saʿīd, and Ibn ʿIdhārī are presumably the means by which someone of his Jewish background would have been able to mount an informed literary attack on Islam and the Prophet. It would also have provided him with the knowledge necessary to engage Ibn Ḥazm in learned disputation regarding the apparent infelicities of language and theology of the Qur'ān.

[59] Ibid., pp. 56–57 (trans. pp. 75–76). See also Moses ibn ʿEzra', p. 66 (35a), whose notice on Yūsuf includes the following statement: "His [extensive] knowledge of Arabica was second only to his surpassing knowledge of Hebraica."

[60] Ibn ʿIdhārī, 3:276.

[61] Al-Ṭurtūshī, 1994, 2:542.

[62] Lévi Provençal, 1934, pp. 238–48; trans. Lewis, 1987, 2:157–65.

Samuel the Nagid's mastery of Arabica is assigned a completely different significance by *Sefer Ha-Qabbalah*. Ibn Daud regards it, of course, as a source of communal pride and as an essential marker of the Andalusi cultural identity he sought to transfer intact to the Jews of twelfth-century (Christian-ruled) Toledo. In the legendary account of his discovery in Malaga, the Nagid's Arabic learning itself is represented as the very means by which he managed to begin his ascent to position and power, attain communal office, and eventually acquire abundant wealth and virtually unlimited authority.[63] And as a rabbinical scholar, the Nagid's purchase of "many books" and his retention of "scribes who would make copies" are construed as evidence of a public campaign he conducted for advanced Jewish literacy (rabbanite as opposed to Karaite), but not for his personal aggrandizement. By comparison, Joseph's commensurate "learning and power" more closely resemble artifacts on view in a palace; they attract attention and wonder in the Jewish world but are not shared with others in the same measure as Samuel's. Indeed, the contrast between father and son as educators and public figures and in the results they achieve is drawn starkly here. While Samuel dispenses both knowledge and largesse, Joseph's "books and treasures" are unfortunately "scattered all over the world."

Ibn Naghrīla's flirtation with *zandaqa*, his amassing an Arabic library of Islamic studies, and engaging the services of many copyists, are thus unmistakable signs of a misappropriation of Islam that complements and deepens his sedition against Islamdom as *wazīr* of Granada. Later Muslim historiographers appear to magnify Ibn Naghrīla's misappropriation of Islamic learning, making even more explicit than Ibn Bassām how the Jew thrashed and maligned the Qur'ān, Islam, and God. Abū l-Ḥasan ʿAlī Ibn Saʿīd al-Maghribī (1213–1286), author of the biographical anthology of Arabic poets *Al-Mughrib fī ḥulā l-maghrib* [*Novel Tidings about the Ornaments of the West*], cites and expands upon the work of the twelfth-century authority Abū Muḥammad ʿAbd Allāh ibn Ibrāhīm al-Ḥijārī, *Al-Muḥsib fī faḍā'il al-maghrib* [*Esteeming the Merits of the West*] to offer a laconic but still damning picture of Ibn Naghrīla:

> Ismāʿīl the son of Yūsuf the son of Naghrīlla the Jew. He was of an eminent Jewish family in Granada. His career was successful to such a degree that Bādīs the son of Ḥabbūs, king of Granada, made him his vizier. Thus he dared make fun of the Muslims and swore that he would versify the whole of the Qur'ān in poems and *muwashshaḥ*s apt to be sung. In the end, however, the Ṣanhāja,

[63] See chapter 1.

> who were the ruling class, killed him, not at the king's order, looting the houses of the Jews and killing them.

The following are verses from the poem in which he versified the Qur'ān:

> It wrote on the cheek a metrical verse from the Book of God: You will not obtain righteousness until you spend of that which you love. (Qur'ān 3:92)[64]

Ibn Bassām attributes to Ibn Naghrīla "a treatise in refutation of the aforementioned scholar of religious law (Ibn Ḥazm) . . . in which he openly expressed calumny against Islam." Ibn Sa'īd retains the literary dimension of the Ibn Naghrīla's public violation of Islam but removes it from the arguably refined station of interfaith polemic among literary and religious intellectuals. Instead, the offense against the Muslims and Islam escalates to irreverent mockery in the public domain. Ibn Naghrīla utilizes his expert knowledge of Arabic and Islam to humiliate Muslims and to demean and satirize God's very own inimitable discourse, transforming it, as it were, into the bawdy stuff of popular entertainment ("he dared make fun of the Muslims and swore that he would versify the whole of the Qur'ān in poems and *muwashshaḥ*s apt to be sung"). As we have seen in other texts, Ibn Sa'īd's report imagines Ibn Naghrīla turning the pecking order of Muslim society and its textual raison d'être topsy-turvy: The Muslim is humiliated and Islam treated disrespectfully by the Jew.

Regarding the elder Ibn Naghrīla's son, *Al-Mughrib* reports:

> His son Yūsuf. He was young when his father was killed in Granada and hanged at the river Genil [*Sanjil*]. He fled to Ifrīqiyā, and sent from there his famous poem to the inhabitants of Granada; the following are verses from it:
>
> O you, lying murdered at the side of the Genil, who are not afraid of the resurrection of the body, having listened to the words of one giving you good advice. The body was thrown to the dust,

[64] Ar. "*fa-stahza'a bil-muslimīn wa-qsama an yanẓama jamī'a l-qur'ān fī ash'ār[in] wa-muwashshaḥāt yughanni bihā*"; Ibn Sa'īd al-Maghribī, 1955, 2:114; trans. Stern, 1963, pp. 255–56. Stern also evaluates the entry according to its reliability and the accuracy of its historical detail.

Regarding the historicity of this episode, Ashtor, 1963, notes, 2:166, "The Moslems grudgingly endured Berber rule but when unbelievers attained dominance, their animosity doubled and redoubled. Moreover, they perceived the open contempt these Jews had for the Moslem faith—time and again their jests were offenses to the sanctity and the honor of the Moslem prophet. Joseph himself scorned much that is written in the Koran." Ashtor, 2:331, thus gives credence to Ibn Sa'īd: "Considering other statements about Joseph in various sources, there is no basis for disqualifying Ibn Sa'īd's account."

> while the spirit became wind over the surface of the earth. Traitors! If you had been loyal and redeemed the slaughtered one, like that other slaughtered one [Ishmael]! If you had killed him without a cause, we have killed before this the Messiah, and a prophet from Hāshim whom we have poisoned, who fell down from eating the shoulder [of a lamb].[65]

As read by S. M. Stern, the poem seems more like a Muslim opponent's lampoon of the assassinated Jewish *wazīr* than a son's lament. The text also appears to allude to Ibn Naghrīla's heretical disbelief in resurrection and divine judgment as reported by Ibn Bassām. Stern also draws attention to the poem's reference to the Jews' perfidy in killing (the prophet) Jesus and their failed attempt to poison Muḥammad, the Messenger of God.[66]

To return to *Al-Dhakhīra*: Ibn Naghrīla's purported conspiracy to replace the drunken and secluded *amīr* with a sympathetic neighboring ally (or stooge) represents the Jew's most serious breach of the boundaries imposed upon *dhimmī* subjects in Islam. In effect, Ibn Naghrīla's collusion with al-Muʿtasim ibn Ṣumādiḥ of Almeria offers the reader incontrovertible evidence of the impairment to Islam and Muslim society wrought by a seditious Jew installed as *ersatz* ruler of Muslim Granada. The text thus takes the trajectory of Jewish empowerment and offense against Islam to the extreme, imagining a Jewish polity supplanting a Muslim one. Ibn ʿIdhārī's aforementioned claim that Ibn Naghrīla planned to establish a Jewish kingdom in Almeria takes the implication of Ibn Bassām's report of the conspiracy with Ibn Ṣumādiḥ to its logical end, amplifying the Jew's subversion of Islam in a different way than Ibn Saʿīd.[67]

Al-Dhakhīra concludes its report on Ibn Naghrīla and 1066 disclosing in matter-of-fact manner the dimension of the destruction wrought by the Muslim populace of Granada against the Jewish usurper and the religious community to which he belonged. Only the concluding comment strikes a celebratory note:

> And they entered the palace through every gate and exposed the Jew's private stash [and plundered it], [leaving him] without cover.

[65] Ibn Saʿīd al-Maghribī, 1955, 2:115; trans. Stern, 1963, p. 257.

[66] Stern, 1963, p. 257.

[67] Almeria had been deeply involved in the internal political affairs of Granada going back to the days of Ḥabbūs first as an ally, then when the *wazīr* Abū l-ʿAbbās sought to bring down Ismāʿīl ibn Naghrīla. See Ashtor, 1992, 2:69. But, as represented in the Arabic historiographical literature, the Jew Ibn Naghrīla's central role as instigator in the conspiracy with Almeria is a departure from the pattern of interference in one another's politics.

> And he was killed, it is said, in one of the coal repositories. . . . So the people took revenge against the Jews,[68] of whom more than 4,000 were killed at that time—one of the slaughters of the Jews by which their abasement was reinstated, may the like of this period be extended![69]

Al-Dhakhīra thus construes the events of eleventh-century Granada to serve as a lesson from the not too distant past, as a cautionary tale regarding Jewish involvement in the affairs of the Muslim state in extremis: the Jew's direct exercise of executive power, his orchestration of affairs in the properly Muslim business of succession of a Muslim sovereign, and his foiled attempt to supplant a Muslim polity with a Jewish one.

What interest and meaning would *Al-Dhakhīra*'s picture of Ibn Naghrīla hold for religious scholars and literary intellectuals living in the thirteenth-century *maghrib* such as Ibn ʿIdhārī (al-Marrākushī) and Ibn Saʿīd al-Maghribī? What reasons would thirteenth-century Maghribi texts have for demonizing one or both eleventh-century Jewish *wazīr*s of Granada? Islam never developed an obsessive image of Jews (or Judaism) akin to what was advanced in medieval Christendom. On the contrary, Islam was largely able to set aside and diminish the historical memory of Jewish resistance to the Prophet and the Message because Muḥammad and Islam emerged victorious from that initial and paradigmatic encounter.[70] Muslims could view Christianity and Christians as constituting an ongoing religious and political "threat" to Islam in Iberia. But there were no longer Christian communities of any significance in the Maghrib.[71] By the thirteenth century the Jew had thus become the essential *dhimmī*, the quintessential religious and social other for the Muslims of North Africa.

Andalusi or Maghribi texts revive representations of the Jews' animus toward Islam or accentuate the danger the Jews pose to Islamdom, on account of the Muslim perception of Islam as no longer triumphant but rendered vulnerable, weakened, or even failing. In C. Vann Woodward's words, "lost causes, especially those that foster lingering loyalties and nostalgic memories, are among the most prolific breeders of

[68] The Arabic *istaṭāla* here translated as "took revenge" has a certain ironic ring because it can also mean "displayed arrogance." Ibn Naghrīla and the Jews are said to have behaved arrogantly toward the Muslims of Granada.

[69] Ibn Bassām, 2:769.

[70] Funkenstein, pp. 34–35.

[71] For this reason Lazarus-Yafeh, 1999, argues that the intensity of Muslim polemics against Christianity outstrip Muslim polemics against Judaism.

historiography—particularly so if the survivors deem the cause in some measure irretrievable."[72] Muslim frustration is projected onto the Jews in the form of narratives about their cunning efforts to interfere with and undermine Islam and take hold of Islamdom. The only "challenge" they could conceivably mount against Islam was internal subversion because the Jews represented neither an external polity hostile to Islam nor a religion capable of enticing or coercing Muslims to convert.

When social and political conditions in al-Andalus and the Maghrib fostered the perception of Islam in peril, sinister forces alighted in the form of highly visible if not always quite so powerful Jews. For this purpose dormant but always available anti-Jewish Islamic topoi could be called into service. Or to put it another way, these topoi could assert themselves in narrative form in the representation of figures and construction of historical events. More often than not, the perception of a Jew or Jews exercising political power over Muslims or the appointment of an influential Jewish official or well-placed physician-confidant seems to have catalyzed the fear of subversion, releasing potent intellectual, political, and religious expressions of frustration and discontent.

In brief, what was the sociopolitical situation in North Africa when Ibn ʿIdhārī and Ibn Saʿīd al-Maghribī produced their accounts of the events of eleventh-century al-Andalus? Marinid rule had replaced the Almohad dynasty in Morocco, and economic ties and social integration between members of the Jewish and Muslim religious communities were renewed and strengthened, as in eleventh-century al-Andalus. Concerns about Jewish position, and close interaction among Muslims and Jews in government circles, would have had a great deal of resonance among pious Muslim religious intellectuals or ambitious notables in thirteenth-century Marinid Morocco. In that context, a selectively although not uniformly more tolerant attitude toward Jews seems to have prevailed,[73] in part because the Jews had come to play an important role in the commercial networks established between the Christian kingdoms of Iberia and Muslim North Africa. Jews were also employed in the Marinid administration at Fez among the few elements of the population not hostile to the dynasty.[74] Even as late as the fifteenth century, Muslim jurists in places such as Tlemçen express ambivalent feelings for members of the local Jewish community. Jews seem to have been fully integrated into the socioeconomic life of Muslim society and Muslim jurists received familiar complaints about Jews dressing and riding like Mus-

[72] Woodward, p. 26, cited by Spiegel, p. 1.
[73] Shatzmiller, 1983, p. 152.
[74] Hunwick, p. 136; Shatzmiller, 1983, p. 156.

lims and keeping company with them in various enterprises,[75] just as we find in eleventh-century Granada.

In the first three chapters we have attempted to touch upon a sample of the rich, complex, and contradictory eleventh- and twelfth-century Andalusi representations of Ismāʿīl ibn Naghrīla as they reflect the Islamic cultural motifs of insubordination and apostasy. We have seen that the historical figure of Ibn Naghrīla is, as it were, enmeshed in imaginative layers of culturally determined representations that tell us more about their producers and consumers than about Ibn Naghrīla himself. Despite differences in tone and approach attributable to genre, these representations all prove to be concerned with issues of sovereignty, power, and knowledge and they resonate with specifically Muslim apprehensions and misgivings and through structures of thought internal to Islam for which the Jew serves as the relational concept.

[75] Hunwick, pp. 137–38.

CHAPTER FOUR

Muslim Counterparts, Rivals, Mentors, and Foes—A Trope of Andalusi-Jewish Identity?

The Problem of Andalusi-Jewish Representations of Muslims

As we have seen in the three previous chapters, Andalusi Muslims freely represented Jewish personalities in historiographical works, literary miscellanies, biographical dictionaries, and other genres. Andalusi-Arabic representations of Jews, particularly their supposed strengths, weaknesses, and religious otherness, we learned, were tropes of Muslim culture and spoke to conflicts of Muslim religion, culture, and identity. For their part, eleventh- and twelfth-century Andalusi-Jewish authors rarely took the liberty of representing Muslim figures. The discipline of their textual practice in this respect might seem to reflect a reluctance to portray Muslim characters or personalities with any degree of detail even though their reading audience was Jewish and the language of their discourse Hebrew or Judeo-Arabic in Hebrew script. In either case such texts would have been inaccessible or of no interest to Muslim readers except for recent and learned converts.[1] By contrast, the Mozarabic Christians of al-Andalus did not stop at taking issue with Islam, its doctrines, and religious praxis in their discourse about the Prophet. Rather, they are also said to have expressed directly and often "the hatred of the unprivileged for the privileged."[2]

Why did Andalusi Jews largely refrain from casting Muslim personalities and figures as characters in the variety of Hebrew and Judeo-Arabic texts they authored? Or, to put it another way, how does the Andalusi-Jewish discursive practice reflect specific dilemmas, challenges, and conflicts they faced as a subcultural minority under Andalusi Islam?

[1] This is an important exception given the prominence of some converts and the notoriety among them of some highly vociferous critics of their former religion. See the remarks of Lewis, 1984a, p. 86; Garcia-Arenal, 1997; and her forthcoming paper on autobiographies of intellectual converts; Stroumsa, 1990; and Lazarus-Yafeh, 1990.

[2] Daniel, 1975, p. 23. For the variety of Mozarabic writings concerning Islam and Muslims, see Burman.

To recall in full Moshe Perlmann's articulation of the different socio-religious positions of Muslims and Jews as it pertains to their textual disinterest or interest in one another: "For Muslims, Jews and Judaism were an unimportant subject. For Jews, Islam was a subject of considerable importance, not so much in and for public debate but rather in numerous, scattered remarks, references, and allusions intended, on the one hand to weaken known Islamic arguments and objections against Jewish texts, beliefs and customs, and on the other hand, to expose to opprobrium matters felt to be weak points of Islam."[3]

With these observations and lines of inquiry in mind it will be useful to recall critical questions such as "who speaks?" and "what difference does it make who is speaking?"[4] Although not what Foucault had in mind in posing these questions—in fact quite the opposite—the study of who is given a voice and is permitted to speak in discourse draws our attention to the reciprocal relationship between power and the power of speech, one of whose most significant forms is the power to represent.[5] Accordingly, we should not assume that the Jews' apparent disinterest in giving Muslim figures a voice or a presence in Jewish texts necessarily reflects a minority's clear-cut strategy of denial, caution, and avoidance in committing itself in discourse to a position vis-à-vis the socially dominant and culturally powerful religious majority. There are many forms of silence and different meanings to be assigned to any such gaps in the text or in the discourse.

The liberties Andalusi-Jewish liturgical poets, biblical exegetes, and theologians sometimes permitted themselves in their remarks about Islam and Islamdom figure hardly at all in the poets' representations of Muslims. Let us consider, for example, a Hebrew elegy on the theme of the Jews' banishment and dispossession from al-Andalus and the Maghrib written by the Andalusi polymath Abraham ibn ʿEzra' (d. 1165). Since Ibn ʿEzra' abandoned al-Andalus in 1140 when he embarked on an odyssey around Mediterranean and European lands,[6] the elegy signi-

[3] Perlmann, 1987, p. 126.

[4] Foucault, 1979, cited by Delany, p. 112.

[5] Foucault, 1981.

[6] Abraham ibn ʿEzra' (1089–1165), a native of Tudela, was a typical Andalusi-Jewish polymath whose career and works are representative of the transition from Jewish society and culture in Muslim al-Andalus to Christian Spain. A Neoplatonic philosopher, astronomer, and astrologer, a prolific poet of both devotional and secular Hebrew verse, and a Hebrew grammarian and seminal biblical exegete, Ibn ʿEzra' spent a significant part of his adult life abroad as an itinerant propagandist for Andalusi-Jewish culture. Through his translations of Arabic texts into Hebrew, his liturgical and secular Hebrew poetry, original grammatical and exegetical as well as scientific works, and with his programmatic attempt to disseminate this body of learning and its approach to knowledge, Andalusi-Jewish culture came to exert a powerful influence over the Jews of other Mediterranean lands.

fies the poet's imaginative literary response to reports that reached him from al-Andalus and North Africa.[7] The historical context in which the text interprets and transforms for Jewish society the experience of displacement and exile is the Almohad invasion and occupation of al-Andalus that began in the mid-1140s. In the wake of this defining event in their history, the Jews of al-Andalus are said to have fled en masse to the refuge of the Christian north "when all the nation passed over [the border]," in the words of Abraham ibn Daud.[8] A smaller number escaped toward the south, their eyes set on the reportedly more hospitable lands of eastern North Africa.

Here is Ibn ʿEzra's elegy in translation:

O woe! Misfortune from heaven has fallen upon Sefarad!
My eyes, my eyes flow with tears!
My eyes weep like ostriches on account of Lucena!
The Exile dwelt there blamelessly in safety
Without interruption for a thousand and seventy years.
But the day came when her people were banished and
she became like a widow,
Without Torah study or biblical recitation, the Mishnah sealed
shut,
The Talmud as though desolate, all its glory vanished.
With murderers and mourners this way and that,
The place of prayer and praise reduced to ill-repute.
That is why I weep and beat my hands, laments forever on my
lips;
I cannot remain silent. Would that my head were a spring of
water.

I shave my head and weep bitterly for the exile of Seville—
For its nobles are corpses and their sons captives,

[7] The text of the poem, "*Ahah yarad ʿal s^{e}farad raʿ min ha-shamayim*" ("O woe! Misfortune from heaven has fallen upon Sefarad!"), may be found in Levin, 1985, pp. 101–103. For earlier printed editions, see Davidson, 1970, 1:62–63. The poem is discussed by Mark R. Cohen, 1994, pp. 182–84, and has been studied by Nahon.

Another elegy on the Almohad persecution that has been ascribed to Ibn ʿEzraʾ but may not belong to him is "*W^{e}-eikh neḥerav ha-maʿarav w^{e}-rafu khol yadayim,*" ("Alas! How Was the Maghrib Destroyed!"), ed. Schirmann, 1939. While "*W^{e}-eikh neḥerav ha-maʿarav*" is devoted exclusively to the fate of the communities of North Africa, it parallels the text of "*Ahah yarad ʿal s^{e}farad*" in style, structure, diction, and tone. Indeed, the first line and the third strophe (dedicated to the communities of Morocco [23–32]) are substantially reproduced in "*W^{e}-eikh neḥerav ha-maʿarav.*" It appears to have been attached to part of "*Ahah yarad ʿal s^{e}farad*" by a later poet. See Hirschberg, 1:123–25. For the view that Ibn ʿEzraʾ is the author of both poems, see Israel Levin, 1969, pp. 18–20, 344; and Pagis, 1968, p. 357.

[8] Abraham ibn Daud, p. 72 (trans. p. 99).

Their elegant daughters handed over to a foreign religion.
How was Cordoba plundered and become like the desolate sea?
There sages and great men died in famine and
Not a Jew besides me is left in Jaen or Almeria.
Majorca and Malaga are without sustenance
And the Jews who remained received a festering blow.
That is why I mourn, learn to wail bitterly, and utter so grievous a lament!
My howls in my anguish—let them melt away like water.

Woe, like a woman in labor I cry out for the community of Sijilmasa,
A city of eminent scholars and sages whose brilliance eclipsed the darkness.
The Talmud's pillar bent, its structure destroyed,
The Mishnah subjected to scorn and trampled underfoot.
The enemy's eye took no pity on precious ones run through.
O woe! The entire community of Fez is naught
Where is the protection of the community of Tlemçen, its glory melted away?
I raise a bitter wail for Ceuta and Meknes
And rent my clothing over Derʿa earlier seized
One Sabbath day, its sons' and daughters' blood shed like water.

What can I maintain? On account of my sin all this has happened
And disaster has overcome me from my God, the Rock of my strength.
For whom can I hope? What can I say? I have done it all by my own hand!
My heart is enraged within me for my soul has been perverse
And from its land, its chosen territory, it has been exiled to an unclean soil
Too shamed and dumb, too weak to relate its catastrophes.
With pain in her heart she hopes for the kindness of her Rock
To ordain redemption from enslavement while she seeks refuge in the shadow of His wings.
Ever imprisoned, she comes alive when she mentions His Name.
Tears on her cheeks, she is held by a maidservant who
Fires a bow directly at her until the Lord looks down from heaven.[9]

[9] "*Ahah yarad ʿal s*^{e}*farad*" is a strophic poem comprising four strophes of ten monorhyming lines each (the last lines in each strophe are linked by a common rhyme) except for the final strophe, which has eleven. It is written in a syllabic meter (twelve

This is not the place to discuss in any detail the lyric's stirring rhetoric and deep pathos, its inventive pacing, the significance of its gender and water-related field of imagery, or its specific construction of exile.[10] What interests us here is the way in which a poem that is supposedly a literary response to specific historical events nevertheless seems to dehistoricize a crucial aspect of those same historical circumstances: The text holds off until the very end any identifying reference to those who wreaked havoc on the Jewish communities surveyed one after another. And even then, the reader will note that the allusion to the perpetrators is oblique. The first "references" to perpetrators, such as they are, come in line 4 ("place of ill-repute") and line 15 ("a foreign religion") but are in no way specific to Islam and Muslims. Lines 42–43 finally refer to the Jews' present tribulations under Islam in al-Andalus and the Maghrib ("Tears on her cheeks, she is held by a maidservant who Fires a bow squarely at her until the Lord looks down from heaven"). But in keeping with the lyric's gender-specific imagery, the text's suggestive but indirect reference to the (Almohad) Muslim persecution mentions only the aggression of the "maidservant," that is, Hagar, mother of Ishmael, the eponymous ancestor of the Muslims according to the well-known rabbinic typology.

The poem's first strophe (ll. 3–12) mourns the desolation of Lucena, the Andalusi city renowned for its venerable rabbinical academy and long tradition of fostering Hebrew learning and letters.[11] The destiny of the communities of other Andalusi towns, Seville, Cordoba, Jaén, and Almeria (the island of Majorca is also included), is taken up

syllables per line divided in tristichs of 3/3/6) common in Andalusi devotional poetry rather than in the Arabic-style quantitative meter characteristic of Andalusi Hebrew secular verse. The name-acrostic, a common feature of liturgical poetry, is also present here. The poet appears to be speaking as the "representative of the congregation" as in a liturgical poem and as the personified voice of the exiled Jewish communities of al-Andalus and the Maghrib. Unlike many of Abraham ibn 'Ezra's devotional poems "*Ahah yarad 'al s^e^farad*" was apparently not incorporated into either the Sefardi or for fast days. Israel Levin does not include the poem in his two-volume edition of Ibn 'Ezra's sacred poetry, *The Religious Poems of Abraham ibn'Ezra'*, placing it instead in the section entitled "Secular Poems" of his *Abraham ibn 'Ezra' Reader.* Masha Itzhaki, who is preparing a critical edition of Ibn Ezra's secular verse, also treats "*Ahah yarad 'al s^e^farad*" as a secular poem. "*Ahah yarad 'al s^e^farad*" was among the texts found in the famous collection of *qinot* preserved in the Lisbon manuscript (no. 86 in that text). See Bernstein, pp. 114–7 (text), 243–45 (notes). For a different translation, see Weinberger, 1997, pp. 96–97.

[10] Brann, 1994, attempts to analyze some of the ways in which cultural determinants and tropes of cultural identity as well as literary tradition inform the construction of dispossession and exile in Abraham ibn 'Ezra's elegy and Abū l-Baqā' l-Rundī's famous Arabic lament on the fall of Seville.

[11] See Ashtor, 1992, 2:143–45.

in rapid succession in the second strophe (ll. 13–22). The effects of the exile are represented by vivid and highly charged figures of social disintegration and individual distress whose images and language all turn on the shocking and deeply distressing contrast between the glorious cultural vitality for which the community was renowned and the desolation that now prevails. In similar fashion, the third strophe (ll. 23–32) surveys the destruction of various communities of the adjacent Maghrib (Derʿa, Sijilmasa, Tlemçen, Ceuta, Meknes, and Fez). The outpouring of grief and its signs in the first and closing verses of each strophe ("O woe"; "I shave my head and bewail"; "Woe I cry") and the well-placed reiteration in the third strophe of the initial note of mourning (l. 28 Heb. "*Ahah*") stand out sharply because the poet deliberately seems to keep in check the direct expression of feelings until the final strophe. Having thus achieved a cathartic recitation of the wreckage in the first three strophes, the poet ceases to depict these miseries and to lament them and turns in the final strophe toward a poetic resolution.

The fourth strophe may be divided into two thematic units. In the first passage (ll. 33–35) the poet suddenly turns penitent. Apparently speaking on behalf of the nation, he accepts the onus of exile as punishment for sin after the fashion of traditional responses to catastrophe. Line 36 marks a dramatic turn in the text that carries to the end of the poem (l. 43). Employing the most candid language in the lament the poet confesses that he (his soul) has been exiled on account of his sinfulness and he decries his failure even to recount the tragedy (ll. 36–38). Line 37 ("*u-me-arṣah mᵉḥoz ḥefṣah lᵉ-ereṣ ṭᵉme'ah galtah*" ["And from its land, its chosen territory, it has been exiled to an unclean soil"]) is arguably the most arresting line in the composition. Is the poet still speaking of his and his people's exile from al-Andalus, thereby rendering explicit the near religious attachment to Sefarad that is implicit in some Andalusi-Hebrew secular lyrics? Or alternatively, has the poet now launched into a lament for the Exile, that is, the historic exile of the Jewish people from the Land of Israel dating back to Roman late antiquity? But for the suggestive allusion in lines 42–43 to the Jews' present tribulations under Islam, the redemption from which the poet speaks in the fourth strophe, seems to pertain to an end to the Exile rather than deliverance from the Muslims. This ambiguity is in fact never resolved. I therefore prefer to think of the final strophe as attempting metonymically to relate the events of the present communal dislocation in al-Andalus and the Maghrib (addressed in the first three strophes) to the Exile of Catholic Israel. Indeed, the poet's persona is replaced as the frustrated speaker in line 36 (the fourth strophe) by the poet's soul. It is his soul that is henceforth identified as the object of abuse, a transformation that points quite literally to the spiritualization of the communal exile from al-Andalus and the Maghrib. Accordingly, the second unit of the final strophe reaffirms hope in the messianic promises set forth by rabbinic tradition and reassures the reader of the anticipated deliverance of the Jews from the Exile itself (ll. 40–43).

The poetic transformation that takes place between the first three strophes and the final strophe of "*Ahah yarad ʿal s^{e}farad*" can be understood as an attempt, in Robert Edwards's words, "to rediscover and enact the values that are presumed to have governed the original order" prior to the exile.[12] In the Hebrew literary imagination such an effort of recollection and recovery can only collapse history, leading the poet away from al-Andalus and the Maghrib and beyond the realm of political history itself toward a projected future in the Promised Land. Thus, despite the lyric's references to a specific time, to certain places, and to a decidedly historical tribulation, the religious identity of the Jews' current persecutors hardly matters at all.[13]

The Jews' sense of detachment from political and social history of which we read in Abraham ibn ʿEzra's lament is also a sign of the sociocultural rupture they experienced during the Almohad persecution. Before 1146–47, the Jewish elites of al-Andalus were simultaneously participants in a shared cultural experience, and socioreligious outsiders in Andalusi Islam. Their predicament, while decidedly premodern, nevertheless corresponds to what Leo Spitzer has called "situational marginality."[14] That is, the contingent nature of the Jews' marginality in al-Andalus varied greatly depending on the social, political, and religious context in which they found themselves operating, as well as on the ambient issues preoccupying Muslim society at any given time or place.

The complexity of the Jews' socioreligious position in al-Andalus and the fullness of their Arabization also contributed greatly toward the cultural production whose loss is mourned in the elegy. Indeed, the Jews' impulse to produce and consume Arabic and Hebrew culture concurrently can be seen as a sign of the ambiguity and conflict central to Andalusi-Jewish identity, of the Jews' closeness to and distance from their Andalusi-Muslim neighbors and counterparts. Andalusi Jewish discourse thus can resist and contest Islam as necessary, while embracing and valorizing Islamic culture, that is, Arabic language and learning. It can also paint the picture of a world in which Muslims seem to have

[12] Edwards, p. 25.

[13] Mark R. Cohen, 1994, p. 183, identifies the poem as the sole "clear-cut example of poetical Jewish reaction to an outbreak of Islamic persecution" during the classical centuries of Islam. On the Jews' representation of historical events in general, see Chazan.

[14] Spitzer. My thanks to Leslie Adelson for drawing my attention to Spitzer's work.

hardly a presence or in which Muslims may speak in textual encounters with Jews controlled by the Andalusi-Jewish author and audience.

Moses ibn ʿEzra, *Kitāb al-Muḥāḍara wal-mudhākara* (*The Book of Conversation and Discussion*) and Judah Halevi, *The Kuzari, Kitāb al-radd wal-dalīl fī l-dīn al-dhalīl* (*The Book of Refutation and Proof on the Despised Faith*).

Perhaps the most prominent paradigm according to which Muslims figure in Andalusi-Jewish texts is exemplified by Moses ibn ʿEzra's (d.c. 1138) famous anecdote about translation recorded in *Kitāb al-Muḥāḍara wal-mudhākara.* The Muslim discussant in this surprisingly frank exchange with polemical undertones is introduced as "a great Islamic scholar who was well-versed in the religious disciplines of Islam [*'baʿḍu l-aʿlām fuqahā' l-muslimīn'*] and most kind towards me." We can think of Ibn ʿEzra's Muslim interlocutor and others like him as a dignified, learned, and sympathetic personality. But he is also slightly misguided in his hope to turn the Jew toward Islam:

> When I was a young man in my native land, I was once asked by a great Islamic scholar, who was well versed in the religious disciplines of Islam and most kind towards me, to recite the Ten Commandments for him in Arabic. I realized his intention: he, in fact, wanted to belittle the quality of their language. So I asked him to recite to me the first *sūra*—the *Fātiḥa*—of his Qur'ān in romance, a language he could speak and understood very well. When he tried to render the *Fātiḥa* in the above-mentioned language it sounded ugly and was completely distorted. He noticed what was in my mind and did not press me further to fulfill his request.[15]

It is noteworthy that the text speaks specifically of the scholar's prominence and his command of the religious disciplines of Islam while drawing the reader's attention to his kindness toward the (then) youthful Ibn ʿEzra'. Clearly a member of the Muslim elite, the scholar's ultimate "intent," of course, is to test the Jew's religious mettle and "belittle the quality" of the language of the Hebrew Decalogue in the hope of turning Ibn ʿEzra' toward Islam.

The reader will note that the literary report of this encounter subtly inverts the roles and results of Muslim accounts of interfaith confrontations such as those involving Abraham ibn ʿAṭā' and Abū ʿImrān al-Fāsī (Introduction), and Ibn Ḥazm and an unidentified Jew (chapter 2). It also differs in tone from the aforementioned Arabic texts. The reader

[15] Moses ibn ʿEzra', p. 42 (24a); trans. Rosenthal, p. 19.

can discern the Jew's tempered satisfaction over his intellectual and religious "triumph," especially because the Jewish novice silences the Muslim master. But it is certainly difficult to detect any expression of smugness or bravado, as opposed to relief, in this tale of the triumph of a Jewish youth over a Muslim sage. Perhaps that is because Ibn ʿEzraʾ knows that victories of this sort are small and only temporary.[16] In the final analysis the anecdote projects the fantasy of an Andalusi-Jewish religious intellectual: A figure, who in fact transformed Jewish tradition with the tools and terminology he absorbed from reading Arabo-Islamic sources, eclipses one of his erstwhile teachers and sources of inspiration. This fantasy may be satisfying and edifying for the Andalusi-Jewish religious intellectual. But it is surely a far cry from the appropriation of Arabic and Islam and the displacement of the Muslim ruler of which we read in the previous chapter.

The typological figure we encountered in Ibn ʿEzra's anecdote—the Muslim savant deserving of intellectual respect but blinded by devotion to Islamic doctrine—makes an appearance in a very important cameo role in Judah Halevi's (d. 1141) dialogic defense of rabbinic Judaism, *The Kuzari* (*Kitāb al-radd wal-dalīl fī l-dīn al-dhalīl*). He is the scholar representing Islam (*ʿālim min ʿulamāʾ l-islām*) before the Khazar monarch (a pagan turned pious "generic monotheist" in search of the perfect way in which to serve God) who succeeds the philosopher and the Christian theologian and immediately precedes the appearance of the Jewish *ḥaver*. Like the Christian scholastic, the Muslim speaks of the universally recognized signs and miracles the Creator executed for the Children of Israel. His interview with the Khazar king, unsuccessful from the Muslim point of view, thus lays the narrative and conceptual groundwork for the king to reconsider what he previously dismissed—inviting a Jewish representative ("I will ask the Christians and Muslims, for either one of their ways of acting is no doubt pleasing [to God]. But as for the Jews, their apparent lowliness, smallness [in number], and the

[16] The inter-religious polemical aspects of Ibn ʿEzra's anecdote are studied by Sadan, 1994a. See also two related and valuable studies by Sadan, 1996 and 1994b, the latter of which also briefly studies the rationale behind the effort of the Andalusi-Christian Ḥafṣ ibn Albar al-Qūṭī to translate the Book of Psalms into poetic Arabic. Drory, 1991 and 1993, sets forth new ground in making the case for considering Moses ibn ʿEzra's, *Kitāb al-muḥāḍara* and Judah al-Ḥarizi's *Taḥkᵉmoni* (studied in chapter 5) in light of the problem of Jewish life in the Christian-ruled states. For our purposes, each of these authors can be considered Andalusi-Jewish intellectuals on account of their educational background. Most students of Moses Maimonides, who lived the better part of his life in Egypt, nevertheless treat him as an Andalusi Jew because of his background, experience, consciousness, and outlook. I have adopted a similar approach to Moses ibn ʿEzraʾ, Judah Halevi, Abraham ibn Daud, and Judah al-Ḥarizi for the same reasons, notwithstanding the time each spent in Christian lands and Drory's very important approach to their work.

hate of all for them is sufficient [reason to ignore them] [1:4]"; "I had decided not to ask a Jew because I knew of the destruction of their traditions and the deficiency of their opinions, since their downfall did not leave them [anything] praiseworthy. [1:12]").[17]

Thus, *The Kuzari* stages an Andalusi-Jewish messianic fantasy far more chimerical than *Kitāb al-Muḥāḍara.* In Ibn 'Ezra', the Muslim scholar is only licked, dismissed, and silenced, albeit by a Jewish novice; in Halevi, the Muslim sage sets up conditions favorable, even essential to the Jew's success and is displaced by his Jewish counterpart. To put it another way, *The Kuzari*'s book-long dramatic enactment of the Khazar king's struggle to understand and embrace Judaism is realized in part because of the groundwork established through his prior engagement with representatives of philosophy, Christianity, and Islam. The Khazar's series of initial interviews end in his determination to become Jewish. This process in fact dramatizes vividly the poetic comparison the *ḥaver* draws (much later in their discussion, 4:23) between Judaism and a seed of grain. Once planted, both the seed and Judaism ultimately, improbably, and miraculously yield splendid results.[18] The sequence of religious scholars appearing before the Khazar ruler also anticipates Moses Maimonides' interpretation of monotheistic religious history. Like Halevi, Maimonides takes the position that the later monotheistic dispensations exist in order to bring all humanity toward the God of Israel: "All these matters relating to Jesus of Nazareth and the Ishmaelite [Muḥammad] who came after him only served to clear the way for King Messiah, to prepare the whole world to worship God with one accord, as it is written, For then will I turn to the peoples a pure language, that they all call upon the name of the Lord to serve Him with one consent (Zeph. 3:9)."[19] Maimonides' more sober messianic projection also compensates for the traumatic historical, political, and religious reality facing the Jews of the twelfth century.

Maimonides

Sefer ha-Qabbalah by Abraham ibn Daud

Let us next turn to a passage in *Sefer ha-Qabbalah* by Abraham ibn Daud, whose importance for the study of Andalusi-Jewish tradition in

[17] Judah ha-Levi, 1977, pp. 8–9 (1:5–10); trans. Berman in Sirat, p. 116.

[18] Judah ha-Levi, 1977, p. 172.

[19] Moses Maimonides, 1975, p. 416 (vol. 17 *Sefer Shoftim, Hilkhot M^elakhim* 11: 4 [uncensored version]); trans. Twersky, 1980, p. 452. The connection between *The Kuzari*'s comparison of Judaism and the seed and Maimonides' is noted, among others, by Pines, pp. 250–51, and Ravitsky, pp. 228–29. Ravitsky also traces the evolution of this idea in Isaac Abrabanel and Abraham Farissol.

general, and Samuel and Joseph the Nagid in particular, we have encountered on more than one occasion in previous chapters. *Sefer Ha-Qabbalah* recounts the apocryphal tale of the "discovery" of Samuel the Nagid in a Malagan spice shop. The agent of the Nagid's discovery is the Andalusi Ibn al-ʿArīf, a *kātib* at the Zirid court.[20] Ibn al-ʿArīf enlists into government service the Jewish scribe endowed with talent and then mentors him behind the scenes. Upon his deathbed Ibn al-ʿArīf confesses dramatically to Ḥabbūs that Samuel was the real source of all his sage advice to the *amīr*. Accordingly, he recommends Samuel to Ḥabbūs in the most glowing terms and without regard for his protégé's religious affiliation:[21]

> This R. Samuel, however, fled to Malaga, where he occupied a shop as a spice-merchant. Since his shop happened to adjoin the courtyard of Ibn al-ʿArīf—who was the *Kātib* of King Ḥabbūs b. Māksan, the Berber king of Granada—the *Kātib*'s maidservant would ask him to write letters for her to her master, the Vizier Abū'l Qāsim ibn al-ʿArif. Consequently, when after a while, this vizier, Ibn al-ʿArīf, was given leave by his King Ḥabbūs to return to his home in Malaga, he inquired among the people of his household: "Who wrote the letters which I received from you?" They replied: "A certain Jew of the community from Cordova, who lives next door to your courtyard, used to do the writing for us." The *Kātib* thereupon ordered that R. Samuel ha-Levi be brought to him at once, and he said to him: "It does not become you to spend your time in a shop. Henceforth you are to stay at my side." He thus became the scribe and counselor of the counselor to the King. . . .
>
> Subsequently, when the *Kātib* Ibn al-ʿArīf took ill and felt his death approaching, King Ḥabbūs paid him a visit and said to him: "What am I going to do? Who will counsel me in the wars which encompass me on every side?" He replied: "I never counseled you out of my own mind, but out of the mind of this Jew, my scribe. Look after him well, and let him be a father and a priest to you. Do whatever he says, and God will help you."[22]

Gerson D. Cohen and Samuel M. Stern identified the tale's sources and analyzed its motifs as they pertain to Ibn Daud's program for the

[20] In ʿAbd Allāh bin Buluggīn, 1986, p. 215, n. 174, Tibi, citing al-Maqqarī, notes that "the *wazīr* is the *kātib*" in al-Andalus.

[21] Compare the different account and sequence of events reported in ʿAbd Allāh bin Buluggīn, 1986, pp. 52–55.

[22] Abraham ibn Daud, pp. 54–55 (trans. pp. 72–73).

transmission of Andalusi-Jewish culture to the Jews of the Christian kingdoms.[23] For our purposes, it is necessary to draw attention to the character of Ibn al-ʿArīf and to consider how its representation in this passage of *Sefer ha-Qabbalah* contributes to the text's sense of Andalusi-Jewish identity. Ibn al-ʿArīf, an Andalusi Muslim, not only has the keen eye to recognize a gifted political and administrative prospect, but also the good sense to enlist him in government service. He is said to mentor Samuel the Nagid as a kindred intellectual spirit without regard for his religious otherness ("It does not become you to spend your time in a shop. Henceforth you are to stay at my side."). There is no hint in Ibn Daud's account of the unusual historical circumstances governing Zirid and *ṭa'ifa* politics, circumstances we know made it possible for the appointment of Jewish officials to positions in Muslim chanceries. Ibn al-ʿArīf is simply so mesmerized by the Jew's talent and skill that it never occurs to him to question the Islamic propriety of drawing Ibn Naghrīla into government service. I think of *Sefer Ha-Qabbalah*'s depiction of Ibn al-ʿArīf as another Andalusi-Jewish imaginative vision in which the Muslim commits himself to a social meritocracy to the benefit of his minority protegé.[24] And on another level, the narrative represents the Muslim as playing an important role, unwittingly, in the unfolding drama of Andalusi-Jewish history and thus the fulfillment of God's purposes. That topos proves central to Samuel's own poetic discourse on his interaction with Andalusi-Muslim society.

Samuel the Nagid

Samuel the Nagid, the quintessentially empowered Andalusi Jew about whom the Muslim authored texts have much to say, seems to take unusual care in representing Muslim figures. Fifty-four poems in the Nagid's *dīwān* depict various aspects of Samuel's engagement in Zirid internal and external political and military affairs. Although the historicity of the "battlefield" poetic reports is highly questionable,[25] three sets of poems represent the Nagid's involvement in open warfare with and alongside Andalusi-Muslim personalities. The pertinent historical episodes the poet reconstructs are: (1) Granada's campaign against its former ally Almeria (1038), (2) Granada's battle with ʿAbbadid Seville (1039), and (3) the suppression of Yiddīr's internal challenge to Bādīs's

[23] Gerson Cohen in Abraham ibn Daud, pp. 269–89; Stern, 1950.

[24] This vision would also have much meaning for Andalusi-Jewish exiles in Abraham ibn Daud's (Christian) Toledo.

[25] Wasserstein, 1993b.

rule (1041).[26] Angel Sāenz-Badillos as well as Israel Levin and Arie Schippers have discussed or analyzed in some detail how the Nagid's "war poems" are highly inventive lyrics. Their application of biblical Hebrew for the Nagid's artistic and ideological purposes is brilliant especially since their form and content are predicated upon the classical Arabic genre (*al-ḥamāsa*).[27] There is great irony in the Nagid's adaptation of this Arabic genre: As cultural mediator, the Hebrew poet appropriates the conventions and style of Arabic verse for his own religious, literary, and political purposes, including publicizing his high rank and accomplishments as a Jewish courtier in Muslim society.

How does the Nagid's Hebrew verse portray the principal parties and players involved in the political strife and military operations between Zirid Granada and its rival Andalusi states during his tenure of government service? "*Eloah ʿOz*,"[28] one of the Nagid's most famous lyrics, depicts in poetic detail the background, conduct, and results of Granada's struggle against the neighboring state of Almeria and the so-called Battle of Alpuente, in 1038, early on in his term of service. The lyric makes reference to the Nagid's political showdown with his counterpart Ibn ʿAbbās, the Andalusi *wazīr* of the kingdom of Almeria ruled at the time by the "Slav" Zuhayr.

The speech and written communications ascribed to Ibn ʿAbbās of Almeria express the Andalusi *wazīr*'s deep-seated hostility toward his Jewish counterpart and rival in Granada. There are even turns of phrase and formulations when Ibn ʿAbbās's "speech" sounds eerily like a Hebrew-language rehearsal of elements found in Ibn Ḥazm's *Refutation* and Abū Isḥāq al-Ilbīrī's furious poetic invective against Yūsuf ibn Naghrīla and its challenge to the Jewish *wazīr*'s Zirid sponsors. In reconstructing his enemy's "thoughts" Samuel the Nagid thus acknowledges the existence, but not the legitimacy, of expressions of indignation that a Jew could attain such high office over Muslims, contrary to the natural order of Muslim society and Islamic law.

The poem may be outlined as follows: invocation and praise of God

[26] There is no single secondary work of historiography to which the reader may turn for a complete picture of the period that would also take into account all of the many difficulties the historian faces in reading the available source material. The best work in both respects is Wasserstein, 1985. See also Handler, for a more accepting view of the Arabic sources. As for Samuel the Nagid, Schirmann, 1979, 1:149–89, and Schirman-(Fleischer), 1995, pp. 183–217, take the reader through the various episodes in the Nagid's life as reflected in his verse, with additional although brief references to external sources.

[27] Sáenz-Badillos, 1983; Israel Levin, 1995, 1:40–76; Schippers, 1994, pp. 217–43.

[28] Samuel ha-Nagid, 1966, 1:4 (ll. 15–16); Schirmann, 1959–60, 1:85; Samuel ha-Nagid, 1988, 1:3–14.

in thanksgiving (ll. 1–6); statement of the poet's personal problem (ll. 7–11); poetic narrative regarding the political situation and struggle (ll. 12–39), setting the stage for an elaborate narrative depiction of the battle followed by the poet's interpretation of its outcome (ll. 40–131). The poem concludes with the poet's instructions to his audience and dedication of the lyric to God (ll. 132–49). Here are the passages relevant to our discussion as they appear in Raymond P. Scheindlin's elegant poetic translation:[29]

> When Prince Zuhair, whose land was by the sea,
> and his vizier, Ibn ʿAbbās, observed
> my status with my king, realized that all
> state counsels and affairs were in my hands,
> noticed that no decree was ever final
> but that the decree had my consent
> they felt resentment over my high rank,
> resolved to see me overthrown at once;
> for how (they said) can aliens like these
> be privileged over Muslim folk
> and act like kings legitimate?[30]
> So this vizier spread awful things about me,
> reckless slanders, brazen wicked gossip,
> had his heinous lies, and plenty of them,
> artfully written up as open letters
> (but God forbid that I should say a word
> that might make anyone think ill of him!).
> He circulated these among the towns
> to put his slanders in the Muslims' mouths,[31]
> inciting them against me with foul words
> as Moses' spies used words that caused much grief.
> It was not only me he hoped to harm
> By framing these malicious, lying words;
> his purpose was to wipe out all the Jews,
> old, young, men, women, children still unborn. . . .
>
> Delighted to see the trouble I was in,
> my foe, gloating sent word to all his friends:
> "This is the day I have been waiting for;
> the only obstacle has been removed.
> With Ḥabbūs dead, this Samuel is finished,
> and all his hopes are ended, done, and gone." (ll. 12–24, 28–30)

[29] Trans. R. Scheindlin in Constable, 1997, p. 84.
[30] Heb. *W^{e}-amru eikh t^{e}hi maʿalah l^{e}-ʿam zar/ʿalei ʿam zeh u-memshalah ashurah.*
[31] Heb. *u-fizzer ba-m^{e}dinot igg^{e}rotaw/l^{e}-shawwot zo't b^{e}-fi ʿammo s^{e}durah.*

Habbūṣ's son and heir, Bādīs, comes to the Nagid's rescue. Ibn ʿAbbās tries again to bring down Samuel by appealing to the *amīr*'s religious sensibility as a Muslim (ll. 33–41):

> Losing no time, my enemy now wrote
> strong letters with peremptory demands:
> "Are you aware that in our Muslim faith
> it is a sin to spare this Samuel's life?[32]
> Never will I let you be in peace
> As long as any breath is left inside this Jew.
> Get rid of him, and that will put an end
> To quarreling and strife; come deal with me.
> But if you won't, just know that all the kings
> of Andalus have formed a league against you."
> Bādīs sent in reply: "If I should do
> what you demand, damnation fall on me!
> Before I yield my servant to his foes,
> I'd see myself a bondsman to my own!"
>
> At this my enemy became enraged,
> and furiously increased hostilities,
> nor did he rest until his troops were massed,
> a league of Slavs and Christians and Arabians
> at Alfuente.

The lyric conveys effectively the seething enmity of the Nagid's enemies, a gang made up of Zuhayr, ruler of Almeria and former ally of Zirid Granada; Ibn ʿAbbās, his Andalusi *wazīr* whose character is defined by his hatred of the Nagid; and the unnamed Zirid "courtiers who disliked me." Just why do they oppose Samuel with such unrelenting resentment? The poet refers to their determined efforts to topple him as an "alien" who trespasses in the political affairs of Granada's Muslims. Furthermore, after Ḥabbūs's death (in 1038) and the ensuing crisis over Zirid succession (in which Samuel apparently played an important role and consolidated his influence and authority under Bādīs), these foes are said to have abandoned their unsuccessful appeals to Ḥabbūs and Bādīs to depose Samuel and terminated their slanderous public campaign against the Nagid in favor of direct military action against Granada. They assembled "a league of Slavs, Christians, and Arabians" ("*ʿAmaleq edom u-vnei qᵉṭurah*" [l. 41]), that is, Zuhayr's own troops from Almeria, along with Christian mercenaries and Andalusi Muslims.[33]

The reader will note that the Hebrew text actually refers to Zuhayr

[32] Heb. *wᵉ-shalaḥ lo hᵃtedaʿ ki shᵉmu'el/ lᵉ-ḥayyoto bᵉ-dateinu ʿaverah.*

[33] Again, compare the account in chapter 3 of ʿAbd Allāh bin Buluggīn, 1986.

as Agag, and Almeria's troops as ʿAmaleq.[34] Agag, of course, is the infamous ʿAmalekite king of Israelite lore (1 Sam. 15; see also the biblical textual antecedents, Exod. 17, Deut. 25:17, 19) and, according to later biblical and rabbinic typology, the incarnation of Israel's most inveterate foe. Identifying Zuhayr with Agag, ancestor of the biblical Haman (Esther 3), the poet establishes one of many ideologically ambitious and explicit links with his namesake, the prophet Samuel, with his Levitic ancestor King David, and with the career and exploits of the late biblical character Mordecai, a Persian-Jewish courtier. The first and last of these figures confronted and defeated an ʿAmalekite representative seeking to annihilate the Israelites/Jews of their time. Samuel the Nagid's classification of his enemies after this fashion exemplifies the poet's patented appeal to typologies of historical recurrence, a maneuver that served the peculiar needs of his ambitious persona as well as the political and historical ethos of the wider audience of Andalusi Jews.[35]

It is significant that in this postbiblical remix, only the figure of Ibn ʿAbbās, Zuhayr's deputy and the Nagid's primary adversary in this episode, retains his own name and identity. Yet Scheindlin's poetic translation inserts the words "Muslim folk" ("*ʿam zar ʿalei ʿam zeh*" = "aliens like these . . . over this folk" [l. 16]) and "Muslims' mouths" ("*b^e-fi ʿammo*" = "in his people's mouth" [l. 20]), presumably to identify clearly and in religious terms the popular audience Ibn ʿAbbās' hoped to enlist and agitate into action against the Nagid. Similarly, in the poet's version of Ibn ʿAbbās' direct appeal to Bādīs's religious sensibility, Scheindlin translates "our Muslim faith" ("*b^e-dateinu*" = "in our faith" [l. 34]). And in the roster of foes aligned against the Nagid and Granada we find "Arabians" (*u-v^enei q^eṭurah*) [l. 41].[36] In fact, *the sig-*

[34] As for the actual as opposed to imagined identity of the "Slavs" in al-Andalus and their place in Andalusi society, see Monroe's study of Ibn Garcia; and Wasserstein, 1985, pp. 58–59. On the *ṣaqāliba* ("Slavs") in general, see Ayalon; on Zuhayr in particular, see Wasserstein, 1993, pp. 129–45; and on "Slavic" Almeria, see Wasserstein, 1985, p. 83.

[35] Brann, 1991, pp. 47–58.

[36] The biblical Qeṭurah (often spelled Keturah) (Gen. 25:1–4) is the patriarch Abraham's third spouse, and the genealogy given for her line of six sons differs clearly from the line of Hagar and Ishmael. Nevertheless, rabbinic traditions, such as Genesis Rabbah 61:4, sometimes identified Qeṭurah with Hagar. Compare the famous legend, Genesis Rabbah 61:7, in which the Ishmaelites and Qeṭurians lay claim to the Land of Israel before Alexander the Great. This latter *aggadah* presents the two peoples as connected yet differentiated. Similarly, in a discussion regarding the circumcision required of all of Abraham's sons, BT Sanhedrin 59b follows the plain sense of the Genesis text. Moses Maimonides, 1975, p. 409, and trans. 1949, pp. 236–37 (*Hilkhot m^elakhim*, 10:8), cites the rabbinic passage but then adds a comment about their joint identity in his time:

> The Rabbis said that the sons of Keturah, who are of the seed of Abraham and who were born after Ishmael and Isaac, are bound to observe the precept of cir-

nifier "Muslim" never appears anywhere at all in the Hebrew lyric. It is as though the poet were handicapped by the prosodic requirements of the Hebrew—a completely dubious proposition given his virtuoso command of Arabicized Hebrew prosody—or as if the poet preferred not to draw attention to the obvious religious identity of his primary adversary.[37]

We should, however, attempt to parse the terms and thus view the construction of events and representation of the participants in a way that accounts for the lyric's limited and idiosyncratic use of identifying markers. Does the Nagid's imagination picture the battle between Granada and Almeria, and between the Nagid and Ibn ʿAbbās, as a conflict between Andalusi Muslims and Jews? It would seem so if we concentrate selectively on the discourse and actions attributed to Ibn ʿAbbās, who certainly appeals to the strictures of Islamic law and to the ruler's conscience as a Muslim. The Jews are deemed "aliens like these"; and the figure of Ibn ʿAbbās asserts that according to "our [Muslim] faith, it is a sin to spare this Samuel's life," "this Jew." The voice of the poet's persona also presents the Nagid's personal fight as Israel's too: "I became furious and the Lord became furious/His anger burned and flamed against ʿAbbās" (l. 31). Ultimately, then, the conflict is God's own, implicating the Jewish religious community of Granada and its "Nagid" in a battle between two sovereign states.[38]

At the same time, other elements in the poem seem to compromise or complicate the reading of the conflict between Ibn ʿAbbās and the Nagid as a struggle between Muslims and Jews. Except for the Nagid and his co-religionists and the Christian mercenaries of Almeria, the poem's entire cast of characters is implicitly Muslim, even if Ibn ʿAbbās is the only party to voice concerns identified with Islam. The reader knows that the sovereign states in question are both Muslim polities. That is, the Jewish *wazīr* serves a Muslim ruler and supposedly fights among Granada's Muslim armed forces against the troops of a rival Andalusi-Muslim state. From this historical perspective, the lyric's interpretation of the conflict between two Muslim polities as a battle between the Jews and Muslims seems a highly subjective gesture even for a poem.[39] Complicating matters further is the response (to Ibn ʿAbbās's

---

cumcision. Since today the descendants of Ishmael are intermingled with the descendants of Keturah ["*w*^{e}*-ho'il w*^{e}*-nitʿarvu ha-yom b*^{e}*nei yishmaʿe'l bi-vnei q*^{e}*ṭurah*"], they are bound to observe the rite of circumcision on the eighth day.

[37] Compare the translation of Weinberger, 1973, pp. 21–28.

[38] This theological interpretation of the Nagid's triumphs and victories is evident in nearly all of the "war poems," in keeping with the poet's (biblical) typologies of historical recurrence.

[39] So too, Ibn ʿAbbās's central adversarial role is undercut somewhat by the "Slav" Zuhayr's identification with Agag/Haman, Israel's most intractable and metaphysical foe.

ultimatum) attributed to the poet's master Bādīs (ll. 38–39): "If I should do what you demand, damnation fall on me! Before I yield my servant to his foes, I'd see myself a bondsman to my own." Once again, the reader encounters a most benevolent Muslim figure who refuses on principle to turn against his Jewish associate in accordance with the religious obligation Ibn ʿAbbās submits to him. This picture of the tripartite "discussion" obscures a significant historical irony: Samuel the Nagid and like-minded Andalusi Jews would have had a more common cultural background with their Andalusi-Muslim counterparts and competitors such as Ibn ʿAbbās than with Andalusi Berbers such as Bādīs with whom they shared political interests.

In order to attain a better grasp of the lyric's ambiguity (the ways in which it seems to operate at cross purposes in defining the nature of the conflict between Granada and Almeria), it will be useful to examine very briefly the poetic treatment of the Nagid's foes in other hostilities. For example, the cycle of poems devoted to Zirid Granada's struggle with ʿAbbadid Seville follows a similar pattern to "*Eloah ʿoz*."[40] "*Hali taʿas*," a thanksgiving poem of praise dating from the campaign of 1039, finds two Andalusi-Muslim enemies bearing similar-sounding names but menacing the Nagid from different quarters:

> but after the death of Ben Abbas,
> Ben Abbad's approach gripped me with fear.
> The two had pursued me—a crown on one,
> and the other of lesser renown;
> the former lifts kings to their kingdoms,
> and it's he who brings them down;
> nobles are set with his seal over lands,
> and then deposed as he pleases;
> to him the Berber princes attend—
> the Arab viziers praise him:
> awaiting his charge as the year's first shower,
> they hope for his word as rain.
> Between him and my king there was envy,
> and each remained in his land. . . .
>
> An insidious people now dwelled in his land,
> Who'd scorned the children of God
> and stoned them with words of abuse.
> They plotted against them, seizing their arms,
> and setting their legs in shackles,

[40] On the political rivalries and military confrontations between the *ṭāʾifa* states, see Kennedy, pp. 130–53; and Wasserstein, 1985, pp. 116–60.

searching out mothers in Israel,
destroying both high and low—
infants suckling along with the weaned. (ll. 10–16, 25–27)[41]

But God intervenes as in the battle with Almeria:

The judgement was set on the second,
and the sentence came down on the fifth;
and you reached in your servant's trial
through Arab and Berber alike,
and shadows grew long as you saved the sons
of Might—in its month—from pagans. (ll. 101–103)[42]

Peter Cole's fine poetic translation identifies the parties who lavish attention upon Granada's adversary, Ibn ʿAbbād of Seville, as "Berber princes" and "Arab viziers" (l. 14). In the Hebrew these troops are signified by the terms "*sarnei p^{e}lishtim*" and "*n^{e}si'ei yishm^{ec}e'lim*," respectively, with "*yishm^{ec}e'lim*" probably better understood as "Andalusi Muslims." And, when the Nagid and Granada triumph with the help of God, "Arab and Berber alike" ("*p^{e}leshet wa-ʿarav*") are judged, saving the "sons of Might . . . (i.e., Israel/the Jews ['*ben eitan*'] from pagans ["*ovdei v^{ee}alim*'])". Phrases such as "an insidious people . . . Who'd scorned the children of God and stoned them with words of abuse" and "as you saved the sons of Might . . . from pagans" signify that the Nagid's if not Granada's conflict with Seville is fundamentally religious: It is construed as a battle against idolatry, comparable to the religious challenges the ancient Israelites faced from their Canaanite neighbors according to the Hebrew Bible.

This is not the place to discuss in detail the unusual history by which the Berbers of North Africa and subsequently al-Andalus came to be called *p^{e}lishtim* (Philistines) in Hebrew.[43] Suffice it to note that the

[41] Text in Schirmann, 1959–60, 1: 94–102; Samuel ha-Nagid, 1988, 1:18–28; Samuel ha-Nagid, 1966, 1:16–26; trans. Cole, pp. 39–40. "*K^{e}var avad b^{e}no ʿabbas*" (Shirmann, 1959–60, 1:102; Samuel ha-Nagid, 1966, 1:27; Samuel ha-Nagid, 1988, 1:29–30; trans. Cole, p. 48) is a three-line "dream poem" of thanksgiving to God. Its background is yet another of the Nagid's conflicts with Andalusi-Muslim figures and also resurrects the figure of Ibn ʿAbbās. In the lyric, the poet foresees the imminent death of his adversary Jaʿafar ibn Abī Mūsā, a Granadan official who apparently conspired with Ibn ʿAbbās against Samuel. So too "*L^{e}kha ʿosher u-mamlakhah*" (Schirmann, 1959–60, 1:103–105 Samuel ha-Nagid, 1966, 1:27–30; Samuel ha-Nagid, 1988, 1:31–35), a lyric that reports on renewed conflict with Almeria and Ibn Abī Mūsā culminating in the realization of the dream.

[42] Cole, p. 44 (ll. 209–10).

[43] Samuel ha-Nagid, 1966, 1:17 (l. 14), 53 (l. 16), 97 (l. 12), 112 (l. 30); Judah Halevi and Abraham ibn Daud also testify to the use of the term after the manner of the

Nagid's own sponsors, the Zirids, are also Berbers, although Ḥabbūs and Bādīs are never designated in his lyrics by the term *p^elishtim*. Similarly, we will not concern ourselves here with the fine points of why North African Arabic historiography regarded the Berbers as descendants of Canaanites, or alternately of Phoenician and Punic settlers of Roman North Africa in late antiquity.[44] For our purposes the various socioethnic and socioreligious appellations for Andalusi players in the Nagid's poetry call for explanation. In part, the designations employed in these lyrics reflect the social setting and a stylistic convention of the classical Arabic poetic genre *ḥamāsa* (heroism; bravery; chivalry) from which Samuel the Nagid's Hebrew lyric is derived.[45] It is, after all, an early Arabic poetic genre whose origins and social setting are traced to the tribal structures, institutions, and values of pre-Islamic Arabia. *Ḥamāsa* was also adapted, transformed, and cultivated in the urban Islam of the Umayyad and ʿAbbāsid periods when new and more complex socioethnic and ideological cleavages and conflicts rooted in Islam supplanted the older tribal ones in poetry as in society.[46] In this respect the Nagid's descriptions of Granada's wars make perfect use of literary convention and draw the reader's attention to the tribal-like, heroic conflicts of eleventh-century al-Andalus.

Literary convention alone does not account for the Nagid's practice. It is possible (but by no means certain) that the poet is sensitive or responding to the supposed divisions and tensions in Andalusi-Muslim society between "Arab" Andalusi identity and Muslims of other ethnic backgrounds, principally Berbers but also "Slavs."[47] By employing eth-

---

Nagid. See "*P^elishtim ne'esafim*," Schirmann, 1959–60, 2:479 (l. 1); Judah ha-Levi, 1994, p. 365; and Abrahahm ibn Daud, p. 57 (trans. p. 76): "*sarnei p^elishtim*" (Berber princes) in the case of Joseph.

Not so for Baer, 1:33–36. Writing in the shadow of the civil war developing among Jews and Arabs in Mandate Palestine, Baer sees the Andalusi opposition to the Zirids and their Jewish *wazīr* as coming from "*religious and nationalist fanatics among the Arabs*." So, too, Baer declares (33): "Yet it was all too conspicuous that a Jew was directing the foreign affairs of Granada, a fact which was *a constant thorn in the side of orthodox Muslims*" (emphases mine).

[44] On the supposed Berber-Canaanite "connection" and the alternative tradition of the South Arabian-Berber link, see the critical comments of Ibn Khaldūn, 1:18–22. Hirschberg, 1:40–48, refers to legendary material identifying the Berbers with Canaanite peoples of antiquity. Shatzmiller, 1988, references the Nagid's usage and studies the course of the legends as they appear in North African Arabic historiography.

[45] The connection is studied by Schippers, 1994, pp. 217–43.

[46] I have in mind the neo-*qaṣīda* panegyrics of al-Mutanabbī and Abū Tammām.

[47] The extent of such divisions and their significance during this period are still very much a matter of dispute among scholars of the period. For a clear presentation of the problems, see Wasserstein, 1985, pp. 55–74. The Nagid relates his final reckoning with Bādīs's rival Yiddīr (1041) in two very long poems, "*Sh^{ee}eh mini ʿamiti w^e-ḥaveri*" (Sam-

nic designations for his patrons and principal adversaries, all of whom were Muslims, the poem succeeds in effectively breaking down religion as the basis for any of Granada's struggles. However, such a rhetorical strategy operates at cross-purposes with the function of the lyric's biblical allusions and Ibn ʿAbbās's discourse (as represented by the Nagid) painting his battle with Samuel as a religious requirement for Muslims. For all Samuel the Nagid's literary bravado, pretensions to Levitic authority and even prophecy, the economy of the representations of Muslims in his lyrics reflects a discourse defined by the consciousness of a subordinate minority. In this respect, the Nagid's silencing of the Muslims is another way of practicing the silence of the Jews, a trope to which we return in the next chapter.

---

uel ha-Nagid, 1966, 1:31–34 [no. 7]; Samuel ha-Nagid, 1988, 1:36–40) and "*Lᵉvavi bᵉ-qirbi ḥam*" (Samuel ha-Nagid, 1966, 1:35–38 [no. 9]; Samuel ha-Nagid, 1988, 1:41–44). Cole, pp. 49–51, translates "*Shᵉnayim mi-nsikhei Sᵉfarad ʿim gᵉdudei ha-ṣᵉmari*" (in "*Sheʾeh minni*") as "two Spanish princes with a troop of Goths."

CHAPTER FIVE

The Silence of the Jews:

Judah al-Ḥarizi's Picaresque Tale of the Muslim Astrologer

Imagine migrating from Iberia and the Muslim West to the Muslim East and composing two texts en route in which are recounted realistic incidents and fanciful escapades in familiar, exotic, and fantastic locales. The two texts, an Arabic rhymed-prose work and a book of Hebrew imaginative prose, have much to relate about the widely dispersed members of a small ecumenical minority, including mention by name of more than 150 communal notables and literary figures encountered during the odyssey. But the texts are noticeably lacking in narrative reports about the dominant culture and society and in depictions of its constituents.

One of the texts in question is a forty-page Arabic *maqāma* ("picaresque rhetorical anecdote") by the Hebrew literary intellectual Judah al-Ḥarizi (ca. 1170–1235)[1] in which the protagonist retraces his (and the author's) itinerary from Toledo in Castile to Iraq for the benefit of the narrator.[2] Because of its realistic tenor and detailed panorama of Jewish life around the Mediterranean this *maqāma* might seem to belong in a book of eyewitness travel narratives such as those produced by Ibn Jubayr (b. 1145), Benjamin of Tudela (c. 1170), or Ibn Baṭṭūṭa (b.1304), the renowned travelers of the age.[3] The other text, also by al-Ḥarizi, is the *Taḥkᵉmoni*, a corpus of fifty diverse and colorful Hebrew *maqāmāt*. It is less apt to be mistaken for a traveler's account though its many descriptive passages include a *maqāma* (the forty-sixth) on the "Men of the Cities" that closely parallels the text of the author's

[1] On al-Ḥarizi, see Schirmann, 1997, pp. 145–221, and the bibliography cited there.

[2] Text: Stern, 1964 and and 1989: 186–210; and Ratzhaby, 1980.

[3] In my opinion, a study of the *Taḥkᵉmoni* by Dishon, errs in reading the *Taḥkᵉmoni* as though it were a kind of travelogue the author used "as a stage for his plots" (p. 12). Dishon asserts that "Alḥarizi was one of the Jewish travelers in the Middle Ages who wrote about his adventures and impressions in a poetical but nonetheless realistic and descriptive way" (p. 11). The *Taḥkᵉmoni* undoubtedly reflects certain realia of the places al-Ḥarizi visited and possibly refers to the experiences or incidents he witnessed on his travels. But to completely separate the realistic from the imaginative is to ignore the way in which these elements are intertwined in the text and to seriously misunderstand the literary character of the *Taḥkᵉmoni*.

Arabic *maqāma*.[4] The relative indifference toward Muslims in two texts that take us from Toledo in the west through Cairo and Jerusalem, and from Damascus to Mosul, Baghdad, and Basra in the Muslim East is striking. *Sefer ha-musar*, a collection of Hebrew *maqāmāt* by the sixteenth-century Yemeni wayfarer Zekhariya al-Ḍahrī that is modeled after the *Taḥkᵉmoni* meaningfully casts Muslim characters in four of its forty-five narratives.[5] By comparison, it is as though the *Taḥkᵉmoni* has all but banished Muslims and the dominion of Islam to the very fringes of consciousness.

Written early in the thirteenth century, the *Taḥkᵉmoni* is probably the best-known work of Hebrew imaginative rhymed prose to have come down to us from the Middle Ages.[6] It is also regarded as the most influential Hebrew adaptation of the medieval Arabic prose form and literary genre famous for its extravagant rhetoric and entertaining charm.[7] Like the Arabic *maqāmāt* of the Eastern belletrists Badīʿ l-Zamān al-Hamadhānī (d. 1008) and al-Ḥarīrī of Basra (d. 1122) that served as its implicit source and explicit model,[8] the *Taḥkᵉmoni* is marked by linguistic resourcefulness, inventive rhetoric, and extensive intertextual allusions. Its witty comedy of social manners and incisive social satire are presented in frequently diverting stories and interspersed with lines of poignant and manneristic verse. The text also introduces an enchanting array of memorable characters such as a loquacious rooster with the mien of a Hebrew prophet (no. 10); a pompous but thoroughly inept *ḥazzan* (no. 24); a nouveau riche merchant with a gauche sense of Near Eastern hospitality (no. 34); a snake charmer who has the power to heal a venomous bite (no. 37); and an elderly and opinionated literary critic with atrocious table manners (no. 3) along with a host of con artists, an assortment of damsels and spinsters and many others includ-

[4] Descriptive and didactic *maqāmāt* became especially prominent in Andalusi-Arabic letters during the twelfth century. See Nemah. The point is also made by Arié in her survey of the Andalusi *maqāma*. For a general introduction to the Arabic *maqāma*, see Brockelman and Pellat.

[5] Zekhariyah al-Ḍahrī, nos. 9, 17, 36, 42.

[6] It is worth recalling that most works of rhymed Hebrew prose are in fact not *maqāmāt* even though they share some of the formal features and conventions of the genre. See Pagis, 1978, pp. 79ff.

[7] The *Taḥkᵉmoni* served as the model for subsequent writers such as Immanuel ha-Romi in fourteenth-century Italy and Zekhariyah al-Ḍahrī in sixteenth-century Yemen. Both ha-Romi, 1:4–5, and al-Ḍahrī , p. 53, explicitly refer to al-Ḥarizi in their works.

[8] Source critical studies have shown at least eight of the *Taḥkᵉmoni*'s *maqāmāt* to be derived from al-Hamadhānī (no. 3 = al-Hamadhānī nos. 1, 15; no. 31 = al-Hamadhānī no. 6; no. 34 = al-Hamadhānī no. 22; no. 21 = al-Hamadhānī no. 12; no. 29 = al-Hamadhānī no. 17; and no. 38 = al-Hamadhānī no. 23. See Dana, 1975; and 1984; Stern, 1946a; Schirmann, 1952; Ratzhaby, 1956.

ing two figures of particular interest to us, a Muslim astrologer and *qāḍī* (see below).

Were the *Taḥkᵉmoni* truly lacking in representations of Muslims among its cast of characters, it would in a sense be in keeping with belletristic Hebrew literature produced during the High Middle Ages in the lands of Islam, principally al-Andalus. Although *piyyuṭīm* (liturgical poetry), midrash, biblical commentaries, and mystical literature openly speak about Islam through extensive discourse on the figure of Ishmael, the eponymous ancestor of the Arabs and Muslims, secular Hebrew poetry and imaginative rhymed prose contain no clear conventions for representing Muslims. As we have seen in the previous chapter, only Samuel ha-Nagid's representations of his and Zirid Granada's trenchant foes survive as very partially realized literary portraits of Muslims in the Hebrew poetry of the Andalusi "Golden Age." Why should so worldly a poetry seem so reluctant to portray Muslims in any light, almost to the point of silence? In addition to the previous chapter's reflections on this question, we should note that the stylized form, conventional content, and Neoplatonic worldview of Andalusi-Hebrew poetry dictated the production and reproduction of stock characters and inhibited the representation of other figures.

The reasons for the *Taḥkᵉmoni*'s reticence in portraying Muslim characters (insofar as the confessional identity of its characters serves a narrative purpose—see below) are not difficult to grasp. The *Taḥkᵉmoni*'s protonational sensibility and ethnocentric focus are in fact typical of imaginative rhymed-prose literature as distinct from medieval Hebrew translations of international lore such as *Kalīla wa-dimna* (*The Panchatantra*), *Mishlei Sendebar* (*Tales of Sendebar*) and the story of Barlaam and Josaphat, *Ben ha-melekh wᵉ-ha-nazir* (*The Prince and Dervish*).[9] Andalusi-Hebrew poetry and to a certain extent the literature produced by subsequent generations of Mediterranean Hebrew writers was largely composed by men of letters for a privileged circle of patrons and peers. As I have tried to show elsewhere, secular Hebrew poetry is an emblem of the particular form of cultural ambiguity unique to Andalusi-Jewish society.[10] It provided members of the elite with (among other things) a transitory means of escape from the condition of cultural marginalization and political domination in Muslim society. Paradoxically, Hebrew literary intellectuals were also given to continuous reflection upon the

[9] Medieval Hebrew "translations" of international lore are generally unconcerned with confessional identity. "National" cultural considerations rarely receive more than perfunctory notice in such works. See, for example, Abraham ibn Ḥisdai's Hebrew version of *Barlaam and Josaphat*, entitled *Ben ha-melekh wᵉ-ha-nazir*; *Mishei Sendebar*, edited and translated by Epstein under the title *Tales of Sendebar*; and Jacob ben Elʿazar's translation of *Kalīla wa-dimna*.

[10] Brann, 1991.

influence of the Islamic environment on their own society and culture on account of their role as outsiders in Muslim society and their acculturation to the norms of Arabic style and expression. Indeed, the impact of living under the aegis of Arabic culture if not always within the domain of Islam is readily apparent throughout the *Taḥkᵉmoni*—in its very form, style, and selection of themes as well as in its detailed reference to Jewish social and economic life under Islam in Mediterranean lands and in the Muslim East. Moreover, the *Taḥkᵉmoni*'s sensitivity to issues of interest to Hebrew literary intellectuals living in the lands of Islam signals its provenance as well as its intended audience.

It is worth recalling that al-Ḥarizi invokes the noble value of promoting Jewish cultural "nationalism" as the goal of the work. In the book's introductory *maqāma* the author's persona describes how, being enamored of the masterful Arabic *maqāmāt* of al-Ḥarīrī, several Hispano-Jewish notables of Toledo cajoled him into translating or, as Ḥayyim Schirmann noted,[11] rendering the Arabic anecdotes into biblical Hebrew.[12] The result of al-Ḥarizi's efforts is *Maḥbᵉrot iti'el*, written between 1205 and 1215.[13] Al-Ḥarizi's persona tells us that this enterprise, while successful, ultimately proved demoralizing, motivating him to compose an original book of Hebrew *maqāmāt* that would eclipse the Arabic *maqāmāt* of al-Ḥarīrī.[14] Al-Ḥarizi undertook the second literary mission, we are told, so as to demonstrate the superior eloquence of Hebrew in relation to Arabic, a value seemingly lost on the Arabic-speaking Jews of Christian Spain and Muslim lands.[15] Furthermore, the language of the introductory *maqāma*, whose parody of philosophical language owes a great deal to Solomon ibn Gabirol's sublime meditative poem "*Keter Malkhut*,"[16] flirts with the notion that the book was prophetically inspired.[17] The introductory *maqāma* therefore suggests,

[11] Schirmann, 1930, p. 18.

[12] Judah al-Ḥarizi, 1952, pp. 3–18. All citations of the *Taḥkᵉmoni* refer to this edition of the work unless noted otherwise. It has been translated by Reichert, Judah al-Ḥarizi, 1973. David S. Segal's long-awaited new translation and annotated study, *The Book of Taḥkemoni*, has been announced by the Littman Library of Jewish Civilization. The *Taḥkᵉmoni*'s introductory *maqāmā* is dedicated to the leader of Damascene Jewry, Samuel al-Barkolī. The technique used by al-Ḥarizi in selecting Hebrew equivalents for the Arabic names is studied by Lavi.

[13] Judah al-Ḥarizi, 1950. Only twenty-seven *maqāmāt* of al-Ḥarizi's translation have survived. Two (the first and twenty-seventh) are in fragmentary form. See Fleischer, 1973.

[14] See Margoliouth and Pellat.

[15] This complaint, which was already uttered during the "Golden Age," is reiterated in the introductory *maqāma* (al-Ḥarizi, 1952, pp. 12, 14) and in the eighteenth and forty-sixth *maqāmāt*.

[16] Mirsky has shown that the prose poem to the Creator and Wisdom in the Introduction owes much to *Keter Malkhut* by Solomon ibn Gabirol.

[17] Judah al-Ḥarizi, 1952, pp. 4–7. See Pagis 1990.

somewhat facetiously, that the task before al-Ḥarizi was one of cosmic significance. The *Taḥkᵉmoni*'s grandiose official agenda, then, is to resuscitate Hebrew language and culture and thereby reconstruct Jewish identity. In other words the *Taḥkᵉmoni* continues and extends the project of Andalusi-Hebrew culture by subversively appropriating another Arabic literary form and style for the purpose of Hebrew cultural "nationalism."

In the highly ironic first *maqāma* al-Ḥarizi's persona credits one of his characters with having tricked him into producing the book.[18] The author's persona reappears in the report of a narrator, called Heman ha-Ezraḥi, one of two recurrent *maqāma* figures familiar from Arabic literature. Heman relates that al-Ḥarizi's persona was accosted by a "Hebrew lad" (*na'ar 'ivri*), a mysterious youth who glorified al-Ḥarīrī's Arabic *maqāmāt* and cynically dismissed the possibility of producing a Hebrew collection to rival and surpass them. Challenged by the young man's disbelief in the project, al-Ḥarizi's persona is galvanized into creating the *Taḥkᵉmoni*. The youth, here named Ḥever ha-Qeni, is then disclosed as the mercurial vagabond, rhetorician, and raconteur who is the second stock character familiar from Arabic *maqāma* literature. Thus in both the introductory and first *maqāmāt* (as well as in the third and eighteenth *maqāmāt*, which take up the history of medieval Hebrew letters),[19] the *Taḥkᵉmoni* contemplates the significance of Hebrew culture under Islam.

The *Taḥkᵉmoni* is a book that clearly means to entertain and dazzle. But its rhetorical excesses and manifestly diverting qualities, especially its robust humor and tendency to satirize, can readily obscure the underlying thoughtfulness of the text. Conversely, its historicism and frequently realistic representation of people and events can easily overshadow its poetic inventiveness and the artfulness of its narratives. Readers who have isolated the *Taḥkᵉmoni*'s humor and satire from other materials in the text or considered its frequently didactic and informative cast apart from its entertaining elements and narrative charm have missed the interplay between the *Taḥkᵉmoni*'s content and its literary form and style. Narrative, as Robert Scholes observes, always displays both an affective and an informative aspect.[20] And in any case, storytelling such as we find in *maqāma* literature, as opposed to historical narrative, is in Hayden White's words "under no obligation to keep

[18] Judah al-Ḥarizi, 1952, pp. 23–28. The first *maqāma* is dedicated to the Exilarch Josiah.

[19] As in al-Hamadhānī's first and fifteenth *maqāmāt*. Judah al-Ḥarizi, 1952, pp. 38–48, 181–96 = Schirmann, 1959–60, 3:103–115, 131–51.

[20] Scholes, pp. 93–94.

the two orders of events, real and imaginary, distinct from one another."[21] That is because the representation of reality in a fanciful narrative is a product of the literary imagination; in historical narrative the representation of reality is shaped by what is perceived and remembered as real.

It is often inadequately appreciated that medieval writers such as al-Ḥarizi were fully conscious of the ambiguities of literary discourse and of the role different readers play in shaping the various meanings a text may have. This is, in part, how we should understand the statement in the *Taḥkᵉmoni*'s introductory *maqāma* that the book is replete with all manner of wisdom and that the audience will be either entertained or enlightened, depending on the intellectual orientation of the individual reader.[22] Similar statements are to be found in many imaginative and didactic works from the period such as *Ḥayy ibn Yaqẓān* by Ibn Ṭufayl (d. 1185),[23] the Hebrew version of *Kalīla wa-dimna* by Jacob ben Elʿazar (d. early thirteenth century),[24] Don Juan Manuel's (d. 1348) *El Conde Lucanor*,[25] *Libro de Buen Amor* by Juan Ruiz (fourteenth century),[26] and Vidal Benveniste's (fl. late fourteenth through early fifteenth century) scatological tale and allegorical postscript *Mᵉliṣat ʿefer wᵉ-dinah*.[27] But though the *Taḥkᵉmoni*'s rich tapestry of Jewish society has been examined, its didactic mien noted, its various literary sources investigated and considered, and Hebrew cultural nationalism frequently discussed, the book's distinctive vision of Jewish life and keen evocation of the Jewish condition in Mediterranean and Middle Eastern lands during the thirteenth century, that is to say, its construction of social mean-

[21] White, pp. 3–4.

[22] Judah al-Ḥarizi, 1952, pp. 13–14. The statement is also a sign of the author's apology for the secular nature of the book. See Brann, 1991, pp. 119ff.

[23] Muḥammad ibn Ṭufayl, p. 92.

[24] Jacob ben Elʿazar, p. 312 (the second introductory poem); and Isaac ibn Sahulah, p. 6. The thirteenth-century Provençal Hebrew writer Qalonymos ben Qalonymos introduces his Hebrew adaption of the fable "*Takwīn al-ḥayawānāt*" from *Rasāʾil ikhwān al-ṣafāʾ* with a similar but more forceful insistence that the text is more than meets the eye. He writes (trans. in Epstein, pp. 12–13):

> Lest anyone lacking in discernment and naked of judgement might think that this book is of the same kind as *Kalilah and Dimnah* or *Mishlei Sendebar* or Hariri and similar books: Heaven forbid! For it is not like them and not even like those which are like unto them. Its purpose rather is to render us consolation and moral lessons; and deep secrets are concealed in it and scattered throughout—which even the wise will not fully comprehend at the first reading.

[25] Keller and Keating, p. 40 (Prologue).

[26] Juan Ruiz, the Archpriest of Hita, *The Book of True Love: A Bilingual Edition*; trans. Daly p. 43.

[27] Vidal Benveniste, fols. 101a (introductory poem); and the author's allegorical postscript, fols. 105b–108a. Critical edition, Huss, pp. 202, 225–33.

ing, have escaped the attention of its many readers.[28] One significant but encoded expression of this vision is found in the *Taḥkᵉmoni*'s representations of the Muslim "other" in whose society most of its narratives take place. If I may apply to our text Bernard Lewis's keen formulation, such representations of Muslims as we find in the *Taḥkᵉmoni* "not only define the outsider but also, and perhaps more particularly, help to define" the Jews of Islam themselves.[29]

Since the *Taḥkᵉmoni* is a corpus of Hebrew *maqāmāt* written for a Jewish audience it would be odd if its principal characters were not presumed to be Jews or recognized as such through their behavior or speech. While this is indeed the case, the confessional affiliation of the various characters serves little narrative purpose in the majority of anecdotes. For instance, in the twenty-first *maqāma*,[30] a story adapted from al-Hamadhānī's "*maqāma* of Baghdad,"[31] Ḥever recounts a tale about his victimization of an amiable but gullible villager. As in several episodes of the *Taḥkᵉmoni*, Ḥever's tale commences with him on the prowl for an easy mark:

> Before I had finished thinking, I looked up and before my very eyes was an Arab arriving from his village riding on his mule. When I saw him I thought to myself: I have found what I hoped for! Oh, this is the day my wish has come true!

The rustic villager is referred to as an Arab, an identification apparently rendered significant by the Arabic superscription referring to the text as "the *maqāma* of the Arab." Riding into town on his donkey with a sack of money obtrusively affixed to his belt, the countryman is a perfect pushover for the city slicker. Ḥever befriends him and lures him into the meat market of the *sūq* where the two devour a sumptuous feast of breads, meats, and sweets. On the pretense of going to fetch some water to quench their thirst, Ḥever disappears, leaving the frantic villager to settle accounts with the impatient meat seller. Meanwhile, Ḥever watches the scene in amusement from behind a corner.

The use of the appellation "Arab" (which is restricted to the Arabic

[28] The *Taḥkᵉmoni* has been subjected to source criticism with some fruitful results. Its rhymed prose has been carefully mined for sociohistorical information concerning the various Jewish communities and dignitaries mentioned in the text. Its widespread use of biblical citation has also been studied. But for all its renown, the *Taḥkᵉmoni* has yet to receive the comprehensive literary critical scrutiny it deserves. For an introduction to the literary character of the book, the reader should refer to Pagis, 1975, pp. 203–215; on al-Ḥarizi and the production of the *Taḥkᵉmoni*, see Schirmann, 1979, 1:353–68.

[29] Lewis, September 1990, p. 49.

[30] Judah al-Ḥarizi, 1952, pp. 208–212 = Schirmann, 1959–60, 3:151–56.

[31] Al-Hamadhānī, pp. 59–62.

title and the passage quoted) in referring to the villager is presumably drawn from Arabic literature in which various authors speak derisively of "Arabs" when referring to Bedouin. As such, the story of a naive villager initiated into the harsh realities of city life pertains to the age-old conflict between the urban and rural worlds as well as than to inter-communal relations. It is interesting to note that a similar attitude toward the villager is found in the *Taḥkemoni*'s "*maqāma* of the Rooster" in which the members of a quaint hamlet are portrayed as Jews.[32] Incidentally, this story is an adaptation of a *maqāma* by the eleventh-century Andalusi writer Abū Ḥafṣ ʿUmar Ibn al-Shahīd, preserved by Ibn Bassām in *Al-Dhakhīra* where the butt of the story is referred to as a Bedouin.[33]

I would now like to turn to the "*maqāma* of the astrologer,"[34] a tale that stands out as especially interesting among the *Taḥkemoni*'s fifty *maqāmāt* because it is the sole narrative in the corpus in which two of the principal characters are Muslims. As told in the report of Ḥever ha-Qeni, a street astrologer and a *qāḍī* (who does not appear until the tale's end) are identified as Muslims. In a splendid illustration of the narrative technique known as "impersonated artistry,"[35] the astrologer and *qāḍī* behave and speak as members of their confessional community even though their discourse is rendered in perfectly elegant medieval Hebrew.

The tale may be summarized as follows: A youthful and carefree Heman ha-Ezraḥi reports that one fine day he chanced upon a deeply troubled Ḥever standing near the city gate. Pained at his companion's anguished expression, Heman inquires about its cause. Ḥever ha-Qeni then relates how, the day before, he and some associates had witnessed

[32] Judah al-Ḥarizi, 1952, pp. 106–114 (no. 10) = Schirmann, 1959–60, 3:123–31.

[33] Ibn Bassām, 1:676ff. Stern, 1946a, studies the parallels.

[34] Judah al-Ḥarizi, 1952, pp. 213–17 (no. 22). The text may be conveniently found in Schirmann, 1959–60, 3:156–61. For another recent study of this tale, see Scheindlin, 1993. In his interpretation of the *maqāma*, Scheindlin comes to similar conclusions. His discussion of the ways in which the *maqāma* manipulates the expectations of the genre, moving from *hazl* to *jidd* (fun to earnest), is especially valuable.

[35] On this concept see Leicester, p. 4. It is worth recalling that al-Ḥarizi comments on the casting of characters before the implicit connection between the author and his literary creation (maintained throughout the introductory *maqāma* and part of the first *maqāma*) breaks down, making way for the "impersonated artistry" that characterizes the remainder of the book. Here is how al-Ḥarizi's persona apprises the reader of the distinction (al-Ḥarizi, 1952, p. 15):

> I have rendered all the words of this book through the tongue of Heman ha-Ezrahi and I have founded and constructed them in the name of Hever ha-Qeni even though neither of them belongs to our generation and *all that I have told in their name never ever was but is simply fiction* ["*mashal*"] [emphasis mine].

Al-Ḥarīrī serves a similar notice in the preface to his collection. See al-Ḥarīrī, 5.

an excited throng assembled at the city gate. The crowd had gathered to hear the words of a "scholarly Arab astrologer" ("*ḥakham me-ḥakhmei ha-ʿaravim ḥozeh va-kohkavim*") who "reveals future events before they happen and relates esoteric matters when they have yet to occur" ("*yᵉgalleh ha-ʿatidot bᵉ-ṭerem heyotam wᵉ-yaggid ha-sodot ʿad loʾ ḥanotam*").[36] Ḥever and his curious cohorts approach and observe an imposing but elderly figure clutching an astrolabe. The man boasts at length of his prowess in reading both the celestial signs and the innermost secrets of individuals, and he invites the crowd to inquire of the mysteries of heaven or to request his guidance on more mundane affairs. Awestricken, many clients approach the astrologer with their personal problems for which they obtain satisfying astrological advice. Ḥever's companions, though, who know a good con when they see one, are skeptical about the astrologer's extraordinary claims as suggested by the parody of Gen. 37:20, "Come now, let's hear his prophecies and see what will become of his dreams."[37] Consequently, Ḥever and his enthusiastic confederates conspire to debunk the astrologer:

[36] It should be noted that al-Ḥarizi, who translated Maimonides' *Guide for the Perplexed*, was an ardent champion of Maimonidean thought. See Judah al-Ḥarizi, 1952, pp. 348–49 (no. 46). His defense of Maimonides is studied by Stern, 1969; and Saenz-Badillos, 1985. Accordingly, al-Ḥarizi certainly ascribed to Maimonides' rejection of the religious and scientific legitimacy of astrology articulated in his *Commentary on the Mishnah*, *ʿAvodah zarah* 4:7; in his *Mishneh Torah*, *Sefer ha-Maddaʿ* (*Hilkhot ʿavodah zarah*, 11:16); in his occasional letter to the rabbis of Provence, edited by Marx, partially translated by Lerner and Mahdi, pp. 227–37; and in *Iggeret teiman*, Moses Maimonides, 1952, pp. 64–65 (trans., p. xiii). For studies of Maimonides' views on astrology, see Lerner; and Langermann. And more generally on Jewish astrology and its Islamic background, see Sela.

Nevertheless, our *maqāma* presents astrology as a veracious science (thought not according to Ḥever and his friends) because this was the prevalent attitude in the twelfth century among Muslims, Christians, and Jews. Benjamin of Tudela reports in his *Sefer massaʿot*, f. 52 and f. 80 (trans. pp 34, 53), that R. Joseph, a head of the Jewish community of Mosul who was given the honorific title *Burhān al-mulk*, served the sultan as a *ḥozeh*, which Adler translated as "astronomer" (English section, pp. 33 and 56). However the context suggests that "astrologer" is the correct meaning of the term. Abraham bar Ḥiyya (d. after 1136) and Abraham ibn ʿEzraʾ (d. 1164) are two of the best-known Jewish scholars of the High Middle Ages to engage in astrological research. See Ibn Ezra's comments (*Sefer yᵉsod moraʾ wᵉ-sod torah*) in Levin, 1985 p. 318, regarding the necessity of astrological knowledge. Bar Ḥiyya refers to astrological data in conjunction with the advent of the Messiah. See chapter 5 of *Mᵉgillat ha-mᵉgalleh*, Abraham bar Ḥiyya, 1967, especially, p. 108. See also Goitein, 1967–93, 5:420–22, where Goitein discusses the place of astrology among the Jews of the Near East during the High Middle Ages. Goitein also cites the important work on astrological almanacs from the Cairo Genizah studied by historians of science David Pingree and Bernard Goldstein. For a survey of the subject, see Barkai.

[37] Judah al-Ḥarizi, 1952, p. 216 = Schirmann, 1959–60, 3:157. Heb. "*Lᵉkhah naʾ wᵉ-nishmᵉʿah nᵉvuʾotaw wᵉ-nirʾeh mah yihyu ḥalomotaw.*"

> Come, let's all agree upon a single question and go to him as one, our minds of one accord. Let's ask about the redemption and when salvation will come to the children of the exile, and whether there is restoration after downfall. We all agreed: It's a great idea![38]

In their haste to discredit the astrologer, Ḥever and his companions believe they have ingeniously conjured the supreme test: The ultimate secret of history, they reason, is surely the redemption of Israel. But in so doing they inadvertently commit themselves to a dangerous course of action in which they, rather than the astrologer or the time of the redemption, will be exposed. When their turn comes they challenge the astrologer to divine the question they have concealed. He consents and proceeds to perform some impressive astrological and geomantic procedures. While manipulating his astrolabe he becomes lost in thought.

> After that, he raised his head and looked at us in amazement. Then he glared at us and said: I swear by Him who created the light that shines, the sun and moon . . . I swear that you are neither Muslims nor Christians but that *you are from a despised and lowly people.* You must be Jews [emphasis mine; "*ki einkhem yishm*ᵉᵉ*'e'lim w*ᵉ*-lo' ʿarelim raq me-ʿam nivzim u-shfalim w*ᵉ*-ulay atem yisr*ᵉ*'elim*"]![39]

The astrologer continues:

> You inquire about a profound secret and ask a most difficult question for it is a secret as deep as the netherworld. Your question concerns the fallen tower [of David], whether it will be rebuilt with turrets; about the scattered sheep [of Israel] and whether they will escape the teeth of lions and go about among the beasts. . . . Your question concerns the ingathering of exiles, the destruction of kingdoms, and the resurrection of the dead. As the Lord lives, you deserve to die because your question concerns the destruction

[38] Judah al-Ḥarizi, 1952, p. 216 = Schirmann, 1959–60, 3:157. The idea to test him is Ḥever's; his companions suggest the test itself.

[39] Judah al-Ḥarizi, 1952, p. 216 = Schirmann, 1959–60, 3:160. The phrase "despised and lowly people" recalls the Arabic title of Judah Halevi's *Kuzari, The Book of Refutation and Proof on the Despised Faith* and the manner in which the Khazar King first refers to the Jews in Judah ibn Tibbon's somewhat free medieval Hebrew translation, (Judah Halevi, 1968, p. 17, "*ki ha-shiflut w*ᵉ*-ha-dalut lo' ʿazvu lahem middah ṭovah*"). Compare the Arabic original, Judah Halevi, 1977, p. 10 (1:10) "But as for the Jews, their apparent lowliness, smallness [in number], and the hate of all for them is sufficient [reason to ignore them] [1:4]"; "I had decided not to ask a Jew because I knew of the destruction of their traditions and the deficiency of their opinions, since their downfall did not leave them [anything] praiseworthy." [1:12] ("*idh al-manḥasa lam tatruk lahum maḥmada*").

> of the world; and you have spoken subversively and conspired against the government.[40]

The astrologer's sweeping indictment thus handed down, the throng seizes hold of Ḥever and his entourage and, with accompanying blows and strokes, hauls them off to the local *qāḍī* before whom the Jews are accused of treason. Fortunately for Hever and his cohorts, the Muslim judge, in the words of the text, "was one of the pious men of the gentiles" ("*me-ḥasidei ummot ha-ʿolam*") and an insightful "man from whom no secret was concealed" ("*w^e-khol sod mimmennu lo' neʿelam*"). Accordingly, the seemingly enlightened *qāḍī* places Ḥever and his friends in protective custody until the mob's fury passes; he then releases them unharmed. The *maqāma* concludes with Ḥever's brief prayer of thanksgiving for his deliverance.

How are we to interpret this engaging yet disquieting tale? What kind of a response might the story elicit from a thirteenth-century audience and what literary techniques are employed to effect the anticipated response? We can begin to address these questions by determining the structural and thematic relationship of the "*maqāma* of the astrologer" with others in the collection and by examining some of its cultural presuppositions. First we must categorize the story among the *Taḥk^emoni*'s various types of narrative discourse: (1) rhetorical anecdotes in which the narrative element exists merely as a setup for rhetorical exercises;[41] (2) *maqāmāt* in which the narrative element is a vehicle for descriptive or didactic discourse;[42] (3) tales involving a ruse or some other form of deception;[43] and (4) accounts of an adventure or a rescue.[44] Since it involves deception, a counter-ruse, and a rescue the "*maqāma* of the astrologer" does not at first appear to be a tale that stands apart. Yet beneath the surface conventions, the story is without parallel in the *Taḥk^emoni*. It reverses the basic pattern of deception found in other *maqāmāt* of its type; its intriguing plot involving the rescue of Jews from grave danger is thematically unique; and most significantly it casts the highly enterprising protagonist in a fundamentally transfigured role.

[40] Judah al-Ḥarizi, 1952, p. 217 = Schirmann, 1959–60, 3:160.

[41] Judah al-Ḥarizi, 1952, pp. 275–81 (no. 33, "Alphabetical Wordplay on Sinners and Saints"); 115–19 (no. 11); 308–311 (no. 39, "Poetic Dispute between Day and Night"); 91–94 (no. 8, A Letter Read Forward As Praise, Read Backward as Reproach").

[42] Judah al-Ḥarizi, 1952, pp. 344–66 (no. 46); 181–96 (no. 18).

[43] Judah al-Ḥarizi, 1952, pp. 74–82 (no. 6, "The Marriage"); 258–62 (no. 31, "The Captured Robber").

[44] Judah al-Ḥarizi, 1952, pp. 258–62 ("The Horseman's Ruse," no. 31); 299–303 ("The Snake Charmer," no. 37) = Schirmann, 1959–60, 3:186–90.

The structure of the tale is disarmingly straightforward. Heman's report (ll. 1–8) frames Ḥever's account of the incident (ll. 9–104), the core of the *maqāma* that can be divided into four parts: (1) the street scene and the astrologer's boast (ll. 9–61), (2) Ḥever's scheme to trip up the astrologer (ll. 62–77), (3) the astrologer's denunciation of the Jews (ll. 78–90), (4) the mob's assault on them and their deliverance by the sympathetic *qāḍī* (ll. 92–103). Finally, Ḥever's short prayer functions as a closing frame (ll. 103–104). Despite its superficial structural affinity with other adventure-rescue *maqāmāt* involving the victimization of Ḥever, some important differences are to be noted. Ḥever's virtual silence during the incident itself and at the conclusion of his account is the most critical sign of the *maqāma*'s exceptional form and content. Though it is conventional for a *maqāma* to end with a poem that comments on the text in some way, Ḥever does not recite a single line of verse; he barely utters a prayer of thanksgiving.[45] And when questioned by the astrologer, the always voluble and glib Ḥever can only muster two words, "You are right!" (l. 81, "*ken dibbarta*") in unison with his companions. The frame report also departs from the familiar pattern of Heman's encounters with Ḥever when the two meet at the beginning of a *maqāma*.[46] In our text the narrator appears in a buoyant frame of mind; the protagonist is uncharacteristically disconsolate, even depressed, and begins to narrate his tale as soon as the two have met. Yet because the significance of Ḥever's sorrow is not explained until the astrologer's outburst (ll. 75ff), the possibility that he is feigning and his story fabricated cannot be completely dismissed until more than midway though the text.

In the morphologically related "*maqāma* of the marriage,"[47] for instance, Heman meets a somber Ḥever who proceeds to tell him a story of outrageous misogyny: A demonic old woman duped him into marrying a grotesque maiden with no trousseau worthy of mention to compensate for her unsightly appearance. Meanwhile, to make matters even worse, the bride's father has bamboozled him on the marriage contract. According to his own account, Ḥever attempts to reverse and avenge his victimization by viciously assaulting his helpless and innocent wife. When all is said and done, the narrator Heman ha-Ezraḥi attempts to play down the brutal and horrifying tale as another of Ḥever's literary

[45] Indeed, the only poem in the text of the *maqāma* (ll. 46–54) belongs to the astrologer.

[46] Pagis, 1975, p. 212, notes two variations of Heman's encounters with Ḥever. The narrator and protagonist either meet at the outset of the *maqāma* or the identity of the latter is withheld from the former until the "surprising" conclusion of the episode.

[47] Judah al-Ḥarizi, 1952, pp. 74–82 (no. 6) = Schirmann, 1959–60, 3:115–23.

inventions.[48] But the discrepancy between what is supposedly real and what is fictitious is not as unambiguous as in other accounts of Ḥever's victimization, such as the *maqāma* of "the merchant's invitation," whose literary model is al-Hamadhānī's famous "*al-Maqāma al-maḍīriyya*."[49]

The first of part of the "*maqāma* of the astrologer" is similarly ambiguous and leaves the reader ill prepared for the seriousness of what ensues. Allusions to the biblical account of Joseph and his brothers,[50] another tale about reading signs, duplicity, and unmasking identity, as well as Hever's own comments on the narrative ("While I, to my ill-luck and the grief that had fallen to my lot . . ." l. 62), hint that the tables will be turned on the cackling conspirators. But the blithe manner in which Ḥever and company plot to entrap and expose the astrologer creates the false impression that this is simply another tale about unmasking a charlatan,[51] comparable, say, to the satirical "*maqāma* of the physician" who claims to possess a cure for love sickness.[52] As the story unfolds and the jeopardy to Ḥever becomes apparent, the unfulfilled humorous expectations brought to the account actually heighten the sense of uncertainty and suspense. The reader's response to the highly dramatic and perilous encounter is thus shock and apprehension followed by relief.

Ḥever's radical transformation makes sense only in the context of the reader's familiarity with the character and the corpus. Like Abū

[48] This tale and other important stories with an overt or covert misogynist orientation are the subject of wonderful and incisive analysis by Tova Rosen in her book on representations of gender in medieval Hebrew literature, *Circumcised Cinderella and Other Gender Trouble: Readings in Medieval Hebrew Literature*.

[49] Judah al-Ḥarizi, 1952, pp. 282–86 (no. 34) = Schirmann, 1959–60, 3:180–85. Heman meets a sullen man who recounts a riotous incident that is supposed to account for his mood. The man relates that he has been victimized by an inhospitable merchant and his brutally zealous servant. When he has concluded his account, the man is revealed to be Ḥever, and the entire episode is deemed a fabrication. Compare al-Hamadhānī, pp. 104–117. Ḥever is also temporarily victimized in the *maqāma* of the robber (Judah al-Ḥarizi, 1952, pp. 258–62 (no. 31) = Schirmann, 1959–60, 3:175–180) but he manages to turn the tables on his aggressor with the aid of a concealed knife. This *maqāma* is noteworthy for its shocking violence and ambiguous conclusion.

[50] In addition to the ironic allusion noted above, the *qāḍī* reassures the Jews quoting Joseph's (who is not what he appears to be) words to his brothers (Gen. 43:23) (l. 99): "All will be well with you. Do not be afraid." (Heb. "*Shalom lakhem al tira'u*").

[51] This motif is also reminiscent of an incident related in the *Sīra of the Prophet* (trans. A. Guillaume, p. 136). Two Qurayshī doubters turn to the rabbis of Medina for help in determining Muḥammad's authenticity as a prophet. The rabbis provide them with three questions to pose to Muḥammad. On Ibn Isḥāq's account of this episode and the relevant Quranic passages, see Wansbrough, pp. 124–26. David S. Powers drew my attention to this text.

[52] Judah al-Ḥarizi, 1952, pp. 373–76 (no. 48) = Schirmann, 1959–60, 3:190–94.

l-Fatḥ and Abū Zayd before him in al-Hamadhānī and al-Ḥarīrī, Ḥever ha-Qeni appears in most of the episodes of the *Taḥkᵉmoni* as the quintessential scoundrel-trickster, the "witty vagabond" (*al-ʿayyār al-ẓarīf*) of medieval Arabic literature. Regardless of the guise he temporarily assumes *his* duplicity is uncovered, his manipulation of reality is exposed, and his success in exploiting others is applauded or deplored.[53] But in the "*maqāma* of the astrologer," another character, not Ḥever, is suspected of deception and the typically venturesome *Ḥever ha-Qeni is cast in the unlikely role of passive victim*. In this his most dire predicament, Ḥever's notorious wiles, extraordinary rhetorical skills, and uncanny resourcefulness are of no avail. He not only fails to act; he fails to speak. And were it not for the seemingly providential intervention of the Muslim magistrate, he would not escape unharmed. The reader is caught completely off guard by Ḥever's victimization, loss of autonomy, and above all his speechlessness, because we have been conditioned to expect that he will prevail and that the circumstances of his success will alternately outrage and delight while always entertaining us.

Fedwa Malti-Douglas has shown that similar role transformations from victimizer to victim are found in the *maqāmāt* of al-Hamadhānī as well as in medieval Arabic *bukhalāʾ* and *taṭfīl* anecdotes about misers and uninvited guests.[54] In such instances, she notes, the primary literary effect of the protagonist's transformation is humor.[55] Comparable transformations and literary effects are also evident elsewhere in the imaginative Hebrew literature of the twelfth and thirteenth centuries, notably in "*Nᵉʾum asher ben yᵉhudah*" ("Asher in the Harem"), the tale of a bumbling courtly lover's misadventures in a harem by Solomon ibn Ṣaqbel (twelfth-century al-Andalus),[56] *Sefer shaʿshuʿim* [*The Book of Delight*], a book-length fantasy of self-discovery by Joseph ibn Zabara (b.c. 1140),[57] and the story known as "*Minḥat yᵉhudah*" ("The Offering of Judah the Misogynist"), a parodic comedy of love by Judah ibn Shabbetai (b. 1168).[58] But unlike Asher's victimization in "*Nᵉʾum asher ben yᵉhudah*," or Zeraḥ's in "*Minḥat yᵉhudah*," the shift in Ḥever ha-Qeni's role from active trickster to passive victim in the "*maqāma* of the

[53] On the various forms of deception in medieval Hebrew narrative art, see Brann, 1991, pp. 137–41.

[54] For this discussion of the shifts in Ḥever ha-Qeni's role, I am indebted to the insights of Fedwa Malti-Douglas, pp. 254ff.

[55] Malti-Douglas, p. 255.

[56] The text of Ibn Ṣaqbel's *maqāma*, which was part of a larger but now lost collection (see Fleischer, 1974, pp. 202–204) may be found in Schirmann's anthology, 1959–60, 2:554–65. A poetic translation by Raymond P. Scheindlin appeared under the title "Asher in the Harem" in Stern and Mirsky, pp. 253–67.

[57] Ibn Zabara (*Sefer shaʿshuʿim*).

[58] Judah ibn Shabbtai (*Minḥat yᵉhudah sone' ha-nashim*, ed. A. Ashkenazi), fols. 1a–12b. Partial translation by Scheindlin, in Stern and Mirsky, pp. 269–94.

astrologer" could hardly have been viewed as the protagonist's comeuppence to which the reader might be expected to register Schadenfreude, sadistic delight. Ḥever is not victimized in the manner in which he repeatedly exploits others such as by preying upon the inexperienced, the gullible, and the pompous or the pious. Rather he is victimized because he is a Jew who has overstepped his bounds. No longer a powerful and elusive liminal figure operating on the margins of society, Ḥever is vulnerable in the "*maqāma* of the astrologer" precisely because he is portrayed as a defenseless Jew in Muslim society.

Two contrasting representations of Muslims are rendered in the text: (1) the supposedly learned but popular astrologer who denounces the Jews as a subversive element in Muslim society; and (2) the sage magistrate whose devotion and mysterious grasp of esoteric knowledge appear to predispose him to act as a protector of the Jews. Because little insight is provided into the characters' motivations, these are by no means fully realized literary portraits but stereotypical characters cast in a literary genre that always depicts reality in a fragmentary manner. But the Muslim characters are more than simplistic stereotypes, because their behavior and roles accurately reflect sociohistorical circumstances. The *munajjim* in our text is not to be confused with a professional astrologer who engages in scientific research and advises the sultan in order to earn a living. Rather, he is one of the shady figures whose exploits are recounted and examined by al-Jawbarī (fl. thirteenth century) in *Kitāb al-mukhtār fī kashf al-asrār wa-hatk al-astār [Revealing the Secrets and Unveiling the Coverings]*, the spellbinding book (cited in the Introduction for its exposé on the fraudulence of Jewish men of learning) devoted to the swindlers, quacks, and tricksters who can be found lurking in every marketplace of medieval urban Islam.[59] Because he operates on the street and not at court, the astrologer is a con artist associated with the faceless masses. Indeed, he shares not only his clients' confidences but also their enmity toward the Jews. Yet the sham astrologer initially does not set out to incite the mob against the Jews with anti-Semitic discourse. When he first realizes that his clients are Jews, he is seemingly astonished and angry.[60] Only when he intuitively apprehends their motive and the unusual nature of their secret query

[59] It is interesting to note that al-Jawbarī, p. 22, mentions a now lost work on the same subject by the eleventh-century Andalusi-Arabic writer Ibn Shuhayd. See Bosworth, 1:107ff.

[60] The reader should take note that the Jews in the story exhibit no outward sign that would betray their identity. While their public anonymity is necessary for the plot, it also reflects a situation in which the legal requirement of *ghiyār*, that *dhimmī*s wear a distinguishing garment or mark, was not enforced, as evident in several pious complaints from Muslims we read in previous chapters. See Goitein 1967–93, 2:285–88; 4:193–96.

does he denounce them as enemies of the state. Even then, he does so primarily in order to safeguard his "professional" reputation. In a sense, then, Ḥever and friends themselves lead the astrologer into his diatribe against the Jews. While poised to expose a fraud, they appear to violate the restrictions imposed upon them as *dhimmī* subjects by Islam. By contrast, the *qāḍī* to whom the Jews are taken is a dignified figure whose representation recalls a tradition in which the biblical Ishmael is said to exemplify kindliness.[61] A high-minded representative of institutional Islam whose portrayal clashes with the tendency in Arabic literature to ridicule men of his office,[62] the local *qāḍī* disdains the intolerance of the masses, presumably because their violent behavior is not in accordance with Islamic law and because of his utter diminishment of the Jews, or alternatively on account of his enigmatic knowledge of esoteric matters.[63] Together, the two contrasting representations of Muslims, one a cunning and underhanded figure easily roused to hostility and associated with the urban masses, the other a seemingly benevolent and ideal figure representative of the religious elite, bespeak of the text's ambivalent attitude toward the sociopolitical experience of the Jews under Islam.

To this point, I have deliberately refrained from placing the tale in a specific historical context in order to concentrate on its literary character and its relationship with Arabic models and other *maqāmāt* in the *Taḥkᵉmoni*. However, since the nature of Jewish messianic aspirations in Muslim society is an issue in the story, it is important to recall that al-Ḥarizi produced the *Taḥkᵉmoni* during a period rife with intense messianic longing, expectations, and activity in al-Andalus and Christian Spain as well as in the Muslim East, that is, about thirty years after the Muslim retaking of Jerusalem from the Crusaders (1187).[64] This

[61] Fenton, p. 85.

[62] In Arabic literature the figure of the local *qāḍī* is often ridiculed. See, for example, the miserly *qāḍī* in al-Ḥarīrī's "*al-Maqāma al-tabrīziyya* [no. 40]," pp. 439ff.

[63] Goitein, *A Mediterranean Society*, 2: 278–80, presents documentary evidence from the Cairo Genizah pertaining to anti-Semitic incidents and the intervention of Muslim officials. One of the anonymous readers assigned by the press comments perceptively that the "*maqāma* of the astrologer . . . illustrates an awareness that Islam followed the rule of its holy law [and that it reflects] Jewish confidence in the Muslim judiciary, as amply evidenced by the documents of the Cairo Geniza."

[64] Gerson Cohen has shown that open messianic speculation was common in Hispano-Jewish society and culture. See Gerson D. Cohen. The same can be said for the extensive messianic activity among the Jewish communities of the Muslim East; see, for example, Maimonides, 1952 (*Epistle to Yemen*), cited above. For a survey of messianic attitudes during the High Middle Ages, see Goitein, 1967–93, 5:391–415. For documentary evidence of messianic movements in the Muslim East during the early twelfth cen-

conquest is in fact discussed in the "Jerusalem *maqāma*,"[65] one of the few episodes in the *Taḥkᵉmoni* besides the "*maqāma* of the astrologer" whose sober theme and serious tone are not compromised by either a frame report or some other narrative artifice. While instructing the pilgrim Heman ha-Ezraḥi in the recent history of Jerusalem, Ḥever explains that the Jews were permitted to return to Zion only when the Muslims repossessed the city. Ḥever then praises the "prince of the Ishmaelites," namely Ṣalāḥ al-Dīn, the Ayyubid sultan of Egypt and Syria, for having served as God's agent in overthrowing the despised Franks and subsequently for encouraging Jewish resettlement of the Holy City. As in the late apocalyptic midrash "*Nistarot shel rabbi shimʿon bar yoḥay*,"[66] the *Taḥkᵉmoni* embraces the sovereignty of Islam over Palestine as a sign of the approaching messianic age:

> Then he [Ṣalāh al-Dīn] commanded that in every city there sound a call to both great and small, saying: "Bid Jerusalem take heart in rebirth, that all seed of Ephraim who desire may return in mirth, who are left in Mosul and Egypt's dearth, and those dispersed to the uttermost ends of the earth. From all sides let them gather unto her and settle within her border."[67]

Ḥever's history lesson thus embodies the same attitude of dependence upon and acceptance of Islamic authority signified in the "*maqāma* of the astrologer."

What does the story of the astrologer tell us about the Jews' messianic hopes and the construction of Jewish identity under Islam? It seems to presume that from the popular Muslim point of view Jewish messianism

---

tury, see the famous "Scroll of Obadiah the Norman Proselyte" (Hebrew), in Norman Golb, pp. 100–101. The events to which Obadiah refers are studied by Goitein, 1952. My thanks to Moshe Gil for calling my attention to the latter texts and studies. For much more on the messianic connections cited in this chapter, see the extensive references to messianism in Gil, 1997.

[65] Al-Ḥarizi, 1952, pp. 245–49 (no. 28) = Schirmann, 1959–60, 3:170–75.

[66] The text may be found in *Midrᵉshei gᵉ'ullah*, pp. 188ff. See also the seventh-century apocalyptic poem, "*Oto ha-yom*" in ibid., pp. 158–60, trans. Lewis, 1974b. By contrast, the eighth-century pseudepigraphic midrash *Pirqei dᵉ-rabbi eliʿezer* presents an unremittingly hostile attitude toward the dominion of Islam. In light of the names of the *Taḥkᵉmoni*'s narrator and protagonist, it is interesting to note that "*Nistarot shel rabbi shimʿon bar yohay*," (p. 190) refers to Abraham by the midrashic appellation "*Eitan ha-ezraḥi*" and understands the biblical Qenites (*ha-Qeni*; cf. Balaam's oracle [Num. 24:21]) as Ishmaelities (i.e., Arabs). On the latter identification, see also *Pirqei dᵉ-rabbi eliʿezer*, 69a (chapter 30).

[67] Al-Ḥarizi, 1952, p. 248 = Schirmann, 1959–60, 3:173–74. The translation here is that of Reichart, al-Ḥarizi, 1973, 2:148. The *maqāma* must have been written before 1229 when Emperor Frederic II occupied Jerusalem.

is seditious and an implicit threat to Islam. Yet Ḥever and his friends do not really expect to uncover the secret of redemption, and, unlike Ismāʿīlī operatives, they hardly represent a menace to Islam unless the messianic aspiration itself is considered sufficiently subversive. Ḥever's scheme is surely imprudent and ill-wrought, because the Jews nonchalantly dabble in "national"-religious discourse in the public eye. In so doing they give the appearance of being openly engaged in a messianic activity whose political dimension—especially the idea of the ingathering of the exiles and the restoration of Jewish sovereignty over the land of Israel—the astrologer instinctively comprehends, represents an implicit threat to state security.[68] Is he correct? A rabbinic (midrashic) interpretation of the Song of Sol. 2:7 ("I adjure you, O maidens of Jerusalem, By gazelles or by hinds of the field: do not wake nor rouse Love until it please!") to which Moses Maimonides alludes at the conclusion of his *Epistle to Yemen*[69] links Jewish messianism with political activity by enjoining the Jews not to force the redemption and not to rebel against the state.[70] It is therefore possible to interpret the story of the astrologer as a subtle critique of engaging in any public discourse on the subject of messianic expectations—as a warning of what can happen when what properly belongs in the category of *bāṭin* (esoteric) is indiscreetly and carelessly treated as though it were *ẓāhir* (exoteric). But the story can be read another way. The astrologer might have dismissed the Jews' question as nothing more than the misguided and religiously absurd doctrine of unbelievers. Instead he finds it useful to appear to take the messianic idea very seriously. And because the magistrate also appears to know some-

[68] The astrologer's "understanding" of Jewish messianism runs the gamut of traditional beliefs as delineated by Saʿadia Gaon, including the notion that resurrection will accompany the advent of the Messiah.

[69] Moses Maimonides, 1952, p. 104 (trans., p. xx). In the same text, pp. 63–64 (trans., p. xii), Maimonides also cites the rabbinic dictum: "May the calculators of the final redemption come to grief" (BT Sanhedrin 97b).

[70] BT Ketubot 111a. In the *Letter on Astrology*, ed. Marx, pp. 50–51; trans. in Lerner and Mahdi, pp. 227–37, reprinted in Twerksy, 1972, pp. 472–73, Maimonides also relates an anecdote about the appearance in Yemen of a deluded individual who announced he had come to prepare the way for the messiah:

> The king of the Arabs who had seized him asked him: "What is this that you have done?" He replied: "What I have done, I have indeed done, and according to God's word." Then he said "What is your authenticating wonder?" He replied: "Chop off my head and I shall revive at once." He said to him: "You (can) have no greater sign than this. Certainly I—and the whole word—shall trust and know that my forefathers have bequeathed a falsehood." At once they killed the poor fellow. May his death be an atonement for him and all Israel. The Jews in most places were punished by fines, and even now there are some ignoramuses there who maintain that presently he will come to life and rise."

thing about the advent of the messianic age, the story would seem to reinforce Jewish hopes for a speedy redemption. Indeed, Maimonides also expresses encouragement for the Jews' political-religious aspirations in their redemption and he repudiates the views of non-Jewish, gentile astrologers to the contrary:

> For while the Gentiles believe that our nation will never constitute an independent state, nor will they [our nation] ever rise above their present condition and all the astrologers, diviners, and augers concur in this opinion, God will prove false their views and beliefs, and will order the advent of the Messiah. . . . This is the correct view that every Israelite should hold, without paying attention to the conjunction of the stars.[71]

In this respect the "*maqāma* of the astrologer," whose astrologer is one of a kind, offers the contemporary reader reassurance and consolation[72] even though in the here and now the contrasting but complementary representations of the Muslim astrologer and *qāḍī* signify resignation and an acceptance of the Jews' loss of power under Islam.[73]

I therefore prefer to think of the dramatic encounter between the Jews and Muslims related in the "*maqāma* of the astrologer" as an unsettling and ambiguous parable of the power relationship between Muslims and Jews in Muslim society of the (European) High Middle Ages. In this reading of the text, the representations of Muslims and Jews in the "*maqāma* of the astrologer" prove central to the significance of the entire collection, especially because the spirit of Arabic letters and Islamic civilization pervades a book in which Muslims are otherwise conspicuously absent. For all the *Taḥkᵉmoni*'s bravura about the superiority of Hebrew culture and its rivalry with Arabic, in the book's only significant tale in which Jews encounter Muslims, the former are represented as defenseless victims who are degraded, rendered powerless, and ultimately silenced by the sociopolitical hegemony of the latter. And since Ḥever ha-Qeni, who prevails over friend and foe throughout the *Taḥkᵉmoni* by virtue of his uncanny skill in manipulating language, is rendered helpless and mute in the "*maqāma* of the astrologer," we can

[71] Moses Maimonides, 1952, pp. 66–68. Mark R. Cohen, 1994, pp. 198–99, discusses Maimonides' prescient sense of the changes in the Jews' historical predicament under Islam.

[72] Cohen, in Abraham ibn Daud, pp. 252, 268 (*Book of Tradition*), has shown that offering such consolation was an important objective of Ibn Daud in writing *Sefer ha-Qabbalah*.

[73] Ḥever's prayer (l. 104), taken from a thanksgiving psalm (Ps. 124:6) is suggestive of national rather than merely personal deliverance: "Blessed is the Lord, who did not let us be ripped apart by their teeth" (Heb. "*Barukh adonai she-lo' nᵉtananu ṭeref lᵉ-shineihem*").

read it as a text that critically comments on itself and the entire corpus of *maqāmāt*. The "*maqāma* of the astrologer" signifies the limitations of the *Taḥkᵉmoni*'s seemingly subversive appropriation of an Arabic literary form and style and denotes the shortcomings of its cultural "nationalism." It suggests that a minority's subcultural production, however enthralling, is an act of resistance that does nothing to undermine the political hegemony of the majority. Read in this fashion the tale of the astrologer signifies that the *Taḥkᵉmoni*'s Hebrew rhetorical eloquence, like Ḥever ha-Qeni's, is no substitute for legitimate power and the political autonomy it yields.[74]

Although the imagined figure Ḥever ha-Qeni is silenced in the "*maqāma* of the astrologer," the Jewish author Judah al-Ḥarizi was able to sustain his voice as a producer of literary culture living under Islam. Joseph Sadan recently discovered an entry devoted to Judah al-Ḥarizi in an Arabic biographical dictionary.[75] Al-Ḥarizi, we now know, left Christian Toledo and journeyed to the Muslim East to settle in an environment where he would feel more culturally at home and where he expected to improve his prospects for securing the support of literary benefactors. In the end, al-Ḥarizi found little backing for his endeavors among the Jews of the East. But he successfully became an Arabic poet and earned his livelihood by offering his services to accepting Muslim patrons in Egypt and Syria.

Sadan's discovery of the Hebrew-turned-Arabic poet's literary fate is all the more striking on account of al-Ḥarizi's avowed and passionate commitment to Hebrew language and letters espoused in *Maḥbᵉrot iti'el* and the *Taḥkᵉmoni*. And yet, unlike other Jewish religious and literary intellectuals who despaired of their people's socioreligious position and found it convenient to profess Islam or became genuine converts, al-Ḥarizi apparently had it both ways by remaining a Jew but earning his living as an Arabic poet. Indeed, al-Ḥarizi's rhetorical and narrative artistry, and the trajectory of his career in a time and place where Muslim elites may not have feared contact with Jewish literary and religious intellectuals, reflect the instability, even permeability of the cultural boundaries between Muslim and Jew erected by the textual representations we have studied from al-Andalus and the Maghrib.

[74] In a provocative study of al-Hamadhānī entitled "Hamadhānī, *Schadenfreude*, and Salvation through Sin," L. E. Goodman argues that al-Hamadhānī's *maqāmāt* celebrate the category of freedom "in a mocking and irreverent way." Applied to the *Taḥkᵉmoni*, Goodman's insight would appear to support my interpretation of "the *maqāma* of the astrologer" as the one *maqāma* in which Ḥever's freedom is forfeited.

[75] Sadan, 1996, reports and discusses this discovery.

Primary Sources

ʿAbd Allāh bin Buluggīn al-Zīrī. *Mudhakkirāt al-amīr ʿabd allāh, al-musammāt bi-Kitāb al-Tibyān*, ed. E. Levi-Provençal (Cairo: Dār al-maʿārif, 1955).

———. *The Tibyān: Memoirs of ʿAbd Allāh b. Buluggīn Last Zirid Amīr of Granada*, trans. Amin T. Tibi (Leiden: E. J. Brill, 1986).

ʿAbd al-Ḥaqq al-Islāmī. *Al-Sayf al-Mamdūd fī l-Radd ʿAlā Aḥbār al-Yahūd*, ed. Esperanza Alfonso (Madrid: Consejo Superior de Investigaciones Cientificas, 1998).

ʿAbd al-Raḥīm al-Jawbarī, *Kitāb al-Mukhtār fī kashf al-asrār wa-hatk al-astār*, ed. ʿIsām Shbāru (Beirut: Dār taḍāmun lil-ṭibāʿa wal-nashr wal-tazwīʿ, 1992).

Abū Isḥāq Ibrāhīm ibn Sahl. *Dīwān ibn sahl al-andalusī*, ed. Yusrī ʿAbd al-Ghānī ʿAbd Allāh (Beirut: Dār al-kutub al-ʿilmiyya, 1988).

Abū Jaʿfar al-Ḍabbī. *Kitāb al-Bughya al-mutamis fī ta'rīkh rijāl ahl al-andalus*, ed. F. Codera and J. Ribera (Madrid: Biblioteca Arabico-Hispana [# 3], 1885).

Abū Nuwās. *Dīwān Abī Nuwās*, ed. Aḥmad ʿAbd al-Majīd al-Ghazālī (Beirut: Dār al-kitāb al-ʿarabī, 1992).

Bar Ḥiyya, Abraham. *M^{e}gillat ha-m^{e}galleh*, ed. Adolf Poznanski (Berlin, 1924; photo-reprint Jerusalem: Sifriyah Le-Maḥshevet Yisra'el, 1967).

Ben Elʿazar, Jacob. *Deux Versions Hebraiques du livre de Kalīlah et Dimnah*, ed. Joseph Derenbourg (Paris: Bibliotheque de L'Ecole Des Hautes Etudes, 1981).

Benjamin of Tudela, *Sefer massaʿot*, ed. and trans. Marcus Adler, *The Itinerary of Benjamin of Tudela* (New York: Feldheim, reprinted 1960).

Benveniste, Vidal. *M^{e}liṣat ʿefer w^e-dinah* (Istanbul, 1516; Jewish Theological Seminary of America, Rare Book Collection, acquisition #94704).

al-Ḍahrī, Zekhariyah. *Sefer ha-Musar*, ed. Yehudah Ratzhaby (Jerusalem: Ben Zvi Institute, 1965).

Guillaume, A. (trans). *The Life of Muḥammad: A Translation of Ibn Isḥāq's Sīrat Rasūl Allāh* (Karachi: Oxford University Press, reprinted 1967).

al-Ḥajarī, Aḥmad ibn al-Qāsim. *Kitāb Nāṣir al-Dīn ʿAlā 'l-Qawm al-Kāfirin*, eds. P. S. Van Koningsveld, Q. al-Samarrai, and G. A. Wiegers (Madrid: Consejo Superior de Investigaciones Cientificas, 1997).

Halevi, Judah. *Sefer ha-Kuzari*, ed. A. Zifroni (Jerusalem-Tel Aviv: Schocken, 1968).

———. *Kitāb al-radd wal-dalīl fī l-dīn al-dhalīl* (*Al-Kitāb al-khazarī*), eds. David H. Baneth and Ḥaggai Ben Shammai (Jerusalem: Magnes Press, Hebrew University and the Israel Academy of Sciences and Humanities, 1977).

———. *Yehuda Ha-Levi: Poemas*, intro., trans., and notes Angel Sáenz-Badillos and Judit Targarona Borras (Madrid: Clasicos Alfaguara, 1994).

al-Hamadhānī, Badīʿ al-Zamān. *Maqāmāt al-hamadhānī*, ed. Muḥammad ʿAbdūh (Beirut: Al-Maṭbaʿa al-kathūlikiyya, reprinted 1965).

Ha-Nagid, Samuel. *Dīwān* (*Ben Tehillim*), ed. Dov Yarden (Jerusalem: Hebrew Union College, 1966).

———. *Šemu'el ha-Nagid, Poemas I: Desde el Campo de Batalla Granada 1038–1056*, Angel Sáenz-Badillos and Judit Targarona Borras, Judit (eds.) (Cordoba: Ediciones El Almendro, 1988).
al-Ḥarīrī, Abū Muḥammad al-Qāsim ibn ʿAlī. *Sharḥ maqāmāt al-ḥarīrī* (Beirut: Dār al-turāth, 1967).
al-Ḥarizi, Judah ben Solomon. *Maḥbᵉrot Iti'el*, ed. Y. Peretz (Tel Aviv: Maḥbarot Lesifrut and Mosad HaRav Kook, 1951).
———. *Taḥkᵉmoni*, ed. Y. Toporowsky (Tel Aviv: Maḥbarot Lesifrut and Mosad HaRav Kook, 1952).
———. *The Taḥkemoni of Judah Al-Ḥarizi*, 2 vols., trans. Victor Emanuel Reichert (Jerusalem: Raphael Haim Cohen's Ltd. Publisher, 1973).
al-Ḥimyarī, Abū ʿAbd Allāh Muḥammad. *Rawḍ al-Miʿṭār fī khabar al-aqṭār*, ed. E. Levi-Provençal (Cairo/Leiden: E. J. Brill, 1937; reprinted Frankfurt-am-Main: Institute for the History of Arabic-Islamic Science, 1993).
al-Ḥumaydī, Abū ʿAbd Allāh Muḥammad ibn Fattūḥ. *Jadhwat al-muqtabis fī dhikr wulāt al-andalus wa-smā' ruwāt al-ḥadīth wa-ahl al-fiqh wal-adab*, ed. Muḥammad b. Tāwīt al-Ṭanjī (Cairo: Dār al-thaqāfa al-islāmiyya, 1953).
Ibn ʿAbd Rabbih, Abū ʿUmar Aḥmad. *Al-ʿIqd al-farīd*, 7 vols., ed. Aḥmad Amīn (Cairo: Lajnat al-ta'līf wal-tarjama wal-nashr, 1962).
Ibn Abī Uṣaybiʿa, Muwaffaq al-Dīn Abū l-ʿAbbās Aḥmad. *ʿUyūn al-anbā' fī ṭabaqāt al-aṭibbā'*, ed. August Muller (Konigsberg: Selbstverlag, 1884; Farnsborough: Gregg International Publishers, reprinted 1972).
Ibn Adret, Solomon ben Abraham. *Ma'amar yishmaʿe'l* in *R. Salomo b. Abraham b. Adereth*, ed. J. Perles (Breslau: Schletter, 1863).
Ibn ʿAqnīn, Joseph ben Judah. *Inkishāf al-asrār wa-ẓuhūr al-anwār*, ed. Abraham S. Halkin (Jerusalem: Mekize Nirdamim, 1964).
Ibn Bassām al-Shantarīnī, Abū l-Ḥasan. *Al-Dhakhīra fī maḥāsin ahl al-jazīra*, 8 vols., ed. Iḥsān ʿAbbās (Beirut: Dār al-thaqāfa, 1979).
Ibn Danān, Saʿadia. "*Ha-ma'amar ʿal seder ha-dorot*," *Ḥemdah gᵉnuzah*, ed. (Zvi) Hirsch Edelmann (Koenigsburg: Gruber and Guphrat, 1856).
———. "'*Ha-ma'amar ʿal seder ha-dorot*' de Seʿadyah ibn Danān: Edición Traducción y Notas," ed. Judit Targarona, *Miscelanea de Estudios Arabes y Hebraicos* xxxv (1986): 81–149.
Ibn Daud, Abraham. *Sefer Ha-Qabbalah* (*The Book of Tradition*), ed. and trans. Gerson Cohen (Philadelphia: Jewish Publication Society, 1967).
Ibn ʿEzra', Abraham. *The Religious Poems of Abraham ibn Ezra* (Hebrew), ed. Israel Levin, 2 vols. (Jerusalem: Israel Academy of Sciences and Humanities, 1975–80).
Ibn ʿEzra', Isaac ben Abraham. *Poems* (Hebrew), ed. Menahem H. Schmelzer (New York: Jewish Theological Seminary of America, 1980).
Ibn ʿEzra', Moses. *Kitāb al-muḥāḍara wal-mudhākara*, ed. A. S. Halkin. (Jerusalem: Mekizei Nirdamim, 1976).
Ibn Gabirol, Solomon. *Secular Poems* (Hebrew), ed. H. Brody and J. Schirmann (Jerusalem: Schocken Institute for Jewish Research, 1974).
Ibn Garcia. *The Shuʿūbiyya in Al-Andalus: The Risāla of Ibn Garcia and Five Refutations*, translation, introduction and notes by James T. Monroe (Univer-

sity of California Publications Near Eastern Studies 13) (Berkeley: University of California Press, 1970).

Ibn Ghiyāth, Isaac. *The Poems of Isaac ibn Ghiyyāt* (Hebrew), ed. Yonah David (Jerusalem: Ah'shav Publishing House, 1987).

Ibn al-Ḥājj al-ʿAbdarī. *Al-Madkhal ilā tanmiyāt al-aʿmāl bi-taḥsīn al-niyāt*, 4 vols. (Cairo: Al-Maṭbaʿa al-miṣriyya, 1929).

Ibn Ḥazm, ʿAlī ibn Aḥmad. *Al-Fiṣal fī l-milal wal-ahwā' wal-niḥal*, 5 vols. in 2 (Photo-reproduction of Cairo ed. 1899–1903; Baghdad, 1964).

———. *Al-Akhlāq wal-siyār fī mudāwāt al-nufūs*, ed. al-Ṭāhir Aḥmad Makkī (Cairo: Dār al-maʿārif, 1981).

———. *Rasā'il ibn ḥazm al-andalusī*, 4 vols., ed. Iḥsān ʿAbbās (Beirut: Al-Mu'assasa al-ʿarabiyya lil-dirāsāt wal-nashr, 1980–83).

———. "*Al-Radd ʿalā ibn al-naghrīla al-yahūdī*," in *Rasā'il ibn ḥazm al-andalusi*, 3:39–70, 1981.

———. *Jamharat ansāb al-ʿarab*, ed. ʿAbd al-Salām Muḥammad Hārūn (Cairo: Dār al-maʿārif, 1982a).

———. *Al-Fiṣal fī l-milal wal-ahwā' wal-niḥal*, 6 vols. (Beirut: Dār al-jīl, 1982b).

———. *Ṭawq al-ḥamāma fī l-ulfa wal-ullāf*, ed. Ṣalāh al-Dīn al-Qāsimī (Baghdad: Dār al-shu'ūn al-thaqāfiyya al-ʿāmma, 1986).

Ibn Ḥisdai, Abraham. *Ben ha-melekh w^{e}-ha-nazir*, ed. A. Habermann (Tel Aviv: Maḥbarot Lesifrut, 1950).

Ibn ʿIdhārī al-Marrākushī, Abū l-ʿAbbās Aḥmad ibn Muḥammad. *Al-Bayān al-mughrib fī akhbār al-andalus wal-maghrib*, ed. E. Levi-Provençal (Beirut: Dār al-thaqāfa, 1930; Dār al-ʿarabiyya lil-kitāb, reprinted 1983).

Ibn Kathīr, ʿImād al-Dīn Ismāʿīl. *Tafsīr al-qur'ān al-ʿaẓīm*, 7 vols. (Beirut: Dār al-andalus lil-ṭibāʿa wal-nashr, 1985).

Ibn Khaldūn, Abū Zayd ʿAbd al-Raḥmān ibn Muḥammad. *The Muqaddimah: An Introduction to History*, 3 vols., trans. Franz Rosenthal (Princeton: Princeton University Press and Bollingen Foundation, 1967).

Ibn Khallikān, Aḥmad ibn Muḥammad Abū l-ʿAbbās Shams al-Dīn al-Barmakī. *Wafayāt al-aʿyān wa-anbā' abnā' l-zamān*, 8 vols., ed. Iḥsān ʿAbbās (Beirut: Dār al-thaqāfa, 1972).

Ibn al-Khaṭib, Lisān al-Dīn. *Kitāb aʿmāl al-aʿlām*, ed. E. Levi-Provençal (Beirut: Dār al-makshūf, 1956).

———. *Al-Iḥāṭa fī akhbār gharnāṭa* (2d rev. ed.), 4 vols., ed. Mohamed Abdulla Enan (Cairo: Al-Khāngī Bookshop, 1973).

Ibn Marzūq, Muḥammad ibn Aḥmad. *El Musnad: hechos memorables de Abū l-Ḥasan, sultán de los benimerines*, study, translation, annotation, annotited indices María J. Viguera (Madrid: Instituto Hispano-Arabe de Cultura, 1977).

Ibn Muyassar, Tāj al-Dīn Muḥammad b. Yūsuf. *Ta'rīkh Miṣr* (*Annales d'Egypte*), ed. Henri Massé (Cairo: Imprimerie de l'Institut Francais d'archéologie orientale, 1919).

Ibn al-Nadīm, Abū l-Faraj Muḥammad ibn Isḥāq. *Fihrist*, 2 vols., trans. Bayard Dodge (New York: Columbia University Press, 1970).

Ibn Nājī. *Maʿālim al-imān fī maʿrifat ahl al-qayrawān*, 4 vols. (Cairo and Tunis: Al-Maktaba al-khānjī and al-Maktaba al-ʿātiqa, 1968–78).

Ibn Qayyim al-Jawziyya, Shams al-Dīn Abū ʿAbd Allāh Muḥammad ibn Abī Bakr. *Aḥkām ahl al-dhimma*, 2 vols., ed. Subḥī Ṣāliḥ (Damascus: Maṭbaʿat jāmiʿa dimashq, 1961).

Ibn Rashīq al-Qayrawānī, Abū ʿAlī al-Ḥasan. *Kitāb al-ʿumda fī maḥāsin al-shiʿr wa-adabihi wa-naqdihi*, ed. Muḥyā al-Dīn ʿAbd al-Ḥamīd (Beirut: Dār al-jīl, 1967).

Ibn Sahulah, Isaac. *M^eshal ha-qadmoni*, ed. Israel Zamorah (Tel Aviv: Maḥbarot Lesifrut, 1952).

Ibn Saʿīd al-Maghribī [al-Andalusī], Abū l-Ḥasan ʿAlī ibn Mūsā. *Al-Mughrib fī ḥulā l-maghrib*, 2 vols., ed. Shawqī Dayf (Cairo: Dār al-maʿārif bi-miṣr, 1955).

———. *Rāyāt al-mubarrizīn wa-ghāyāt al-mumayyazīn*, ed. Naʿmān ʿAbd al-Matʿāl al-Qāḍī (Cairo: Al-Ahram Press, 1973).

Ibn Shabbtai, Judah. "*Minḥat y^ehudah sone' ha-nashim*," ed. A. Ashkenazi, in *Ṭaʿam z^eqenim* (Frankfurt am Main: Verlag der hebraischen-antiquarischen Buchhandlung, 1854).

Ibn Ṭufayl, Abū Bakr Muḥammad ibn ʿAbd al-Malik. *Ḥayy ibn yaqẓān*, ed. Jamīl Ṣalība and Kāmil ʿAyyād (Damascus: Maṭbaʿat jāmiʿat dimashq, 1962).

Ibn Zabara, Joseph. *Sefer shaʿshuʿim*, ed. Israel Davidson (New York: Jewish Theological Seminary of America, 1914).

Ibn al-Zaqqāq, Abū l-Ḥasan ʿAlī. *Dīwān Ibn al-Zaqqāq*, ed. Afīfa Maḥmud Dirānī (Beirut: Dār al-thaqāfa, 1964).

Koran, The (with parallel Arabic text), trans. N. J. Dawood (London: Penguin Books, revised 1995).

al-Maghribī, Samau'al. *Ifḥām al-yahūd*, ed. and trans. Moshe Perlmann, *Proceedings of the American Academy of Jewish Research* 32 (1964).

Maimonides, Moses. *The Code of Maimonides* [Book 14]: *Book of Judges*, trans. A. M. Hershman (New Haven: Yale University Press, 1949).

———. *Iggeret teiman l^e-rabbenu moshe ben maimon* (*Epistle to Yemen*), ed. Abraham S. Halkin and trans. Boaz Cohen (New York: American Academy for Jewish Research, 1952).

———. *The Guide of the Perplexed*, 2 vols., trans. Shlomo Pines (Chicago and London: University of Chicago Press, 1963).

———. *Commentary on the Mishnah* (Arabic and Hebrew), 3 vols., ed. Joseph Qāfiḥ (Jerusalem: Mosad HaRav Kook, 1965).

———. *Mishneh Torah*, 6 vols. (Jerusalem: Mosad HaRav Kook, 1975).

al-Maqqarī, Shihāb al-Dīn Aḥmad ibn Muḥammad. *Nafḥ al-ṭīb min ghusn al-andalus al-raṭīb*, 8 vols., ed. Iḥsān ʿAbbās (Beirut: Dār ṣādir, 1968).

al-Masʿūdī, Abū l-Ḥasan ʿAlī ibn al-Ḥusayn. *Kitāb al-tanbīh wal-ishrāf*, ed. M. J. De Goeje (Leiden: E. J. Brill, 1894).

Midr^eshei g^e'ullah: Pirqei ha-apoqalipsah ha-y^ehudit me-ḥatimat ha-talmud ha-bavli w^e-ʿad re'shit ha-elef ha-shishshi, ed. Judah Kaufman (Yehudah Even Shemu'el) (2d rev. ed. Jerusalem: Bialik Institute-Massadah Publishing Co., 1953).

Pirqei d^e-rabbi eliʿezer, ed. Raham Horowitz (Jerusalem: Makor, 1972).

Pirqei d^e-rabbi eliʿezer (Warsaw, 1851; New York: Om Publishing, reprinted 1946).

Qalonymos ben Qalonymos. *Iggeret baʿalei ḥayyim*, ed. I. Toporowsky (Tel Aviv: Mahbarot Lesifrut, 1949).
ha-Romi, Immanuel. *The Cantos of Immanuel of Rome* (Hebrew), 2 vols. ed. Dov Jarden (Jerusalem: Mosad Bialik, 1957).
Saʿadia Gaon, *The Book of Beliefs and Opinions*, trans. Samuel Rosenblatt (New Haven: Yale University Press, 1948).
Ṣāʿid ibn Aḥmad al-Andalusī. *Ṭabaqāt al-umam*, ed. Louis Cheiko (Beirut: Al-Maṭbaʿa al-kathūlikiyya lil-abā' al-yasuʿiyyin, 1912).
al-Shāfiʿī, Muḥammad ibn Idrīs. *Kitāb al-umm* (Būlāq: Al-Maṭbaʿa l-kubrā al-amīriyya, 1321–25 A.H.).
al-Shahrastānī. Muḥammad ibn ʿAbd al-Karīm. *Al-Milal wal-niḥal*, 3 vols. in 1, ed. ʿAbd al-ʿAzīz Muḥammad al-Wākil (Cairo: Mu'assasa l-ḥalabī lil-nashr wal-tawzīʿ, 1968).
al-Silāfī, Aḥmad b. Muḥammad. *Akhbār wa-tarājim al-andalusiyya*, ed. Iḥsān ʿAbbās (Beirut: Dār al-thaqāfa, 1964).
al-Suyūṭī, Jalāl al-Dīn Abū l-Faḍl ʿAbd al-Raḥmān ibn Abī Bakr. *Ḥusn al-Muḥāḍara fī akhbār miṣr wal-qāhira*, ed. Muḥammad Abū l-Faḍl Ibrāhīm (Cairo: Dār iḥyā' l-kutub al-ʿarabiyya, 1967–68).
al-Ṭabarī, Muḥammad ibn Jarīr. *Ta'rīkh al-rusūl wal-mulūk*, ed. M. de Goeje et al. (Leiden: E. J. Brill, 1879–1901).
al-Thaʿālibī, Abū Manṣūr ʿAbd al-Malik ibn Muhammad. *Al-tamthīl wal-muḥāḍara*, ed. ʿAbd al-Fattāḥ Muḥammad al-Hulūw (Cairo: ʿĪsā al-bābī l-ḥalabī, 1961).
al-Ṭurtūshī, Muḥammad ibn al-Walīd. *Kitāb al-ḥawādīth wal-bidʿa*, ed. Maribel Fierro (Madrid: Consejo Superior de Investigaciones Cientificas, 1993).
———. *Sirāj al-mulūk*, ed. Muḥammad Fatḥī Abū Bakr (Cairo: Al-Dār al-miṣriyya al-lubnāniyya, 1994).
al-Wansharīsī, Aḥmad ibn Yaḥyā. *Kitāb al-Miʿyār al-muʿrib wal-jāmiʿ ʿan fatāwā ahl ifrīqiyā wal-andalus wal-maghrib*, 13 vols. ed. Muḥammad Ḥājjī (Rabat: Wizārat al-awqāf wal-shu'ūn al-islāmiyya lil-mamlaka al-maghribiyya, 1981).

Secondary Works

Abbott, Nadia. *Arabic Literary Papyri* (Volume 2: Qur'ānic Commentary and Tradition) (Chicago: University of Chicago Oriental Institute Publications, 1967).
———. "Wahb b. Munabbih: A Review Article," *Journal of Near Eastern Studies* 36 (1977): 103–12.
Abrahams, Israel. *Hebrew Ethical Wills*, 2 vols. (Philadelphia: Jewish Publication Society, 1926).
Abramson, Shraga. *Rav Nissim Ga'on: Ḥamishah sᵉfarim* (Jerusalem: Mekize Nirdamim, 1965).
Abū Laylah, Muḥammad. "Ibn Ḥazm's Influence on Christian Thinking in Research," *Islamic Quarterly* 31 (1987): 103–115.
———. *In Pursuit of Virtue: The Moral Theology and Psychology of Ibn Ḥazm al-Andalusī* (London: Taha Publishers Ltd., 1990).

Abun-Nasr, Jamil M. *A History of the Maghrib* (2d ed.) (Cambridge: Cambridge University Press, 1975).
Adang, Camilla. *Islam frente a Judaismo. La polemica de Ibn Ḥazm de Cordoba* (Madrid: Aben Ezra Ediciones, 1994).
———. "Ibn Ḥazm's Criticism of Some "Judaizing" Tendencies among the Malikites," *Medieval and Modern Perspectives on Muslim-Jewish Relations* (Studies in Muslim-Jewish Relations 2), ed. Ronald L. Nettler (Amsterdam: Harwood Academic Publishers, 1995), 1–15.
———. Muslim Writers on Judaism and the Hebrew Bible: From Ibn Rabban to Ibn Ḥazm (Leiden: E. J. Brill, 1996).
al-Ahwānī, Aḥmad Fu'ād. *Al-Taʿlīm fī ra'y al-qābisī min al-alūsī* (Beirut: Dār alfikr, 1979).
Alcalay, Ammiel. *After Jews and Arabs: Remaking Levantine Culture* (Minneapolis: University of Minnesota Press, 1993).
Alfonso, Esperanza. *Los Judíos en el Islam Medieval: La Percepcion de lo islamico en la construccion de la intentidad.* Ph.D. diss., Universidad Complutense, Madrid, 1998.
———. "ʿAbd al-Karīm al-Mağīlī: Un paralelo magrebi a los acontecimientos de 1066 en Granada," *Jewish Studies in Europe at the Turn of the Twentieth Century*, ed. Angel Sáenz-Badillos and Judit Targarona (Leiden: E. J. Brill, 1999), 1:370–78.
———. "ʿAbd al-Karīm al-Mağīlī (n. c. 1440): El contexto socio-literario de un poema contra los judios," forthcoming.
Allard, Michel. *Textes apologetique de Juwaini* (Beirut: Dār al-Machreq, 1968).
Allony, Nehemya. "Songs of Zion in the Poetic Works of R. Shmuel Hanagid" (Hebrew), *Sinai* 68 (1971): 210–34.
Arberry, A. J. (trans.). *Ibn Ḥazm: The Ring of the Dove* (London: Luzac, 1953).
———. (trans.). *The Koran Interpreted* (New York: Collier Books/MacMillan Publishing, reprinted 1986).
Arié, Rachel. "Notes sur la *maqāma* andalouse," reprinted in *Etudes sur la civilization de l'Espagne musulmane* (Medieval Iberian Peninsula Texts and Studies Volume 6) (Leiden: E. J. Brill, 1990), 207–223.
Arnaldez, Roger. "Controverse d'Ibn Ḥazm contre Ibn Nagrīla le juif," *Revue de l'occident musulman et de la Mediterranée* 13–14 (1973): 41–48. Reprinted in *Aspects de la pensée musulmane* (Paris: J. Vrin, 1987).
———. "Ibn Ḥazm," *EI*², 3:790–99.
Ashtor, Eliyahu. *Qorot ha-yᵉhudim bi-sfarad ha-muslimit.* 2 vols. (Jerusalem: Kiryat Sefer, 1960).
———. "The Number of Jews in Moslem Spain" (Hebrew) *Zion* 28 (1963): 34–56.
———. [Strauss]. "Saladin and the Jews," *Hebrew Union College Annual* 27 (1965): 305–326.
———. *The Jews of Moslem Spain*, trans. Aaron Klein and Jenny Machlowitz Klein with an introduction by David J. Wasserstein. 3 vols. in 2 (Philadelphia: Jewish Publication Society, reprinted 1992).
Ayalon, David. "On the Eunuchs in Islam," *Jerusalem Studies Arabic and Islam* 1 (1979): 92–124.

Baer, Yitzhak. *A History of the Jews in Christian Spain*, 2 vols., trans. Louis Schoffman with an introduction by Benjamin R. Gampel (Philadelphia: Jewish Publication Society, reprinted 1992).

Barkai, Ron. "L'Astrologie juive médiévale: aspects théoretiques et practiques," *Moyen Age* 93 (1987): 328–48.

Baron, Salo W. *A Social and Religious History of the Jews*, 17 vols. 2d rev. ed. (New York and Philadelphia: Columbia University Press and the Jewish Publication Society, 1952–83).

Bashear, Suliman. "Abraham's Sacrifice of His Son and Related Issues," *Der Islam* 67 (1990): 243–77.

Bat Ye'or. *The Dhimmi: Jews and Christians under Islam* (Rutherford, NJ: Fairleigh Dickenson University Press; and London and Toronto: Associated University Presses, 1985).

———. "Islam and the *Dhimmis*," *Jerusalem Quarterly* 42 (1987): 83–88.

Bellamy, James A. "Qasmūna the Poetess: Who Was She?" *Journal of the American Oriental Society* 103 (1983): 423–24.

Benaboud, M'hammad. "The Socio-Political Role of the Andalusian ʿUlamā' during the Fifth through Eleventh Centuries," *Islamic Studies* 23 (1984): 103–141.

———. "Religious Knowledge and Political Power of the ʿUlamā' in Al-Andalus during the Period of the Taifa States," in *Saber Religioso Y Poder Politico En El Islam* (Actas del Simposio Internacional [Granada, 15–18 octubre 1991]) (Madrid: Agencia Espanola de Cooperacion Internacional, 1994), 39–51.

Ben-Shammai, Ḥaggai. "Jew-Hatred in the Islamic Tradition and the Koranic Exegesis," *Antisemitism through the Ages*, ed. Shmuel Almog and trans. Nathan H. Reisner. Vidal Sassoon International Center for the Study of Anti-Semitism, Hebrew University of Jerusalem (Oxford: Pergamon Press, 1988), 161–69.

Bernstein, Simon. *ʿAl naharot s^e^farad* (Tel Aviv: Maḥbarot Le-Sifrut, 1956).

Bland, Kalman. "An Islamic Theory of Jewish History: The Case of Ibn Khaldūn," *Journal of Asian and African Studies* 18 (1983): 129–97.

Blanks, David R. "Cross-Cultural Encounters: Past and Present," *Images of the Other: Europe and the Muslim World before 1700*, ed. David Blanks (Cairo Papers in Social Science Volume 19, No. 2) (Cairo: American University in Cairo Press, 1997), 1–6.

Bosworth, Clifford Edmond. *The Medieval Islamic Underworld: The Banū Sāsān in Arabic Society and Literature* (Part 1) (Leiden: E. J. Brill, 1976).

Brann, Ross. *The Compunctious Poet: Cultural Ambiguity and Hebrew Poetry in Muslim Spain* (Baltimore: Johns Hopkins University Press, 1991).

———. "Constructions of Exile in Hispano-Hebrew and Hispano-Arabic Elegies" (Hebrew), *Israel Levin Jubilee Volume* (Studies in Hebrew Literature 1), eds. Reuven Tsur and Tova Rosen (Tel Aviv: Tel-Aviv University, Katz Research Institute for Hebrew Literature, 1994), 45–61.

———. "The Arabized Jews," in Maria R. Menocal, Raymond P. Scheindlin, Michael Sells, eds. *The Cambridge History of Arabic Literature: Al-Andalus* (Cambridge: Cambridge University Press, 2000), 435–54.

Bravmann, M. "A propos de Qur'ān IX, 29," *Arabica* 10 (1963): 94–95.

Brinner, William M. "The Image of the Jew As *Other* in Medieval Arabic Texts," *Israel Oriental Studies* 14 (1994): 227–40.
Brockelman, C., and Pellat, Ch. "Maḳāma," *EI*² 6:107–115.
Burman, Thomas E. *Religious Polemic and the Intellectual History of the Mozarabs, c. 1050–1200* (Leiden: E. J. Brill, 1994).
Burshatin, Israel. "The Moor in the Text: Metaphor, Emblem, and Silence," in Henry Louis Gates (ed.), "*Race*," *Writing, and Difference* (Chicago and London: University of Chicago Press, 1986), 117–39.
Butterworth, Charles E., trans. *Averroes' Middle Commentary on Aristotle's Poetics* (Princeton: Princeton University Press, 1986).
Cahen, C. "Qur'ān IX, 29," *Arabica* 9 (1962): 76–79.
———. "Ibn Muyassar," *EI*² 3:894.
Carmi, T. *The Penguin Book of Hebrew Verse* (Hammondsworth: Penguin, 1981).
Carpenter, Dwayne E. *Alfonso X and the Jews: An Edition of and Commentary on Siete Partidas 7.24 "De los judios"* (University of California Publications: Modern Philology) (Berkeley: University of California Press, 1986).
———. "Social Perception of Literary Portrayal: Jews and Muslims in Medieval Spanish Literature," in *Convivencia: Jews, Muslims, and Christians in Medieval Spain*, ed. Vivian B. Mann, Thomas F. Glick, Jerrilyn D. Dodds (New York: George Braziller in association with the Jewish Museum, 1992), 61–81.
Catlos, Brian. "To Catch a Spy: The Case of Zayn al-Dīn and Ibn Dukhān," *Medieval Encounters* 2 (1996): 99–113.
Chazan, Robert. "Representation of Events in the Middle Ages," in *Essays in Jewish Historiography*, ed. Ada Rapaport-Albert (Atlanta: Scholars Press, 1991), 40–55.
Chejne, Anwar G. *Ibn Ḥazm* (Chicago: Kazi Publications, 1982).
Cheyette, Bryan (ed.). *Between Race and Culture: Representations of "the Jew" in English and American Literature* (Stanford: Stanford University Press, 1996).
Cohen, Gerson D. "Messianic Postures of Ashkenazim and Sephardim prior to Shabbethai Zvi," ed. M. Kreutzberger, *Studies of the Leo Baeck Institute* (1967): 115–65.
Cohen, Jeremy. *Living Letters of the Law: Ideas of the Jews in Medieval Christianity* (Berkeley: University of California Press, 1999).
Cohen, Mark R. "Islam and the Jews: Myth, Counter Myth, History," *Jerusalem Quarterly* 38 (1986): 125–37.
———. "The Neo-Lachrymose Conception of Jewish-Arab History," *Tikkun* (May–June 1991), 55–60.
———. *Under Crescent and Cross: The Jews in the Middle Ages* (Princeton: Princeton University Press, 1994).
———. "What Was the Pact of ʿUmar? A Literary-Historical Study," *Jerusalem Studies in Arabic and Islam* 23 (1999): 100–157.
Cole, Peter (trans.). *Selected Poems of Shmuel HaNagid* (Princeton: Princeton University Press, 1996).
Collins, Roger. *The Arab Conquest of Spain*, 710–797 (Oxford: Basil Blackwell, 1989).
Constable, Olivia Remie, *Trade and Traders in Muslim Spain: The Commercial*

Realignment of the Iberian Peninsula, 900–1500 (Cambridge: Cambridge University Press, 1994).
——— ed. *Medieval Iberia: Readings in Jewish, Christian and Muslim Sources* (Philadelphia: University of Pennsylvania Press, 1997).
Coope, Jessica A. *The Martyrs of Cordoba: Community and Family Conflict in an Age of Mass Conversion* (Lincoln and London: University of Nebraska Press, 1995).
Corriente, F. *A Dictionary of Andalusi Arabic* (Leiden: E. J. Brill, 1997).
Courbage, Youssef, and Fargues, Philippe. *Christians and Jews under Islam*, trans. Judy Marbo (London and New York: I. B. Tauris, 1997).
Dagenais John. *The Ethics of Reading in Manuscript Culture: Glossing the Libro de buen amor* (Princeton: Princeton University Press, 1994).
Daly, Saralyn R. (trans.). *The Book of True Love* [Juan Ruiz, the Archpriest of Hita]: *A Bilingual Edition*, ed. Anthony N. Zahareas (University Park and London: Pennsylvania State Press, 1978).
Dana, Joseph. "On the Source of the *Taḥkᵉmoni*" (Hebrew), *Tarbiz* 44 (1975): 172–81.
———. "Al-Hamadhānī As a Source of R. Judah al-Ḥarizi" (Hebrew), *Dappim: Research in Literature* 1 (1984): 79–89.
Daniel, Norman. *The Arabs and Mediaeval Europe* (London and Beirut: Longman and Librairie du Liban, 1975).
———. *Islam and the West: The Making of an Image* (Oxford: One World Press, revised 1993).
Davidson, Israel. *Thesaurus of Mediaeval Hebrew Poetry*, 4 vols. (New York, 1924; reprinted with an introduction by J. Schirmann, New York: Ktav Publishing, 1970).
Delany, Sheila. *Medieval Literary Politics: Shapes of Ideology* (Manchester and New York: Manchester University Press, 1990).
Dishon, Judith. "Medieval Panorama in the Book of Taḥkemoni," *Proceedings of the American Academy for Jewish Research* 56 (1989): 11–27.
Dozy, Reinhart P. *Supplement aux dictionnaires arabes*, 2 vols. (Leiden: E. J. Brill, 1881; reprinted Paris: G. P. Maisonneuve et Larose, 1967).
———. *Spanish Islam: A History of the Moslems in Spain*, trans. F. G. Stokes (London, 1913; reprinted London: Frank Cass, 1972).
Drory, Rina. "The Hidden Context: On Literary Products of Tri-Cultural Contacts in the Middle Ages" (Hebrew), *Peʿamim* 46–47 (1991): 9–28.
———. "Literary Contacts and Where to Find Them: On Arabic Literary Models in Medieval Jewish Literature," *Poetics Today* 14 (1993): 277–302.
Edelmann, (Zvi) Hirsch (ed.). *Ḥemdah gᵉnuzah* (Koenigsburg: Gruber and Guphrat, 1856).
Edwards, Robert. "Exile, Self, and Society," *Exile in Literature*, ed. Maria-Ines Lagos-Pope (Lewisburg: Bucknell University Press, 1988).
Epstein, Morris (ed. and trans.). *Tales of Sendebar* (Philadelphia: Jewish Publication Society, 1967).
Fahd, T. "Saḥbān Wā'il," *EI*², 8:830.
Fattal, Antoine. *Le Statut legal des non-musulmans en pays d'Islam* (Beirut: Imprimerie Catholique, 1958).

Fenton, Paul B. "Jewish Attitudes to Islam: Israel Heeds Ishmael," *Jerusalem Quarterly* 29 (1983): 84–102.

Fierro, Maribel (Isabel). "Andalusian 'Fatāwā' on Blasphemy," *Annales Islamologiques* 25 (1990): 103–17.

———. "Ibn Ḥazm et le *zindīq* juif," *Revue du monde musulman et de la Mediterranée* 63–64 (1992a): 81–89.

———. "Religious Beliefs and Practices in al-Andalus in the Third through Ninth Centuries," *Rivista degli Studi Orientali* 66 (1992b): 15–33.

———. "The *Qāḍī* As Ruler," in *Saber Religioso Y Poder Politico En El Islam* (Actas del Simposio Internacional [Granada, 15–18 octubre 1991]) (Madrid: Agencia Espanola de Cooperacion Internacional, 1994), 71–116

———. "Christian Success and Muslim Fear in Andalusi Writings During the Almoravid and Almohad Periods," *Israel Oriental Studies* 17 (1997): 155–78.

Finkel, Joshua. "An Eleventh-Century Source for the History of Jewish Scientists in Mohammedan Land (Ibn Ṣāʿid)," *Jewish Quarterly Review* 18 (1927a): 45–54.

———. "A Risāla of al-Jāḥiẓ," *Journal of the American Oriental Society* 47 (1927b): 311–34.

Fischel, Walter J. *Jews in the Economic and Political Life of Mediaeval Islam* (London: Royal Asiatic Society, 1937).

———. "The *Resh Galuta* in Arabic Literature" (Hebrew), in *The Magnes Anniversary Book*, ed. F. I. Baer et al. (Jerusalem: Hebrew University Press, 1938), 181–87.

Fleischer, Ezra. "An Overlooked Fragment of the Translation by Yehudah al-Ḥarizi of the Maqāmas of al-Ḥarīrī," *Journal of Jewish Studies* 24 (1973): 179–84.

———. "*ʿInyᵉnei piyyuṭ wᵉ-shirah*," *Meḥqᵉrei sifrut mugashim lᵉ-shimʿon halkin*, ed. Ezra Fleischer (Jerusalem: Magnes Press, 1974), 183–204.

Foucault, Michel. "What Is an Author?" *Textual Strategies*, ed. Josué Harari (Ithaca: Cornell University Press, 1979), 141–60.

———. *Power/Knowledge: Selected Interviews and Other Writings, 1972–1977*, ed. Colin Gordon (New York: Pantheon Books, 1981).

Funkenstein, Amos. "Jews, Christians and Muslims: Religious Polemics in the Middle Ages," *The Jews in European History: Seven Lectures* (Cincinnati: Hebrew Union College Press in association with the Leo Baeck Institute, 1994), 23–37.

Garcia-Arenal, Mercedes. "The Revolution of Fās in 869–1465 and the Death of Sultan ʿAbd al-Ḥaqq al-Marīnī," *Bulletin of the School of African and Oriental Studies* 41 (1978): 43–66.

———. "Jewish Converts to Islam in the Muslim West," *Israel Oriental Studies* 17 (1997): 227–48.

———. "Dreams and Reason: Autobiographies of Converts in Religious Polemics," forthcoming.

Garcia Gomez, E. "Polemica religiosa entre Ibn Ḥazm e Ibn al-Nagrīla," *Al-Andalus* 4 (1936–39): 1–28.

———. *Un alfaqui español: Abū Isḥāq de Elvira* (*Texto arabe de su Dīwān*) (Madrid-Granada: Consejo Superior de Investigaciones Cientificas, 1944).

Gardet, L. "Fitna," *EI*², 2:930.
Gates, Henry Louis Jr. (ed.) "*Race*," *Writing, and Difference* (Chicago and London: University of Chicago Press, 1986).
Gerber, Jane S. *The Jews of Fez 1450–1700. Studies in Communal and Economic Life* (Leiden: E. J. Brill, 1980).
———. "Anti-Semitism and the Muslim World," *History and Hate: The Dimensions of Anti-Semitism*, ed. David Berger (Philadelphia: Jewish Publication Society, 1986), 73–93.
Gil, Moshe. *The Tustaris: Family and Sect* (Hebrew) (Tel Aviv: Disapora Research Institute, Project Moreshet for the Research of Oriental Jewry, 1981).
———. *A History of Palestine, 634–1099*. Trans. from the Hebrew by Ethel Broido (Cambridge: Cambridge University Press, 1992).
———. *Bᵉ-malkhut yishmʿ e'l bi-tqufat ha-gᵉ'onim*. 4 vols. (Tel Aviv: University of Tel Aviv and the Ministry of Defense, and Jersuaelm: Mosad Bialik, 1997).
Goitein, S. D. "A Report on Messianic Troubles in Baghdad in 1120–21," *Jewish Quarterly Review* 43 (1952): 57–75.
———. "Three Letters from Qayrawān Addressed to Joseph ben Jacob ben ʿAwkal" (Hebrew), *Tarbiz* 34 (1965): 162–82.
———. *Studies in Islamic History and Institutions* (Leiden: E. J. Brill, 1966).
———. *A Mediterranean Society: The Jewish Communities of the Arab World As Portrayed in the Documents of the Cairo Geniza* (6 vols.) (Berkeley: University of California Press, 1967–93).
———. "The Constitution of Medina: A Reconsideration," *Israel Oriental Studies* 4 (1974): 44–66.
———. "Banū Isrā'īl," *EI*², 1:1020–22.
Golb, Norman. "Scroll of Obadiah the Norman Proselyte" (Hebrew), *Studies in Genizah and Sephardi Heritage Presented to Shelomo Dov Goitein* (on the occasion of his eightieth birthday), ed. Shelomo Morag and Issachar Ben-Ami (Jerusalem: Magnes Press, 1981), 100–101.
Goldziher, Ignaz. "Uber muhammedanische Polemik gegen Ahl al-kitāb," *Zeitschrift der Deutschen Morgenlandischen Gesellschaft* 32 (1878): 341–87.
———. "Renseignements de source musulmane sur la dignité de *Resch-Galuta*," *Revue des études juives* 8 (1884): 121–25.
———. "Usages juifs d'apres la litterature religieuse des Musulmans," *Revue des études juives* 28 (1894): 75–94.
———. *Muslim Studies*, 2 vols., ed. S. M. Stern, trans. C. R. Barber and S. M. Stern (London: George Allen and Unwin Ltd., 1967).
———. "Monotheisme dans la vie religieuse des Musulmans," reprinted in *Gesammelte Schriften*, 6 vols., ed. Joseph DeSomogyi (Hildesheim: Olms Verlag, 1967–73), 2:173–81.
———. The Ẓāhirīs. Their Doctrine and Their Theory: *A Contribution to the History of Islamic Theology*, trans. Wolfgang Behn (Leiden: E. J. Brill, 1971).
———. [A.M. Goichon]. "Dahriyya," *EI*², 2:95–97.
Goodman, Lenn E. "Hamadhānī, *Schadenfreude*, and Salvation through Sin," *Journal of Arabic Literature* 19 (1988): 27–39.
Gottheil, Richard. "An Answer to the Dhimmīs," *Journal of the American Oriental Society* 41 (1927): 383–457.

Granara, William. "*Jihād* and Cross-Cultural Encounter in Muslim Sicily," *Harvard Middle Eastern and Islamic Review* 3 (1996): 42–61.

Grossman, Avraham. *The Babylonian Exilarchate in the Gaonic Period* (Hebrew) (Jerusalem: Merkaz Zalman Shazar, 1984).

———. "The Economic and Social Background of Hostile Attitudes toward the Jews in the Ninth and Tenth Century Muslim Caliphate," *Anti-Semitism through the Ages*, ed. Shmuel Almog and trans. Nathan H. Reisner. Vidal Sassoon International Center for the Study of Anti-Semitism, Hebrew University of Jerusalem (Oxford: Pergamon Press, 1988), 171–87.

Halkin, Abraham S. "On the History of the Almohad Persecution" (Hebrew), *Joshua Starr Memorial Volume: Studies in History and Philology* (*Jewish Social Studies* Publications Number 5) (New York: Conference on Jewish Relations, 1953), 101–110.

———. "The Judeo-Islamic Age," in *Great Ages and Ideas of the Jewish People*, ed. Leo W. Schwarz (New York: Modern Library, 1956), 213–63.

———. *Crisis and Leadership: Epistles of Maimonides* (Philadelphia: Jewish Publication Society, 1985).

Halkin, Hillel. "The First Post-Ancient Jew," *Commentary* (September 1993): 43–50.

Halperin, David. J. *Faces of the Chariot: Early Jewish Responses to Ezekiel's Vision* (Tubingen: Mohr, 1988).

Halperin, David J., and Newby, Gordon D. "Two Castrated Bulls: A Study in the Haggadah of Kaʿb al-Aḥbār," *Journal of the American Oriental Society* 102 (1982): 631–38.

Handler, Andrew. *The Zirids of Granada* (Coral Gables: University of Miami Press, 1974).

Hirschberg, H. Z. (J. W.). *A History of the Jews in North Africa* (Vols. 1–2). 2d rev. ed. translated from the Hebrew (Leiden: E. J. Brill, 1974).

Hodgson, Marshall G. S. *The Venture of Islam: Conscience and History in a World Civilization*, 3 vols. (Chicago: University of Chicago Press, 1974).

———. "ʿAbd Allāh b. Saba'," *EI*², 1:51.

Horovitz, Joseph. "ʿAbd Allāh b. Salām," *EI*², 1:52.

———. "Wahb ibn Munabbih," *EI*¹, 4: 1084–85.

Horowitz, Yehoshua. "The Attitude of R. Shmuel ha-Nagid toward the Geonim" (Hebrew), *Proceedings of the Eleventh World Congress of Jewish Studies* (Div. C, Vol. 1) (Jerusalem: World Union of Jewish Studies, 1994), 185–90.

Humphreys, R. Stephen. *Between Memory and Desire: The Middle East in a Troubled Age* (Berkeley: University of California Press, 1999).

Hunwick, John O. "Al-Maghīlī and the Jews of Tuwāṭ: The Demise of a Community," *Studia Islamica* 61 (1985): 155–83.

———. "The Rights of *Dhimmī*s to Maintain a Place of Worship: A Fifteenth Century *Fatwā* from Tlemçen," *Al-Qanṭara* 12 (1991): 133–55.

Huss, Matti. "*Mᵉliṣat ʿefer wᵉ-dinah*." Master's thesis, Hebrew University, Jerusalem, 1984.

Idel, Moshe. "Saturn and Sabbatai Zevi: A New Approach to Sabbateanism," in *Toward the Millenium: Messianic Expectations from the Bible to Waco*, eds. Peter Schafer and Mark Cohen (Leiden: E. J. Brill, 1998), 173–202.

Idris, Hadi Roger. "Deux Maitres de l'ecole juridique Kairouanaise sous les Zirides (xie siecle): Abū Bakr b. ʿAbd al-Raḥmān et Abū ʿImrān al-Fāsī," *Annales de l'institut d'études orientales* 13 (1955): 30–60.

———. *La Berberie orientales sous les Zirides, X^e^–XIIIe siecle*, 2 vols. (Paris: A. Maisonneuve, 1962).

———. "Les Zirides d'Espagne," *Al-Andalus* 29 (1964): 39–137.

———. "Les Tributaires en occident musulman médiéval d'apres le "Miʿyār" d'al-Wansharīsī," in *Mélanges d'Islamogie* (Volume dedicated to the memory of Armand Abel), ed. Pierre Salmon (Leiden: E. J. Brill, 1974), 172–96.

———. *Al-Dawla al-ṣanhājiyya, ta'rīkh ifrīqiyyā fī ʿahd banī zīrī min al-qarn 10 ilā l-qarn 12 m.* (Beirut: Dār al-gharb al-islāmī, 1992).

Kassis, Hanna. "Roots of Conflict: Aspects of Christian-Muslim Conflict in Eleventh-Century Spain," *Conversion and Continuity: Indigenous Christian Communities in Islamic Lands Eighth to Eighteenth Centuries*, eds. Michael Gevers and Ramzi Jibran Bikhazi (Toronto: Pontifical Institute of Mediaeval Studies, 1990), 151–60.

———. "Arabic-Speaking Christians in al-Andalus in an Age of Turmoil (Fifth through Eleventh Centuries until A.H. 478–A.D. 1085)," *Al-Qanṭara* 15 (1994): 401–422.

Katz, Sarah. "*Biqquro shel rav nissim mi-qayrawān bi-granaṭah*," *Sinai* 96 (1985): 114–43.

Keller, John E. and Keating, L. Clark (trans.). *The Book of Count Lucanor and Patronio: A Translation of Don Juan Manuel's El Conde Lucanor* (Lexington: University of Kentucky Press, 1977).

Kennedy, Hugh. *Muslim Spain and Portugal. A Political History of al-Andalus* (London and New York: Longman, 1996).

Khālid, Ṣalāḥ. *Muḥammad ibn ʿAmmār: Dirāsa adabiyya ta'rīkhiyya* (Baghdad: Maṭbaʿat al-hoda, 1957).

Kister, M. J. "*Ḥaddithū ʿan banī isrā'īla wa-lā ḥaraja*," *Israel Oriental Studies* 2 (1972): 215–39.

———. The Massacre of the Banū Qurayza: A Re-Examination of a Tradition," *Jerusalem Studies in Arabic and Islam* 8 (1986): 61–96.

———. "Do not Assimilate Yourselves . . . *Lā tashabbahū*," *Jerusalem Studies in Arabic and Islam* 12 (1989): 321–71.

Koningsveld, P. S. van, Sadan, J, and al-Samarrai, Q. *Yemenite Authorities and Jewish Messianism* (Leiden: E. J. Brill, 1990).

Kraemer, Joel L. "Heresy versus the State in Medieval Islam," *Studies in Judaica, Karaitica and Islamica Presented to Leon Nemoy on His Eightieth Birthday*, ed. S. R. Brunswick (Ramat-Gan: Bar Ilan University Press, 1982), 167–80.

———. *Humanism in the Renaissance of Islam: The Cultural Revival during the Buyid Age* (Leiden: E. J. Brill, 1986).

LaCapra, Dominick. *Representing the Holocaust: History, Theory, Trauma* (Ithaca: Cornell University Press, 1994).

Langermann, Y. Tzvi. "Maimonides' Repudiation of Astrology," *Maimonidean Studies* 2 (1991): 123–58.

Lassner, Jacob. "The Covenant of the Prophets: Muslim Texts, Jewish Subtexts," *Association for Jewish Studies Review* (1990a): 207–238.

———. "The Origins of Muslim Attitudes towards the Jews and Judaism," *Judaism* 39 (1990b): 494–507.

———. "The 'One Who Had Knowledge of the Book' and the 'Mightiest Name' of God: Qur'anic Exegesis and Jewish Cultural Artifacts," *Studies in Muslim Jewish Relations* 1 (1991): 59–74.

——— (rev. and ed.). *A Mediterranean Society by S. D. Goitein: An Abridgement in One Volume* (Berkeley: University of California Press, 1999).

Lavi, Abraham. "The Rationale of al-Ḥarizi in Biblicizing the *Maqāmāt* of al-Ḥariri," *Jewish Quarterly Review* 74 (1984): 280–93.

Lazarus-Yafeh, Hava. *Studies in Al-Ghazzali* (Jerusalem: Magnes Press, Hebrew University, 1975).

———. *Some Religious Aspects of Islam* (Leiden: E. J. Brill, 1981).

———. "The Contribution of a Jewish Convert from Morocco to the Muslim Polemic against Jews and Judaism" (Hebrew), *Peʿamim* 42 (1990): 83–90.

———. *Intertwined Worlds: Medieval Islam and Bible Criticism* (Princeton: Princeton University Press, 1992).

——— (ed.). *Muslim Authors on Jews and Judaism: The Jews among their Muslim Neighbors* (Hebrew) (Jerusalem: Zalman Shazar Center for Jewish History, 1996).

———. "Some Remarks on Medieval Muslim Polemics against Christianity" (Hebrew), *Hamizraḥ Heḥadash* 40 (1999): 33–37.

Lecker, Michael. "The Bewitching of the Prophet Muhammad by the Jews: A Note à Propos ʿAbd al-Malik B. Ḥabīb's *Mukhtasar fī l-Ṭibb*," *Al-Qanṭara* 13 (1992): 561–69.

Lehmann, Matthias B. "Islamic Legal Consultation of the Jewish-Muslim "*Convivencia*"—Al-Wansharīsī's *Fatwā* Collection As a Source for Jewish Social History in al-Andalus and the Maghrib," *Jewish Studies Quarterly* 6 (1999a): 25–54.

———. "The Jews of Muslim Spain and the Maghrib: Al-Wansharīsī's Collection of *Fatwa*s As a Source for Jewish Social History," in *Jewish Studies in Europe at the Turn of the Twentieth Century*, eds. Angel Sáenz-Badillos and Judit Targarona (Leiden: E. J. Brill, 1999b), 1:440–46.

Leicester, H. Marshall Jr. *The Disenchanted Self: Representing the Subject in the Canterbury Tales* (Berkeley: University of California Press, 1990).

Lerner, Ralph. "Maimonides' Letter on Astrology," *History of Religions* 8 (1968): 143–58.

Lerner, Ralph, and Mahdi, Muhsin (eds.). *Medieval Political Philosophy* (Glencoe, Il: Free Press, 1963; reprinted Ithaca: Cornell University Press, 1972).

Le Tourneau, Roger. *Fez in the Age of the Marinids*, trans. Besse Alberta Clement (Norman: University of Oklahoma Press, 1961).

Levin, Israel. *Avraham ibn ʿEzra': ḥayyaw wᵉ-shirato* (Tel Aviv: Hakibbutz Hameuhad, 1969).

———. *Samuel the Nagid: His Life and Poetry* (Hebrew) (n.p.: Hakkibutz Hameuhad, 1973).

———. *Abraham ibn ʿEzra' Reader* (Hebrew) (New York and Tel Aviv: Israel Matz Hebrew Classics and Edward I. Kiev Library, 1985).

———. *The Embroidered Coat: The Genres of Secular Hebrew Poetry in Spain*,

3 vols. (Hebrew) (Tel Aviv: Hakibbutz Hameuchad Publishing House [Katz Research Institute for Hebrew Literature Tel Aviv University], 1995).

Levi-Provençal, E. "Un Nouveau Text d'historire merinide: Le Musnad d'Ibn Marzūq," *Hesperis* V (1925): 1–82.

———. "Un Document sur la vie urbaine et les corps des métiers a Seville au debut du XIIieme sìecle: le traité d'Ibn ʿAbdūn," *Journal Asiatique* 224 (1934): 238–48.

Levtzion, Nehemia. "Toward a Comparative Study of Islamization," in *Conversion to Islam*, ed. N. Levtzion (New York: Holmes and Meier, 1979).

Levy, Leonard W. *Blasphemy: Verbal Offense against the Sacred, from Moses to Salman Rushdie* (Chapel Hill: University of North Carolina Press, 1993).

Lewis, Bernard. "Some Observations on the Significance of Heresy in the History of Islam," *Studia Islamica* 1 (1953): 43–63.

———. "On That Day: A Jewish Apocalyptic Poem on the Arab Conquests," in Pierre Salmon, ed. *Mélanges D'Islamologie: Volume dédié à la memoire de Armand Abel.* (Leiden, E. J. Brill: 1974), 197–200.

———. *The Jews of Islam* (Princeton: Princeton University Press, 1984a).

———. "Usurpers and Tyrants: Notes on Some Islamic Political Terms," in *Logos Islamicos: Studia Islamica in Honorem Georgii Michaelis Wickens*, eds. Roger M. Savory and Dionisus A. Agius (Toronto: Pontifical Institute of Mediaeval Studies, 1984b), 259–67.

———. *Islam from the Prophet Muhammad to the Capture of Istanbul*, 2 vols. (Oxford: Oxford University Press, 1987).

———. "The Roots of Muslim Rage," *The Atlantic Monthly* (September 1990) (a version of Lewis's "Western Civilization: A View from the East," The Jefferson Lecture in the Humanities delivered May 1990).

———. "The Other and the Enemy: Perceptions of Identity and Difference in Islam," *Religions-gespräche im Mittelatler* (Wiesbaden: Otto Harrsassowitz, 1992), 371–82.

———. *Islam in History: Ideas, Men, and Events in the Middle East*, rev. ed. (Chicago and La Salle: Open Court, 1993).

Lichtenstadter, Ilse. "And Become Ye Accursed Apes," *Jerusalem Studies in Arabic and Islam* 14 (1991): 153–75.

Loewe, Raphael. *Ibn Gabirol* (New York: Grove Weidenfeld, 1988).

Lotman, Yuri M. *Universe of the Mind: A Semiotic Theory of Culture* (Bloomington: Indiana University Press, 1990).

Madelung, Wilferd. "Mulḥid," EI^2, 5:546.

Makki, Mahmoud. "The Political History of al-Andalus," in *The Legacy of Muslim Spain*, ed. Salma Khadra Jayyusi (Leiden: E. J. Brill, 1992), 3–87.

Malti-Douglas, Fedwa. "*Maqāmāt* and *Adab*: "*Al-Maqāma al-Maḍīriyya*" of al-Hamadhānī," *Journal of the American Oriental Society* 105 (1985): 247–58.

Margoliouth, D. S., and Pellat, Ch. "al-Ḥarīrī," EI^2, 3:221.

Marin, Manuela. "*Inqibād ʿAn Al-Sulṭān*: ʿUlamāʾ and Political Power in Al-Andalus," in *Saber Religioso Y Poder Politico En El Islam* (Actas del Simposio Internacional [Granada, 15–18 octubre 1991]) (Madrid: Agencia Española de Cooperacion Internacional, 1994), 127–39.

Marx, Alexander. "The Correspondence between the Rabbis of Southern France and Maimonides about Astrology," *Hebrew Union College Annual* 3 (1926): 349–58.

Masuzawa, Tomoko. "Culture," in *Critical Terms for Religious Studies*, ed. Mark C. Taylor (Chicago and London: University of Chicago Press, 1998), 70–93.

Melville, Charles, and Ubaydli, Ahmad (eds.) *Christians and Moors in Spain* (vol. 3) (Warminster: Aris and Philips Ltd., 1992).

Mirrer, Louise. *Women, Jews and Muslims in the Texts of Reconquest Castile* (Ann Arbor: University of Michigan Press, 1996).

Mirsky, Aharon. "Al-Ḥarizi's Introduction to the *Taḥkemoni*" (Hebrew), "*Ha-Aretz*" (9/28/1952), reprinted in *Ha-Piyyuṭ* (Jerusalem: Magnes Press, 1990), 699–704.

Mitchell, W. J. T. "Representation," *Critical Terms for Literary Study*, eds. Frank Lenticchia and Thomas McLaughlin (Chicago: University of Chicago Press, 1990), 11–22.

Mones, Hussein. "Le Rôle des hommes de religion dans l'histoire de l'Espagne musulmane jusqu'a la fin du Califat," *Studia Islamica* 20 (1964): 47–88.

Monroe, James T. *Hispano-Arabic Poetry: A Student Anthology* (Berkeley: University of California Press, 1974).

Nahon, Gerald. "La Elegia de Abraham ibn Ezra sobre la persecucion de los Almohades, Nuevas Perspectivas," *Abraham Ibn Ezra y su tiempo*, ed. Fernando Diaz Esteban (Madrid: Asociacion Espanola de Orientalistas, 1990), 217–24.

Nemah, H. "Andalusian Maqāmāt," *Journal of Arabic Literature* 5 (1974): 83–92.

Netton. Ian Richard. *Text and Trauma: An East-West Primer* (Surrey: Curzon Press, 1996).

Newby, Gordon D. *A History of the Jews of Arabia from Ancient Times to Their Eclipse under Islam* (Columbia: University of South Carolina Press, 1988).

Nichols, James Mansfield. "The Arabic Verses of Qasmūna Bint Ismā'īl ibn Bagdālah," *International Journal of Middle Eastern Studies* 13 (1981): 155–58.

Nykl, A. R. *Hispano-Arabic Poetry and Its Relations with the Old Provençal Troubadours* (Baltimore: Hispanic Society of America, 1946).

Ortega, Jose, and del Moral, Celia. *Dictionarrio de escritores granadinos* (siglos 7–20). (Granada: Universidad de Granada, 1991).

Pagis, Dan. "Dirges on the Persecutions of 1391 in Spain" (Hebrew), *Tarbiz* 37 (1968): 335–73.

———. *Change and Tradition in the Secular Poetry: Spain and Italy* (Hebrew) (Jerusalem: Keter Publishing, 1975).

———. "Variety in Medieval Rhymed Narratives," *Scripta Hiersolymitana* 27 (1978): 79–98.

———. "The Poet As Prophet in Medieval Hebrew Literature," in James L. Kugel (ed.), *Poetry and Prophecy: The Beginnings of a Literary Tradition* (Ithaca: Cornell University Press, 1990), 140–50.

Palacios, Asin M. *Abenhazam de Cordoba y su historia critica de las ideas religiosas*, 5 vols. (Madrid: Real Academia de la Historia, 1927–32).

Patai, Raphael. *The Seed of Abraham: Jews and Arabs in Contact and Conflict* (Salt Lake City: University of Utah Press, 1986).

Pellat, Ch. "Note sur l'Espagne musulmane et al-Jāḥiẓ," *Al-Andalus* 21 (1956): 277–84.

———. "Al-Jāḥiẓ," in *ʿAbbasid Belles-Lettres* (The Cambridge History of Arabic Literature), eds. Julia Ashtiany, T. M. Johnstone, J. D. Latham, R. B. Serjeant, and G. Rex Smith (Cambridge: Cambridge University Press, 1990), 78–95.

———. "al-Aḥnaf b. Ḳays," *EI²*, 1:303–4.

———. "Ḳuss b. Sāʿida," *EI²*, 5: 528–29.

Penny, Ralph. "Uncanny Foreigners: Does the Subaltern Speak through Julia Kristeva?" *The Psychoanalysis of Race*, ed. Christopher Lane (New York: Columbia University Press, 1998).

Pérès, Henri. *La Poésie andalouse en arab classique au xiᵉsiecle*, 2d ed. (Paris: Adrien-Maisonneuve, 1953).

Perlmann, Moshe. "ʿAbd al-Ḥaḳḳ al-Islāmī, a Jewish Convert," *Jewish Quarterly Review* 31 (1940): 171–91.

———. "Eleventh-Century Andalusian Authors on the Jews of Granada," *Proceedings of the American Academy for Jewish Research* 18 (1948–49): 269–80.

———. "Ibn Ḥazm on the Equivalence of Proofs," *Jewish Quarterly Review* 40 (1949–50): 279–90.

———. "A Legendary Story of Kaʿb al-Aḥbār's Conversion to Islam," *Jewish Social Studies* 5 (1953): 85–99.

———. *Examination of the Three Faiths* (Berkeley: University of California Press, 1971).

———. "Notes on the Position of Jewish Physicians in Medieval Muslim Society," *Israel Oriental Studies* 2 (1972): 315–19.

———. "The Medieval Polemics between Islam and Judaism," in *Religion in a Religious Age*, ed. S. D. Goitein (Cambridge: Association for Jewish Studies, 1974), 103–38.

———. "Judeo-Islamic Polemics," *The Encyclopedia of Religion*, ed. M. Eliade (New York: Macmillan, and London: Collier Macmillan, 1987), 11:396–402.

———. "Ghiyār," *EI²*, 2:1075–76.

Peters, F. E. *Jerusalem* (Princeton: Princeton University Press, 1985).

———. *A Reader on Classical Islam* (Princeton: Princeton University Press, 1994).

Pines, S. "Shīʿite Terms and Conceptions in Judah Halevi's *Kuzari*," *Jerusalem Studies in Arabic and Islam* 2 (1980): 165–251.

Powers, David S. "Reading/Misreading One Another's Scriptures: Ibn Ḥazm's Refutation of Ibn Nagrella al-Yahūdī," in W. M. Brinner and S. D. Ricks (eds.), *Studies in Islamic and Judaic Traditions* 1 (Atlanta: Scholars Press, 1986), 109–121.

Pulcini, Theodore. *Exegesis As Polemical Discourse: Ibn Ḥazm on Jewish and Christian Scriptures* (Atlanta: Scholars Press, 1998).

Ratzhaby, Yehudah. "On the Sources of the *Taḥkᵉmoni*" (Hebrew), *Tarbiz* 23 (1956): 424–39.

———. "An Arabic Maqāma by Alḥarizi" (Hebrew), *Criticism and Interpretation* 15 (1980): 5–51.

———. "The Image of R. Samuel the Nagid and Joseph His Son in the Arabic Sources" (Hebrew), *Criticism and Interpretation* 31 (1995): 25–35.

Ravitsky, Aviezer. "'To the Utmost Human Capacity': Maimonides on the Days of the Messiah," in *Perspectives on Maimonides: Philosophical and Historical Studies*, ed. Joel L. Kraemer (Oxford: Oxford University Press for the Littman Library, 1991).

Rejwan, Nissim. *Israel's Place in the Middle East: A Pluralist Perspective* (Gainesville: University Press of Florida, 1998).

Rosen, Tova. *Circumcised Cinderella and Other Gender Trouble: Readings in Medieval Hebrew Literature* (forthcoming).

Rosenthal, Franz, *The Classical Heritage in Islam*, trans. from the German by Emile and Jenny Marmorstein (Berkeley and Los Angeles: University of California Press, 1965).

Roth, Norman. "Some Aspects of Muslim-Jewish Relations in Spain," in *Estudios en homenage a Don Claudio Sanchez Albornoz en sus 90 anos* (Buenos Aires: Instituto de Historia de Espana, 1982), 2:179–214.

Rozen, Minna. "Pedigree Remembered, Reconstructed, Invented: Benjamin Disraeli between East and West," in Martin Kramer, ed. *The Jewish Discovery of Islam: Studies in Honor of Bernard Lewis* (Tel Aviv: Moshe Dayan Center for Middle Eastern and African Studies, 1999), 49–75.

Rubin, Uri. "Apes, Pigs and the Islamic Identity," *Israel Oriental Studies* 17 (1997): 89–105.

Sadan, Joseph. "Some Literary Problems Concerning Judaism and Jewry in Medieval Arabic Sources," in *Studies in Islamic History and Civilization in Honour of David Ayalon*, ed. Moshe Sharon (Jerusalem and Leiden: Cana and E. J. Brill, 1986), 353–98.

———. "The Image of the Jew in Classical Arabic Literature" (Hebrew), *Mahanaim* 1 (1991): 196–207.

———. "Biblical Poetics As Seen by Medieval Christians, Jews, and Muslims: The View of al-Ḥārith ibn Sinān and of Jewish Writers" (Hebrew) in *Israel Levin Jubilee Volume* (Studies in Hebrew Literature 1), eds. Reuven Tsur and Tova Rosen (Tel Aviv: Tel-Aviv University, Katz Research Institute for Hebrew Literature, 1994a), 195–239.

———. "Identity and Inimitability: Contexts of Inter-Religious Polemics and Solidarity in Medieval Spain, in the Light of Two Passages by Moshe Ibn ʿEzra' and Yaʿaqov Ben Elʿazar," *Israel Oriental Studies* 14 (1994b): 325–47.

———. "Judah Alḥarizi As a Cultural Junction—An Arabic Biography of a Jewish Writer As Perceived by an Orientalist" (Hebrew), *Peʿamim* 68 (1996a): 16–67.

———. "Polemics as Religious and Literary Writing (Al-Jāḥiẓ and Later Authors)" (Hebrew) in H. Lazarus-Yafeh (ed.). *Muslim Authors on Jews and Judaism: The Jews among Their Muslim Neighbors* (Hebrew) (Jerusalem: Zalman Shazar Center for Jewish History, 1996b), 37–58.

Sáenz-Badillos, Angel. "La Poesia belica de Šemu'el ha-Nagid: una muestra de convivencia judeo-musulmana," *Actas del I Congresso Internacional "Encuentro de las tres culturas" 3–7 octubre 1982* (Toledo: Ayuntamiento de Toledo, 1983), 219–35.

———. "Yehudah al-Ḥarizi, Admirador de Maimonides," *Micelanea de Estudios Arabicos y Hebraicos* 34 (1985): 61–70.

———. "Jewish Tradition in Arabic Form in the War Poetry of Shemuel HaNagid," in *From Iberia to Diaspora: Studies in Sephardic History and Culture*, eds. Yedida K. Stillman and Norman A. Stillman (Leiden: E. J. Brill, 1999), 264–81.

Sáenz-Badillos, Angel, and Targarona, Judit. *Diccionario de autores judios (Sefarad. Siglos 10–15)* (Cordoba-Madrid: Ediciones El Almendro, 1988).

Salem, Semaʿan I., and Kumar, Alok. *Science in the Medieval World* (Austin: University of Texas Press, 1991).

Sartain, E. M. "Medieval Muslim-European Relations: Islamic Juristic Theory and Chancery Practice," *Images of the Other: Europe and the Muslim World before 1700*, ed. David Blanks (Cairo Papers in Social Science Volume 19, No. 2) (Cairo: American University in Cairo Press, 1997), 81–95.

Scales, Peter. C. *The Fall of the Caliphate of Cordoba: Berbers and Andalusis in Conflict* (Leiden: E. J. Brill, 1994).

Scheindlin, Raymond P. "The Jews in Muslim Spain," in *The Legacy of Muslim Spain*, ed. Salma Khadra Jayyusi. (Leiden: E. J. Brill, 1992), 188–200.

———. "Al-Ḥarizi's Astrologer: A Document of Jewish-Islamic Relations," *Studies in Muslim-Jewish Relations* 1 (1993): 165–75.

———. *The Gazelle: Medieval Hebrew Poems on God, Israel and the Soul* (Oxford: Oxford University Press, 1999a).

———. *Wine, Women and Death: Medieval Hebrew Poems on the Good Life.* (Oxford: Oxford University Press, 1999b).

Schippers, Arie. *Spanish Hebrew Poetry and the Arabic Literary Tradition: Arabic Themes in Hebrew Andalusian Poetry* (Leiden: E. J. Brill, 1994).

———. "Literacy, Munificence and Legitimation of Power during the Reign of the Party Kings in Muslim Spain," in *Tradition and Modernity in Arabic Language and Literature*, ed. J. R. Smart. (Richmond, Surrey: Curzon Press, 1996), 75–86.

Schirmann, Jefim (Ḥayyim). *Die Hebraïsche Uebersetzung der Maqamen des Ḥarizi* (Frankfurt a. Main: J. Kaufmann, 1930).

———. "*Qinot ʿal ha-gezerot b*ᵉ*-ereṣ yisra'el, afriqah, s*ᵉ*farad, ashkenaz w*ᵉ*-ṣorfat*," *Qoveṣ ʿal yad* (new series) 3 (1939): 31–35.

———. "Le Dīwān de Šemu'el Hannagid consideré comme source pour l'histoire espagnole," *Hesperis* 35 (1948): 163–88.

———. "Samuel Hannagid, the Man, the Soldier, the Politician," *Jewish Social Studies* 13 (1951): 99–126.

———. "Researching the Sources of the *Taḥk*ᵉ*moni*" (Hebrew), *Tarbiz* 23 (1952): 198–202.

———. *Hebrew Poetry in Spain and Provence* (Hebrew), 4 vols. (Jerusalem-Tel Aviv: Mosad Bialik-Dvir, 1959–60).

———. *New Hebrew Poems from the Genizah* (Hebrew) (Jerusalem: Israel Academy of Sciences and Humanities, 1965).

———. *Studies in the History of Hebrew Poetry and Drama* (Hebrew), 2 vols. (Jerusalem: Mosad Bialik, 1979).
———. *The History of Hebrew Poetry in Muslim Spain* (Hebrew), ed., suppl., and annot. Ezra Fleischer (Jerusalem: Magnes Press, Hebrew University, and Ben-Zvi Institute, 1995).
———. *The History of Hebrew Poetry in Christian Spain and Southern France* (Hebrew), ed., suppl., and annot. Ezra Fleischer (Jerusalem: Magnes Press, the Hebrew University, and Ben Zvi Institute, 1997).
Schlossberg, Eliezer. "The Attitude of Maimonides toward Islam" (Hebrew), *Pe'amim* 42 (1990): 38–60.
Schmitz, M. "Ka'b al-Aḥbār," *EI*², 4:316–17.
Scholes, Robert. *Structuralism in Literature* (New Haven: Yale University Press, 1975).
Sela, Shlomoh, *Astrology and Biblical Exegesis in Abraham ibn Ezra's Thought* (Hebrew) (Ramat-Gan: Bar Ilan University Press, 1999).
Septimus, Bernard. "Better under Edom than under Ishmael: The History of a Saying" (Hebrew), *Zion* 47 (1962): 103–11.
Shatzmiller, Maya. "Les Juifs de Tlemçen aux XIVᵉ sìecle," *Revue des Etudes Juives* 137 (1978): 170–77.
———. "An Ethnic Factor in a Medieval Social Revolution: The Role of Jewish Courtiers under the Marinids," in *Islamic Society and Culture: Essays in Honour of Professor Aziz Ahmad*, eds. Milton Israel and N. K. Wagle (New Delhi: Manohar, 1983), 149–63.
———. "The Legacy of the Andalusian Berbers in the Fourteenth-Century Maghreb: Its Role in the Formation of Maghrebi Historical Identity and Historiography," in *Relaciones de la Peninsula Iberica con el Maghreb, siglos 13–16* (Actas del Coloquio), eds. M. Garcia Arenal and M. J. Vigera (Madrid: Consejo Superior de Investigaciones Científicas, Instituto de Filología; Instituto Hispano-Arabe de Cultura, 1988), 205–236.
Shemesh, Hanna. "Ibn Ḥazm's '*Al-Radd 'alā Ibn Al-Naghrīla*'" (Hebrew) in *Muslim Authors on Jews and Judaism: The Jews among Their Muslim Neighbors*, ed. Hava Lazarus-Yafeh (Jerusalem: Zalman Shazar Center for Jewish History, 1996), 83–118.
Shinar, Pesah. "Saturn and Judaism, Venus and Islam in the Mirror of an Eleventh-Century Arabic Handbook of Astrological Magic," *Hamizraḥ Heḥadash* 40 (1999): 9–32.
Signer, Michael A. *The Itinerary of Benjamin of Tudela* (*Travels in the Middle Ages*) (Malibu: Joseph Simon Pangloss Press, 1983).
Simon, Emilio de Santiago. "Unos Versos Satiricos de al-Sumaysir contra Bādīs B. Ḥabūs de Granada," *Miscelanea de Estudios Arabes y Hebraicos* 24 (1975): 115–18.
Sirat, Colette. *A History of Jewish Philosophy in the Middle Ages* (Cambridge: Cambridge University Press, and Paris: Editions de la maison des sciences de l'homme, 1985).
Sklare, David E. *Samuel Ben Ḥofni Gaon and His Cultural World.Texts and Studies* (Leiden: E. J. Brill, 1996).

Smith, Colin. *Christians and Moors in Spain*, 2 vols. (Warminster: Aris and Phillips Ltd. 1988–89).

———. "*Convivencia* in the *Estoria de Espana* of Alphonso X," in *Hispanic Studies in Honor of Samuel G. Armistead*, eds. E. Michael Gerli and Harvey K. Sharrer (Madison: Hispanic Seminary of Medieval Studies, 1992), 291–301.

Smith, Jonathan Z. "What a Difference a Difference Makes," in *'To See Ourselves As Others See Us': Christians, Jews and 'Others' in Late Antiquity*, eds. Jacob Neusner and Ernest S. Frerichs (Chico: Scholars Press, 1985), 3–48.

Smith, Paul Julian. *Representing the Other: 'Race,' Text, and Gender in Spanish and Spanish American Narrative* (Oxford: Clarendon Press, 1992).

Speight, R. Marston. "Muslim Attitudes toward Christians in the Maghrib during the Fatimid Period, 297/909–358/969," in *Christian-Muslim Encounters*, eds. Yvonne Yazbeck Haddad and Wadi Z. Haddad (Gainesville: University Press of Florida, 1995), 180–92.

Sperl, S. M. "Islamic Kingship and Arabic Panegyric Poetry in the Early Ninth Century," *Journal of Arabic Literature* 8 (1979): 20–35.

Sperl, Stefan, and Shackle, Christopher (eds.), *Qaṣīda Poetry in Islamic Asia and Africa*, 2 vols. (Leiden: E. J. Brill, 1996).

Spiegel, Gabrielle M. *Romancing the Past: The Rise of Vernacular Prose Historiography in Thirteenth-Century France* (Berkeley: University of California Press, 1993).

Spitzer, Leo. *Lives in Between: Assimilation and Marginality in Austria, Brazil, and West Africa, 1780–1945* (Cambridge: Cambridge University Press, 1989).

Spivakovsky, Erika. "The Jewish Presence in Granada," *Journal of Medieval History* 2 (1970): 215–37.

Steinschneider, Moritz. *Polemische und apologetische Literature in arabischer Spräche: zwischen Muslimen, Christen und Juden*. 1877 edition (reprinted Hildesheim: Georg Olms Verlag, 1966).

Stern, David, and Mirsky, Mark Jay. *Rabbinic Fantasies: Imaginative Narratives from Classical Hebrew Literature* (Philadelphia: Jewish Publication Society, 1990).

Stern, Samuel M. "The Arabic Original of Al-Ḥarizi's "*Maqāma* of the Rooster" (Hebrew), *Tarbiz* 17 (1946a): 87–100.

———. "Two New Data about Ḥasdai B. Shapruṭ" (Hebrew), *Zion* 11 (1946b): 141–46.

———. "On the History of Samuel ha-Nagid" (Hebrew), *Zion* 15 (1950): 135–45.

———. "Arabic Poems by Spanish-Hebrew Poets," *Romanica et Occidentalia: Etudes dediées à la memoire de Hiram Peri*, ed. Moshe Lazar (Jerusalem: Magnes Press, 1963), 254–63.

———. "A New Description by al-Ḥarizi of His Journey to Iraq" (Hebrew), *Sefunot* 8 (1964): 147–56.

———. "R. Judah al-Ḥarizi in Praise of Maimonides" (Hebrew) in *Hagut ʿivrit b^e-eiropah*, ed. M. Zohari (Tel Aviv: Yavneh, 1969), 91–103.

———. "An Unpublished *Maqāma* by al-Ḥarizi," *Papers of the Institute of Jewish Studies* (Volume 1), ed. J. G. Weiss. (Jerusalem: Magnes Press, 1964; reprinted Lanham, MD: University Press of America, 1989 [Brown Classics in Judaica, ed. J. Neusner]), 186–210.

Stetkevych, Suzanne Pinckney. *Abū Tammām and the Poetics of the ʿAbbasid Age* (Leiden: E. J. Brill, 1991).

———. "The *Qaṣīdah* and the Poetics of Ceremony: Three ʿĪd Panegyrics to the Cordoban Caliphate," in *Languages of Power in Islamic Spain*, ed. Ross Brann (Occasional Publications of the Department of Near Eastern Studies and the Program of Jewish Studies, Cornell University, Number 3) (Bethesda, MD: CDL Press, 1997), 1–48.

Stillman, Norman, A. "Aspects of Jewish Life in Islamic Spain," *Aspects of Jewish Culture in the Middle Ages*, ed. Paul E. Szarmach. Albany: State University of New York Press, 1979a), 51–84.

———. *The Jews of Arab Lands: A History and Source Book* (Philadelphia: Jewish Publication Society, 1979b).

———. "Myth, Countermyth, Distortion," *Tikkun* (May–June 1991): 60–64.

Stock, Brian. "History, Literature, and Medieval Textuality," *Yale French Studies* 70 (1986): 7–17.

Strothman R.-[Moktar Djebli], "Taḳiyya," *EI²*, 10: 134–36.

Stroumsa, Sarah. "From Muslim Heresy to Jewish-Moslem Polemics: Ibn al-Rāwandī's Kitāb al-Dāmigh," *Journal of the American Oriental Society* 107 (1987): 767–72.

———. *Dāwūd ibn Marwān al-Muqammiṣ's "Twenty Chapters"* [*ʿIshrūn Maqāla*], ed., trans., and annot. Sarah Stroumsa (Leiden: E. J. Brill, 1989).

———. "On Jewish Intellectual Converts to Islam in the Early Middle Ages" (Hebrew) *Peʿamim* 42 (1990): 61–75.

———. "The Blinding Emerald: Ibn al-Rāwandī's Kitāb al-Zumurrud," *Journal of the American Oriental Society* 114 (1994): 163–85.

———. "Jewish Polemics against Islam and Christianity in the Light of Judeo-Arabic Texts," *Studies in Muslim-Jewish Relations* 3 (Judaeo-Arabic Studies, ed. Norman Golb) (Amsterdam: Harwood Academic Publishers, 1997), 241–50.

———. *Freethinkers of Medieval Islam: Ibn al-Rāwandī, Abū Bakr al-Rāzī, and Their Impact on Islamic Thought* (Leiden: E. J. Brill, 1999).

Ṭāha, ʿAbdulwāḥid Dhanūn. *The Muslim Conquest and Settlement of North Africa and Spain* (London and New York: Routledge, 1989).

Tolan, John Victor. *Petrus Alfonsi and His Medieval Readers* (Gainesville: University Press of Florida, 1993).

———. "Mirror of Chivalry: Ṣalāḥ al-Dīn in the Medieval European Imagination," in David Blanks, ed. *Images of the Other: Europe and the Muslim World before 1700* (Cairo Papers in Social Science 19:2) (Cairo: American University in Cairo Press, 1997), 7–38.

Tottoli, Roberto. "Origin and Use of the Term *Isrāʾīliyyāt* in Muslim Literature," *Arabica* 46 (1999): 193–210.

Tritton, Arthur S. *The Caliphs and Their Non-Muslim Subjects: A Critical Study*

of the Covenant of 'Umar (London: Oxford University Press, 1930; reprinted London: Frank Cass, 1970).
Twersky, Isadore. *A Maimonides Reader* (New York: Behrman House, 1972).
———. *Introduction to the Code of Maimonides* (New Haven: Yale University Press, 1980).
Udovitch, Abraham L. "The Jews and Islam in the High Middle Ages: A Case of the Muslim View of Differences," in *Gli Ebrei nell'Alto Medioevo* (Spoleto: Centro italiano di studi sull'alto medioevo, 1980), 2: 655–711.
Vaglieri, L. Veccia. "'Abd Allāh ibn 'Abbās," *EI²*, 1:40–41.
Vajda, Georges. "Juifs et musulmanes selon le *ḥadīth*," *Journal Asiatique* 209 (1937): 57–127.
———. "Un Traite maghrebin 'Adversus Judaeos': 'Aḥkām ahl al-dhimma' du shaykh Muhammad b. 'Abd al-Karīm al-Maghīlī," *Etudes d'orientalism dediées à la memoire de Levi Provençal* (Paris: G. P. Maisonneuvre et Larose, 1962), 2:805–813.
———. "Isrā'īliyyāt," *EI²*, 4:211–12.
Viré, F. "Ḳird," *EI²*, 5:131.
Wansbrough, John. *Quranic Studies: Sources and Methods of Scriptural Interpretation* (Oxford: Oxford University Press, 1977).
Wasserstein, David J. *The Rise and Fall of the Party-Kings: Politics and Society in Islamic Spain, 1002–1086* (Princeton: Princeton University Press, 1985).
———. *The Caliphate in the West: An Islamic Political Institution in the Iberian Peninsula* (Oxford: The Clarendon Press, 1993a).
———. "Samuel Ibn Naghrīla ha-Nagid and Islamic Historiography in al-Andalus," *Al-Qanṭara* 14 (1993b): 109–125.
———. "Jewish Elites in Al-Andalus," in *The Jews of Medieval Islam: Community, Society, and Identity*, ed. Daniel Frank (Leiden: E. J. Brill, 1995), 101–110.
———. "The Muslims and the Golden Age of the Jews in al-Andalus," *Israel Oriental Studies* 17 (1997): 179–96.
Wasserstrom, Steven M. *Species of Misbelief: A History of Muslim Heresiography of the Jews*. Ph.D. diss., University of Toronto, 1985.
———. " 'The Shī'is Are the Jews of Our Community: An Interreligious Comparison within Sunnī Thought," *Israel Oriental Studies* 14 (1994): 297–324.
———. *Between Muslim and Jew: The Problem of Symbiosis under Early Islam* (Princeton: Princeton University Press, 1995).
———. "Šahrastānī on the Maġāriyya," *Israel Oriental Studies* 17 (1997): 127–54.
Weinberger, Leon J. *Jewish Prince in Moslem Spain: Selected Poems of Samuel ibn Nagrela* (Tuscaloosa: University of Alabama Press, 1973).
———. *Twilight of a Golden Age: Selected Poems of Abraham ibn Ezra* (Tuscaloosa and London: University of Alabama Press, 1997).
Wensinck, A. J. "Kunya," *EI²*, 5:395–96.
White, Hayden. *Tropics of Discourse: Essays in Cultural Criticism*. Baltimore and London: Johns Hopkins University Press, 1978.
Wolf, Kenneth Baxter. *Christian Martyrs in Muslim Spain* (Cambridge: Cambridge University Press, 1988).

Wolfson, Harry A. *The Philosophy of the Kalam* (Cambridge: Harvard University Press, 1976).

Woodward, C. Vann "The Lost Cause," *New York Review of Books* (30 January 1986): 26–29.

Yerushalmi, Yosef Haim. "Exile and Expulsion in Jewish History," in Benjamin R. Gampel, ed. *Crisis and Creativity in the Sephardic World, 1391–1648* (New York: Columbia University Press, 1997), 3–22.

Zucker, Moshe. "*Berurim b^{e}-toldot ha-vikkuḥim ha-datiyim she-bein ha-yahadut w^{e}-ha-islam*," in *Festschrift Armand Kaminka* (Vienna: Maimonides Institute, 1957), 31–48.

Zwartjes, Otto. *Love Songs from al-Andalus: History, Structure and Meaning of the Kharja* (Leiden: E. J. Brill, 1997).

INDEX

CPSIA information can be obtained at www.ICGtesting.com
Printed in the USA
BVOW041210170113

310838BV00003B/63/P